THE FIRST AMENDMENT BUBBLE

THE FIRST AMENDMENT BUBBLE

How Privacy and Paparazzi Threaten a Free Press

Amy Gajda

HARVARD UNIVERSITY PRESS
Cambridge, Massachusetts
London, England
2015

Library of Congress Cataloging-in-Publication Data

Gajda, Amy, author.
  The First Amendment bubble: how privacy and paparazzi threaten a free press /
Amy Gajda.
      pages cm
  Includes bibliographical references and index.
  ISBN 978-0-674-36832-3
  1. Freedom of the press—United States. 2. Freedom of information—United States.
  3. United States. Constitution. 1st Amendment. 4. Privacy, Right of—United States.
  5. Paparazzi—United States. I. Title.
  KF4774.G35 2015
  342.7308'53—dc23   2014014450

For Louise, whose appreciation for the daily morning newspaper and the nightly evening news helped to inspire my career path.

For Marie and Margaret, who taught me to appreciate the rich culture of the Old Country and the exciting media of the New.

And for Clare, who led the way.

Contents

Preface

I am now a law professor, but for a significant part of my adult life, I was tasked with news judgments.

When I worked as a television news anchor and producer at the PBS station in Harrisburg, Pennsylvania, in the 1980s, our camera crew was on the scene when the state treasurer killed himself during a news conference. We decided to air part of the video—but only to the point where he took the gun from his briefcase. The fact that such a high-ranking public official had committed suicide in front of others was national news, but to show anything more than a small part of the news conference seemed utterly without benefit and potentially harmful to his family and to our viewers.

Similarly, when I worked for the NBC station in Charlottesville, Virginia, a man had a heart attack on the plaza just outside our offices and a camera-person recorded the man's medical care. The man eventually died. Some in the newsroom pushed to make that video a part of our nightly newscast, arguing that there was news value in watching hardworking EMTs serve the public. Others, like me, disagreed, weighing the family's privacy more heavily. It did not air.

And when I worked at the ABC station in Salisbury, Maryland, with tangential help from an inside source we confirmed the dalliances of an elected official that surely would have been of interest to the community. We decided not to pursue the story, however, weighing the person's privacy more strongly than the story's newsworthiness. That was only one of a number of secrets and alleged secrets my colleagues and I learned throughout my career but did not report or investigate for privacy's sake.

Before becoming a law professor, I worked in journalism in some capacity for nearly a decade, and, throughout that time, had to make newsworthiness determinations nearly daily. My career in journalism took me from Ann Arbor, Michigan, to Toledo, Ohio, to Salisbury, Maryland, to Charlottesville, Virginia, to Harrisburg, Pennsylvania, and to Detroit, and I covered car crashes, drownings, fatal fires, political life, and kittens stuck in pipes. Once I started teaching law, I worked as the weekly legal commentator for Illinois Public Radio and there, too, had to decide what information was appropriate for broadcast and what was not. I taught journalism for part of that time; my joint appointment at the University of Illinois meant that my teaching load routinely included both Reporting I and Journalism Ethics.

Since I traded work as a full-time journalist for law practice and teaching, the work of editors and reporters in deciding what is newsworthy and how to report it has become harder still. Economic pressures in traditional media have left newsrooms with far fewer resources to evaluate developing stories and increasing competitive pressures to capture the fleeting attention of readers and viewers. The rise of digital media and the twenty-four-hour news cycle have ratcheted up the demand for instant decisions; and the explosion of new media and "citizen journalists," often playing by their own rules, means that editors know that any story they sit on will work its way into the public eye by other means. (Indeed, the graphic footage of the Pennsylvania treasurer's suicide that we elected to withhold from viewers in 1987 is now freely available on at least a half-dozen websites, ranging from YouTube to Best Gore.) And, finally, significant advances in technology have shifted popular notions of what is beyond the pale of public exposure, at once giving rise to an unprecedented culture of self-disclosure through social media and otherwise, but also stoking growing anxieties about the need to draw clearer privacy-related boundaries through law.

My experiences helped to shape my research agenda. They also inspired this book. I write from significant personal experience, knowing how little journalism understands law, but also how little law understands journalism.

THE FIRST AMENDMENT BUBBLE

An Introduction

Hulk Hogan, born Terry Bollea, is a professional wrestler. His bigger-than-life personality, halo of long white hair, and career that includes professional wrestling and reality television—both of which can be as far from real as can be—have made him an American icon.

They have also made him a media magnet.

In fall of 2012, Gawker, a website that boasts that its gossip today will make mainstream news headlines tomorrow, posted parts of a hidden camera video with audio of Hulk Hogan fully nude and engaging in sexual activity with a woman on a bed in somebody else's house. Approximately thirty seconds of the tape featured explicit sex. Gawker headlined the story "Even for a Minute, Watching Hulk Hogan Have Sex in a Canopy Bed Is Not Safe For Work, but Watch it Anyway."[1] At last count, more than four million people had, making the story the third most clicked on Gawker that year.

Then a judge ordered that the tape be taken down on privacy grounds.

Gawker grudgingly removed the tape, but left up its writer's full description, suggesting that both the video and its accompanying play-by-play essay were newsworthy and, therefore, constitutionally protected. "[T]he Constitution does unambiguously accord us the right to publish true things about public figures," a Gawker writer wrote, "[a]nd [the judge's] order requiring us to take down not only a very brief, highly edited video excerpt from a 30-minute Hulk Hogan [expletive] session but also a lengthy written account from someone who had watched the entirety of that [expletive] session, is risible and contemptuous of centuries of First Amendment jurisprudence."[2]

Whether Gawker is correct regarding the First Amendment and, if not, where the law should draw the line between free disclosure and legally punishable invasions is part of the larger question that this book explores. What legal and ethical restrictions exist, and should exist, regarding the publication of truthful news and information in today's privacy-interested yet over-exposure society?

Gawker's interpretation of its First Amendment protection is not that ludicrous. Previously, law and social understandings had been premised on a certain bargain: Journalists were accorded broad latitude to decide for themselves what was sufficiently newsworthy and to publish accordingly. Individuals, in turn, were entitled to keep their private affairs to themselves and to guard against unwarranted intrusions unless they actively sought publicity or somehow became entangled in a newsworthy event.

This bargain rested on the assumptions that journalists could be trusted to regulate themselves through professional norms and standards, and that ordinary individuals would naturally take care to preserve their own privacy. On these assumptions, courts felt secure in construing the First Amendment broadly to favor truthful public disclosure by the press and to quash the temptation to second-guess the editorial judgment of journalists. The highly influential Restatement of Torts, capturing the prevailing sentiment under both common and constitutional law, helpfully defined news as any information "of more or less deplorable popular appeal" and stopped short only at the point of "morbid and sensational prying for its own sake."[3] With such a capacious definition, courts understandably rarely found a violation.

In recent years, however, there has been an erosion of both fundamental assumptions underlying this balance between press rights and personal rights. Journalism as a whole has become less reliably professional as its ranks have expanded to include push-the-envelope websites like Gawker and other new media—and even traditional media outlets have buckled ethically in response to intense competition. Evolving public tastes and market pressures have led to a melding of news and entertainment, reshaping programming decisions in ways that discourage self-restraint and encourage use of unfiltered, audience-generated content. Citing constitutional freedoms, reporters have welcomed or begrudgingly accepted free-wheeling websites and untrained bloggers within their protective First Amendment shield. At the same time, the sense of decorum or fear of social sanctions that once inhibited individuals from sharing intimate details of their private lives is giving ground to a stream of confessional internet posts and reality television shows. Rapid technological advances, meantime, are accelerating both of these trends, making possible unprecedented new harmful intrusions and enabling their world-wide dissemination in an instant.

The result is that courts and other legal actors are beginning to rethink the balance between privacy rights and public interests in free disclosure. The deference that once shielded journalists from editorial control by the government is eroding as courts are showing a new willingness to limit public disclosure of truthful information. Increasingly, personal privacy seems deeply vulnerable and deserving of new, more potent protections, just as the expansive new practices and identity of media are stretching the credibility of journalism's claim to occupy a distinctive and privileged place in democratic life. The combined effect creates a sort of First Amendment bubble, in which constitutional protection for press and news media continually expands to the breaking point, jeopardizing future protection not only at the margins but also for the core.

This much is clear: the *New York Times*, in contrast, did not publish the Hulk Hogan sex tape on its website. Lending significant credibility to Gawker's motto about it sourcing mainstream news, however, the venerable newspaper published a graphic containing risqué celebrity tweets about it above a single short paragraph suggesting that the tape was "horrible" to watch but "delightful to discuss."[4] The fact that it did not publish or link to the tape was to be expected; today's mainstream media maintain privacy-based ethics provisions that would caution against such publication, even if a single journalist's internal ethics code would push for it, and even if its attorneys would approve such coverage. The fact that the *Times* published others' humorous tweets, however (including one that suggested that Hogan had already gone "one-on-one" with someone who was "faking it," another about him "finishing" without using wrestling moves, and a third commenting on Hogan's "performance"), reflects the pressure that mainstream publications feel in covering sensational stories published by other, less ethically bound publications. Today, even the loftiest of reads must fight for the four-million Gawker readers, and others who know of the Hulk Hogan sex tape, and wonder why mainstream publications have not reported on it in a significant way.

The law, meantime, is playing catch-up. It grew responsively in a decades-old world where journalism was credited with pushing democracy forward and where Supreme Court Justices wrote in their powerful opinions that law that was too restrictive would chill journalists who needed significant breathing space to report robustly. Given that sort of legal and journalistic history, it is not surprising that the law today remains deferential. But the jurists who wrote and followed those words in their opinions had not faced a First Amendment-based argument that an explicit sex tape was in the public interest for its news value and therefore should be allowed to remain on a gossip website, no matter its celebrity star's apparent embarrassment and his wishes that it be taken down. Courts in such situations, then, are left with flowery pro-press language but a decreasing sense that such press deserves support. The Hulk Hogan case is not the Pentagon Papers case, one that involved the publication of information about war, after all; it involves an act so intimate that even the media-protective Restatement suggests that celebrities should be able to keep their sex lives private.

Abner Mikva, a retired judge who once sat on the federal appeals court for the District of Columbia, predicted that this would be our future, and that there would come an anti-media shift in the courts. He warned in a 1995 law review article that changes were afoot in First Amendment doctrine because of what judges perceived as an "irresponsible" press:

> I think that I can say that a feeling is abroad among some judges that the Supreme Court has gone too far in protecting the media from defamation actions resulting from instances of irresponsible journalism. That sounds like a scary message for me to deliver. . . . I have been a judge for fifteen years, and now that I have taken off my robes, one of the first things I must say is: "Watch out! There's a backlash coming in First Amendment doctrine."[5]

That backlash and the resulting impact may well be here—and the Hulk Hogan case itself offers a circuitous example.

A New Newsworthiness

The Florida state court judge's order to Gawker to take down the Hulk Hogan sex tape was not the first or last legal proceeding arising from the publication of the video. Hulk Hogan had initially brought his claim to federal court, arguing that the court should suppress publication of the tape on invasion-of-privacy grounds. Gawker argued in response that it should be allowed to leave the tape up because, among other things, it showed a television star engaging in sexual activity in a very human way, a contribution to public understanding that Gawker considered newsworthy.

Perhaps not as shockingly as it might otherwise be, given strong First Amendment protection for journalism, the federal district court judge sided with Gawker. The judge explained that he was hesitant to do anything that might violate constitutionally protected expression and refused to grant what he considered an unconstitutional prior restraint.[6] The court's analysis offered a window into the power of the press and the related danger of seeking celebrity today. It found that the sex videotape itself was newsworthy, in part, based upon Hogan's work as a reality television star:

> Plaintiff's public persona, including the publicity he and his family derived from a television reality show detailing their personal life, his own book describing an affair he had during his marriage, prior reports by other parties of the existence and content of the Video, and Plaintiff's own public discussion of issues relating to his marriage, sex life, and the Video all demonstrate that the Video is a subject of general interest and concern to the community.

The court explained that strong legal precedent led it to defer to Gawker's editorial discretion in posting the explicit tape, quoting an earlier deferential court in a very different case that had held that "the judgment of what is newsworthy is primarily a function of the publisher, not the courts." Any other outcome, the Florida federal court implied in line with that earlier case, would cause Gawker to suffer a loss of First Amendment press freedom that, based on years of precedent, rightly trumps such an individual's privacy concerns. The decision to post the Hulk Hogan sex tape, it found, was "appropriately left to [Gawker's own] editorial discretion" and, in keeping with older legal precedent, the court refused to sit as a sort of superior editor and order that it be taken down.

That decision, if not completely surprising given strong legal precedent, was notable. It marked the first time that a court had decided that a plaintiff who would normally be protectively cloaked heavily in privacy—a man explicitly pictured nude and engaged in sexual activity in a video taken surreptitiously in a private bedroom—must defer to a proudly push-the-envelope news website that had decided that such information was appropriate for excerpted but otherwise unedited public viewing.

The decision also shows the lasting legacy of First Amendment jurisprudence built when the *New York Times* and news organizations of its kind were

the defendants who stood before the courts. To defer to a respected and generally respectful publication and its well-trained journalists took little effort
when a story had real news value; protective language remains from the
Pentagon Papers case, for example, when the *New York Times* successfully
argued that it had the First Amendment right to publish a trove of documents
on the conduct of a controversial war. In fact, when Hogan brought a second,
copyright-based claim in federal court against Gawker, the court similarly
rejected it, noting that even though the sex tape depicted "explicit sexual
activity" and nudity against his wishes, "[t]he Supreme Court has repeatedly
recognized that even minimal interference with the First Amendment freedom
of the press causes an irreparable injury."[7] The court then cited as support for
that principle two cases that involved unconstitutional prior restraints on
crime-related news, traditionally among the most newsworthy of stories.

Some evidence in the Hogan case of the backlash of which Judge Mikva
warned came when Hogan brought his privacy claims to a Florida state trial-
level court. There, in contrast, the judge granted Hogan's request for a preliminary injunction and ordered Gawker to take the tape down. Gawker's
attorney is quoted in the court hearing's transcript—published as part of a
Gawker webpage titled "A Judge Told Us to Take Down Our Hulk Hogan
Sex Tape Post. We Won't"[8]—as arguing that the judge was "not permitted to
make an editorial judgment" about what news is publishable and what is not.
But the court rejected that longstanding First Amendment argument and
sided with what it said was the "public interest" in protecting the plaintiff's
"private sexual encounter."

In doing so, of course, the court flatly rejected in spirit if not in language
the federal district court's constitutional worries and that court's reliance on
past Supreme Court precedent, lifting an individual's privacy, at least for the
moment, above Gawker's strident and traditionally powerful First Amendment
press freedom arguments.

This may have been a very good thing for individual privacy, but it was also
a very, very bad thing for the press. After all, a decision admonishing Gawker
and granting an extraordinarily rare preliminary injunction to a plaintiff on
privacy grounds could well have had far-reaching effects for all media, even in
cases involving different and perhaps far less heinous facts.

In early 2014, privacy, in turn, suffered a loss. A Florida state appeals court
reversed the trial court's decision and, in doing so, supported in part Gawker's
claim that it could publish whatever truthful thing it wished regarding

celebrities. The court wrote that such "arguably inappropriate and otherwise sexually explicit content" could well be of legitimate public interest because it addressed "matters of public concern"—and that Gawker enjoyed the "editorial discretion" to publish the explicit tape. This court too blamed Hulk Hogan in large part for making his sex life of public interest, pointing to media appearances and—in a surprisingly broad critique that affects expression of a different sort—his autobiography in which he had written about an affair in a repentant and decidedly innocuous way.[9]

Should that reasoning stand as the case continues, it could well be that any public figure's private life in its most explicit sense will be fair game should the celebrity be seen as courting media interest or discussing personal relationships. The privacy implications for many are enormous.

No matter the outcome, the Hulk Hogan case exemplifies the clash between a bolder media and the privacy it can decimate. Consider this: Gawker's founder and owner, Nick Denton, boasted in 2014 that his website routinely published private information that an ethics-abiding newspaper would not and suggested that the crowd-sourced ratting out of anyone and the "spilling of secrets" including sex pictures would be healthy for most people.[10] Just a few months earlier, in contrast, U.S. Supreme Court Justice Sonia Sotomayor had written in her autobiography that with her ascent to the nation's highest court had come the "notorious," "profoundly disconcerting" and "overwhelming" experience of being suddenly propelled into the public eye, a life that brought with it what she called "psychological hazards."[11]

The one behind the computer keyboard with the power of the press, therefore, buoyantly works toward an end to privacy while the one behind the bench with the power to interpret that freedom considers privacy necessary for personal well-being.

It seems clear which power will ultimately triumph.

"There is still a tendency among members of the media to view the courts in somewhat romantic terms," constitutional law scholar David Pozen said in 2014, nearly twenty years after Judge Mikva's warning and within a few months of Gawker's claim that it had the right to publish whatever truthful information it wanted. "I'm not confident that remains a descriptively accurate view of the courts."[12]

Selfies and Our Current Conceptions of Privacy

The Hulk Hogan saga has an interesting and relevant twist. Just a few months after Hogan had successfully argued that the sex tape should be removed from Gawker, Hogan himself posted his own set of differently graphic pictures. According to news accounts, Hogan tweeted to his followers on the Internet that a radiator had exploded on his hand—and attached a photograph of the injury. "Would you like it rare?" he asked his Twitter readers, referring to his burned and bloodied hand.[13]

After receiving several complaints, Hogan took the images down. "I apologize for posting my burned hand photos," he wrote, "with all the feedback I now realize I really should take a moment before I make a decision [to tweet]." That a star who continued to defend himself in court against Gawker's desire to post his sexually explicit tape needs such a lesson seems inconsistent.

And yet, in a privacy sense, it is the story of many Facebook "friends," Instagram users, and Twitter tweeters and, therefore, has relevance here. As media invades privacy more often with resulting criticism and backlash from courts, many people continue to willingly share information about themselves online with little regard for their own privacy and the potential public response. Consider, as a second example, journalist Geraldo Rivera's Twitter self-photograph, taken in front of a bathroom mirror with a towel only slightly covering his groin, sent to followers in summer 2013. He later removed the photo, explaining that he had learned his lesson.[14] Congressmen Chris Lee and Anthony Weiner, each of whom sent into the world highly embarrassing photographs of themselves—colloquially known as "selfies"—and each of whom were outed by what might be called quasi-journalists (a term I will use here to differentiate them from more traditional, mainstream journalists) could have told him that.

We are, therefore, at a doubly interesting time in terms of privacy and media. As some courts seem to be growing more protective of privacy, weighing it above freedom-of-the-press and freedom-of-information interests, many individuals are protecting their own privacy less, sharing personal information with the world, oblivious that there are never-friends and former friends who might want to see it and publicize it. Privacy law scholar Anita Allen has rightly called this "the era of revelation."[15] At the same time that courts are grappling with press and privacy interests in graphic sex tapes, then, they also must consider the issue of whether a sex picture freely posted to a limited group of people or even the world can and should ever again be private.

The answers are not easy. Consider, for example, the arguments in favor of a so-called right to be forgotten, an idea now codified as law in some sense in some parts of the world. At its most protective, such a concept creates liability for those who publish photographs and information that the subjects wish removed, even if the subjects had once willingly posted it themselves. Privacy law scholar Jeffrey Rosen has written that the right to be forgotten "represents the biggest threat to free speech on the Internet in the coming decade."[16] Those in favor argue that young people do silly things that can harm their reputations as they get older; fifteen-year-olds who post to certain friends on Facebook sexually graphic information or teens who post photos of themselves with hardcore drugs would likely want those photos suppressed should they ever decide to become a teacher, run for Congress, or apply to the FBI. Those who support the right to be forgotten or the related right to erasure argue that, indeed, the bell should be able to be unrung so that we have a chance to make mistakes when we are young and then change our lives for the better. As memories fade, the argument goes, so should reminders of indiscretion. There are those who support a similar law in the United States.

And there are many in the United States who might wish to avail themselves of the opportunity to unring the bell. A 2013 Pew survey found that the number of young people who post information about themselves on social media sites is growing. According to a Pew poll released in 2013, this is what young people share with their, on average, 300 "friends"—and, for a significant minority, the world:

- 91 percent post a photo of themselves, up from 79 percent in 2006.
- 71 percent post their school name, up from 49 percent.
- 71 percent post the city or town where they live, up from 61 percent.
- 53 percent post their email address, up from 29 percent.
- 20 percent post their cell phone number, up from 2 percent.[17]

Researchers also asked several new questions and the answers are similarly revealing:

- 92 percent post their real name to the profile they use most often.
- 84 percent post their interests, such as movies, music, or books they like.

- 82 percent post their birth date.
- 62 percent post their relationship status.
- 16 percent have set their accounts to show their location information automatically.
- 24 percent post videos of themselves.

What this means is that many young people reveal much about themselves online and, while 60 percent of the teens have set their accounts to "private," 40 percent had made at least part of their profile public. Another 60 percent had deleted or edited a post or photograph that they later regretted, which means that many of those items had already been published to the world.

Consider the related example of a high school student who in 2010 and 2011 openly posted on a college admissions forum where most posters remain anonymous, her full name, her high school, her Facebook web page, her desire to go to college at one of the top schools in the United States, her psychotherapy treatment for anxiety, that she liked to "party"—and, one time, the fact that she was at that moment driving eighty miles per hour on a highway and posting to the website at the same time because, as she suggested, she was bored. Right before she signed off of the forum, presumably forever, she had excitedly noted that a representative from her dream university had called her teacher to ask about her and, among other things, how she handled anxiety. Shortly thereafter, apparently learning about her honest and highly identifiable and informational posts on the forum, her college counselor ordered her to stop posting immediately. A Google search showed that she ultimately matriculated at a different college. Poignantly, she had responded to concerns that she had revealed too much about herself by explaining she had confidence that the website allowed people to remain anonymous.[18]

What the numbers and that story seem to show is that self-publishing teens believe that 300 "friends" will keep their secrets or that others simply won't be interested given their seeming insignificance among the world's billions of internet users. But in today's world, the teens who feel that way are sometimes wrong, and they could eventually become the strongest supporters of a right to be forgotten and, in years to come, the fuel for an even greater push toward privacy.

In 2012, as another more notorious example, just after President Obama was elected a second time, a Tumblr account calling itself "Hello There, Racists!" posted multiple tweets and Facebook posts from young people around the country who were responding to the election's outcome. The posts were indeed offensive and racist and seemed meant for a small group of followers; "I hate black people. Go back to Africa where you belong" is part of an additionally hateful post that remained on Hello There, Racists! many months later.[19] Some readers of the racist tweets or racist posts had apparently sent helpful links to persons running the Tumblr account and, suddenly, what was meant for some became available to the world.

Many of the racist posters, however, were still in high school. One of them, a girl named Kayla, is pictured atop her racist post, smiling for the camera and looking all of fourteen. The Hello There Racists! Tumblr website gives her full name, the small town where she lives, the name of her high school, her boyfriend's full name, and links to her now-deactivated Twitter and Facebook accounts. On the remaining page of the now apparently dormant Tumblr, nearly twenty different young people are outed by name, location, high school, other identifiers, and their racist posts.

Eventually, those in mainstream media—whose ethics codes would likely have prevented such outings by name—took notice. A writer for Slate, for example, posted a piece she titled "Hey Internet, Quit Outing Kids for Racism"[20] and quoted another Slate contributor: "[T]hese sites are pinning kids like butterflies as permanent racists. These idiotic, repulsive remarks will follow them for years and have potential effects on their ability to go to college, to get jobs. We need to tread very lightly with the privacy of minors." As of 2014, the Hello There Racists! website remained online.

Or take as related examples those who have sent nude photographs of themselves to others before breaking off the relationships and those who have had such photographs stolen from computers or cell phones. Several so-called "revenge porn" sites publish those nude photographs. One, IsAnybodyDown, linked identifying information to some photos and offered prizes for help in identifying the people pictured in others. In an interview with the NPR program *On the Media* in 2012, the owner of the website explained that he believed that laws involving nudity in the United States should be changed, that he hoped nude photographs of everyone would be public in ten years, and that his website was a "progressive cause" in that direction. "These are not victims," he explained, "these are people who have decided to publically transmit their information" over the Internet. Important here, he also explained that he had always wanted to be a journalist and that, after a failed job search, the website was "a last resort."[21]

In these examples, mainstream media would likely have published the information differently, if at all. Ethics codes remind journalists to tread carefully in identifying young people in any story, let alone one where their posts could haunt them forever. And mainstream ethics codes would certainly prevent the worldwide publication of a nude photograph meant for one. Even if a mainstream journalist would want to include such information in a story, the newspaper's editors, following traditional newsroom ethics provisions on privacy, would not allow it.

One wonders what effect these sorts of websites have had on judges' perceptions of media and the value of privacy, given recent warnings about constitutional limits for irresponsible journalism. It is not too far-fetched to imagine that judges today would be pushed even further away from traditional constitutional protections. In other words, even though those websites might not be considered mainstream journalism, their activity could well create a greater paternalistic sense that we must act to protect privacy and a corresponding sense that media irresponsibility must be curbed.

The People and the "Press"

In September 2012, a reader wrote a letter to the editors of *Vanity Fair* in response to an earlier piece in the magazine on tabloid journalism. In the letter, she blamed many societal problems on media, suggesting that "[s]itcoms, reality shows, tweets, most contemporary print news, and broadcast news—infotainment—are responsible for [the] massacre of our brain cells, the English language, and what's left of our collective intelligence."[22]

The judges' opinions that favor privacy over press freedoms and plaintiffs over publications, then, reflect that opinion on a broader and more powerful scale: that media is spinning out of control, creating harm that is both individual and collective, and that something needs to be done about it legally before we suffer tremendous societal loss.

The most recent poll numbers seem to show that many Americans would agree that current law must become more responsively restrictive to changes in media. In 2013, the Newseum Institute's First Amendment Center released a First Amendment survey in which it reported that 34 percent of Americans today believe that the First Amendment goes "too far."[23] Relevant to the future of First Amendment freedoms, nearly half of younger Americans aged eighteen to thirty believe that the First Amendment is too expansively protective.

A similar survey, done in 2005, focused more specifically on the press itself, asking respondents directly if the press had too much, too little, or just the right amount of freedom. Nearly 40 percent answered that journalists had too much freedom.[24] Even though that specific question was not asked in 2013, the 2013 results reflected a related sensibility: nearly half of those surveyed believed that journalists should give up their sources to make America safer, only 1 percent responded that Freedom of the Press was the most important freedom that Americans enjoy, and only 14 percent could name Freedom of the Press as a First Amendment right.

Recent opinion polls about the quality of today's journalism show a similar lack of enthusiasm for the press. A 2011 poll done by the Pew Center for the People and the Press showed that "[n]egative opinions about the performance of news organizations now equal or surpass all-time highs on nine of 12 core measures," including favoritism, political biases, and inaccuracies, that the Center has been tracking since 1985. In that same poll—and in contrast to older laudatory Supreme Court language about journalism's key role in democracy—42 percent of Americans reported that they felt that the press actually harms democracy (the same percentage said it helped). This was the first time Americans had answered the democracy question in such a negative fashion.

Perhaps this is because America's newsrooms are changing and seemingly moving away from traditional news coverage and story depth. Certainly the number of mainstream journalists continues to fall. The Pew Research Center's Project for Excellence in Journalism 2013 report found that newsrooms had lost 30 percent of their staff since 2000 and that two newspaper chains and eighteen individual newspapers had closed all of their foreign bureaus, with additional outlets trimming staff overseas. In Washington, D.C., too, the seat of government and a hotbed for stories of important public interest, the report showed that news organizations had also "drastically reduced their coverage."[25] Shortly after the release of the Pew report, the American Society of News Editors confirmed that in the one-year period from 2011 to 2012 alone, there were 2,600 fewer full-time professional editors working at newspapers in the United States.[26] And coverage seems to have been affected; Pew called it a "shrinking reporting power." Its report on journalism showed, for example, that local broadcast news coverage of crime and trials had dropped from 29 percent of stories in 2005 to 17 percent of stories in 2012 and that politics and government stories had decreased from 7 percent to 3 percent. Meantime, coverage of "bizarre" stories and accidents had increased from 5 percent to 13 percent and weather, traffic, and sports news grew to 40 percent of a typical newscast. Such stories require less effort than would investigative pieces, for example.

What all this means is that now is a troubling time for the press not only in the courts, but also in the court of public opinion, reflected in the numbers just stated and in the letter to the editor linking media's decline with a decline in our collective intelligence. But the *Vanity Fair* writer made another important, albeit unintentional point. When she criticized media, she did so by lumping everything together in her condemnation, equating newspapers with reality television shows and sitcoms. The same phenomenon can be seen elsewhere, including a Huffington Post article from 2013 that condemned "media" for criticism that went too far and included in its examples the satirical humor newspaper the *Onion*, the sensational gossip website created by blogger Perez Hilton, Donald Trump, and the *New York Times*.[27] When 40 percent of Americans say that the press has too much freedom, they could well be thinking of media in a general sense: as much of Honey Boo Boo as Bob Woodward or as much of The Dirty, a website that seems to specialize in hypercriticism of women's bodies, as the *Los Angeles Times*.

In an article in a legal magazine about British tabloids accused of tapping into public figures' voicemail messages, as another example, the condemnation and calls for a change in legal response reached stateside. The behavior by the tabloids in England, the article noted, had changed perceptions that media in the United States are "the good guys" wearing white hats, as many law school classes portray them. Instead, as one constitutional law professor explained, the phone-tapping scenario should awaken all to "the political and social power of the media" with a reminder that "[t]he First Amendment has never been read to confer upon reporters and editors the right to break the law." Collectively, the article notes "[t]he news media, already faltering in both financial and social status in the post-Internet era, faces another hit to its overall reputation."[28]

In other words, many different types of publications in many different places come under the "media" umbrella today and attempting to define the "press" has become increasingly difficult. Today, in the United States alone, traditional print journalism has morphed into broadcast news that has morphed into *60 Minutes* that has morphed into *Dateline NBC* that has morphed into real-life crime programming like *The First 48* or *Cops* that has morphed into *Bait Car* (a program depicting real-life incidents of car theft using hidden video) that has morphed into *Cheaters* (a program that follows people suspected of infidelity using hidden cameras) that has morphed into *The Real Housewives of New Jersey* and beyond. The point at which the publication's focus loses its journalistic value and is no longer "press" or "journalism" or even truly "real" is not clear—especially because each is supposedly nonfiction and is said to reveal at least some truthful information. Traditional news, then, may be suffering not only from its own troubles and its own news judgment, but also from the choices made by push-the-envelope reality programming that many find distasteful. All merge together as the "media" we condemn.

A study released in 2013 showed this on a different but still very relevant level. The study's researchers created a news blog on which they posted a story about nanotechnology. They then posted what they called "rude" and "nasty" comments after the story—including suggestions by commenters that those who did not support the technology were "idiots" or "stupid"—and they exposed half of the sample group to that story and those comments. The other half of the sample group was given the same story with far more civilized comments after it. The rude comments, the researchers reported, actually changed the participants' interpretation and understanding of the news story, causing readers to believe more strongly in the technology. In other words, participants seemingly blended the news in the news item with comments that followed from their anonymous peers and read them as one. "This study's findings," the researchers wrote, "suggest perceptions towards science are shaped in the online blog setting not only by 'top-down information,' but by others' civil or uncivil viewpoints, as well."[29]

That study could well affect public perception of most mainstream journalism websites. The *New York Times*, for example, once reported that Tiger Woods had apologized to his then-wife for personal failings. The newspaper then left up as the first (perhaps defamatory) comment from a reader that "[s]he shouldn't have hit him so hard." This suggested that a blow from a golf club in Woods' wife's hand had given Woods a concussion that had led him to crash the car at the end of their driveway,[30] a gossipy allegation not covered in the story. A reader could then have unknowingly blended the comment with the reported information and remembered incorrectly that the newspaper itself had engaged in what might be called tabloid journalism. Or a viewer may consider *Bait Car*'s coverage of car theft the equivalent of crime-related journalism, even though *Bait Car* uses a sometimes mocking tone, video from hidden cameras, and a microphone placed within the car. That difficulty in drawing a line, between facts and comments, and between journalism and quasi-journalism, is highly relevant in today's privacy cases.

The Prosecutor and His Privacy

One of the best recent examples of dissatisfaction with media in a broad sense and how it can affect privacy jurisprudence stems from the television program *To Catch a Predator*, a series aired on NBC as part of its *Dateline NBC* programming. Producers for *To Catch a Predator* worked closely with Perverted Justice, a group of concerned adults who pretended to be very young teens in internet chat rooms, awaiting what often turned out to be a graphically sexual come-on from a much older man. The "teen" would then suggest that they meet in person, the man would show up at a prearranged location (usually a house rented by NBC) often with condoms or alcohol, at which point the "teen," an actor, would quickly excuse himself or herself. As the program progressed, its host, Chris Hansen, would appear and would confront the man, asking him detailed questions about the explicit internet chats. As the uncomfortable conversation continued, previously concealed photographers and sound technicians would reveal themselves, swarming around the man in the kitchen, and Hansen would explain that he worked for NBC. At that point, the man usually would attempt to leave and waiting police would promptly arrest him.

William Conradt, a once-elected fifty-six-year-old county prosecutor from Texas who had unsuccessfully run for judge and then had returned to prosecution, was one of the men who chatted explicitly with a boy he thought was thirteen. Online, Conradt pretended to be a nineteen-year-old college student; unbeknownst to Conradt, of course, the thirteen-year-old boy was really an adult Perverted Justice worker. Over the course of several days, Conradt sent the boy explicit photographs, including at least one of a penis, and shared multiple graphic sexual descriptions and specific sexual desires with the boy, both in messaging and in phone calls.[31]

Conradt and the thirteen-year-old then agreed to meet. But Conradt failed to arrive at the house despite his assurances that he would. At that point, as

Perverted Justice would later explain on its website: "We began to notice that information was disappearing—Conradt was deleting profiles—and when we advised the police of this, they chose to act then on the information, as Conradt had already broken the law"[32] by communicating in such a manner with someone he seemingly presumed to be an underage child. NBC's journalists meantime had covered much of the interaction between Conradt and the child and had interviewed police about their decision to arrest Conradt. Some pundits would later criticize them for playing far too active a role in that attempted arrest.

After receiving a warrant, police officers and a SWAT team arrived at Conradt's home. The *To Catch a Predator* camera crew, including Hansen, also arrived. Most watched from the sidewalk and some recorded the police activity. But this arrest was not as easy as others: when the police entered Conradt's home, he shot and killed himself.

It is not known if Conradt had realized that journalists had outed him, if he even knew that journalists were somehow involved with his impending arrest, or if he realized that he would soon be featured on *To Catch a Predator*. Perverted Justice later posted on its website that police had found "a large child pornography collection" on his computers. Obviously, with police at his door, Conradt likely would have known or would have at least suspected that his chats and the lurid photographs he had sent days before had been made available to police and he also would have known that any child pornography in his possession would be discovered: he had prosecuted cases involving child sex abuse himself and understood the forensic investigation that was necessary for a solid case against a perpetrator. He also would have known that his arrest would be big news even if no journalists were there to record it because he himself had given interviews to media after similar arrests.[33]

But William Conradt's sister wanted NBC to pay for what she considered its misdeeds leading to her brother's suicide. She sued the network for invasion of privacy and intentional infliction of emotional distress on behalf of her brother's estate. By showing up at the arrest and by playing such an active role, she argued, NBC had invaded Conradt's privacy and had caused him great emotional harm that had led to his suicide.

Arguably, such claims would have been dismissed out of hand by courts in the past. Arrests—especially the arrest of a prosecutor, a public official, charged with the sexual solicitation of a child—are newsworthy. As early as 1931, the U.S. Supreme Court had written as much, crediting the press for reporting wrongdoing, especially the wrongdoing of public officials: "'The importance of this [kind of reporting] consists, besides the advancement of truth[,] . . . [in providing means] whereby oppressive officers are shamed or intimidated, into more honourable and just modes of conducting affairs,'" the Justices wrote, citing historic language.[34] And the highly influential Restatement states specifically that *any* arrest is of legitimate public interest and, therefore, newsworthy.[35]

But, the federal trial court hearing the *Conradt* case decided that the intentional-infliction-of-emotional-distress claim was a valid one, and rejected NBC's call to dismiss the case.[36] It did so with surprisingly strong language and with surprising precedent. Initially, the court rejected the privacy claim but only because legal precedent meant that the right to sue for privacy invasions of such a sort dies with the plaintiff. The emotional distress claim, however, had no such restriction, and the court upheld it even though the claim decidedly sprang from the same privacy-related concerns.

First, NBC's actions, the court wrote with a decidedly and almost naïvely pro-plaintiff tone, caused a blurring of news and law enforcement that had harmed Conradt. "[T]o avoid public humiliation," the court wrote, "an otherwise law-abiding man was shamed into committing suicide, before he had been charged by any court, before he had any opportunity to be heard." NBC, in contrast, was in a "position of power" and should have known of Conradt's potential for emotional distress.

Second, the court focused on one of the necessary and most difficult elements to prove in any emotional distress claim: outrageous behavior on the part of the defendant, frequently defined as behavior that is utterly intolerable in a civilized society. In the *Conradt* case, the court found the potential for such outrageousness in NBC's journalistic choices and how it felt those choices compared with journalism ethics. "[T]he failure to abide by . . . journalistic standards may indeed be relevant" to the jury, the court wrote, and pointed to various provisions it had found within the Society of Professional Journalists Code of Ethics, provisions not mandatory but aspirational and voluntarily accepted by journalists as a guide for ethical behavior.[37] The *Conradt* court, however, used them as a demarcation point for liability, finding that they could be used to prove outrageousness of behavior, including the ethics provisions that suggest that journalists should:

- Recognize that gathering and reporting information may cause harm or discomfort.

- Show good taste. Avoid pandering to lurid curiosity.
- Recognize that private people have a greater right to control information about themselves than do public officials and others who seek power, influence or attention. Only an overriding public need can justify intrusion into anyone's privacy.

Any reasonable jury, the court wrote, could have found that the *To Catch a Predator* journalists had violated all three provisions "by failing to take steps to minimize the potential harm to Conradt, by pandering to [the American public's] lurid curiosity, . . . and by manufacturing the news rather than merely reporting it." Jurors, the court found in deciding that the case should continue, could well decide that "NBC [had] created a substantial risk of suicide or other harm, and that it [had] engaged in conduct so outrageous and extreme that no civilized society should tolerate it."

Many would agree that some of the journalistic procedures used by *To Catch a Predator* were distasteful; a well-respected journalism ethics organization, for example, criticized the program as "not good journalism."[38] But consider the implications of the court's decision, its readiness to sit as a kind of super-editor, and its reliance on ethics code provisions for news media today. First, any newsgathering and presumably actual news coverage that causes "discomfort" could well become the basis for an intentional-infliction-of-emotional-distress claim. Second, any time newsgathering and presumably actual news coverage fails in a judge's or jury's mind to "show good taste" and merely panders to "lurid curiosity," the subject of that news coverage will have a valid claim. Third, even someone who is a public prosecutor, a man who was once elected to his post and who had previously run for judge, should be considered a "private person" who has a right to "control information" about himself.

Finally, and perhaps most troubling, the court implied that a news item's newsworthiness should be determined by public "need" as opposed to public "interest"—and that the arrest of a public prosecutor on child sex solicitation charges would not necessarily fit into the former category. If the standard becomes one of "need," the definition for legally acceptable news becomes much narrower. Perhaps the public needs to know about matters involving government and schools and war and the environment and other weighty news items. But convincing a court that the public needs to know about arrests, members of Congress who send nude photos to younger Facebook friends, or even celebrity marriages would indeed be a challenge.

Conradt, therefore, turns traditional media law on its head by holding that coverage of a public official's arrest could indeed be the basis for tort liability because it potentially had made the public official feel bad. Not surprisingly, that legal outcome has also led to copycat cases in other jurisdictions, filed by men who had been outed on the *To Catch a Predator* series. Three of the claims were at least initially successful.[39] The *Conradt* case itself settled just after the trial court judge released his decision and, therefore, never reached a jury.

But even if such cases are eventually dismissed or eventually settled, they have the very real potential to change journalistic practices. A media attorney might now tell journalists to be cautious about reporting arrests, even an arrest of a public official. After all, there is good reason to be cautious if the liability standard is that a news item caused the subject "discomfort" or if it might be considered in bad taste or if there arguably is little public "need" for the information.

After the *Conradt* decision and its focus on ethics, the Society of Professional Journalists quickly moved to add a statement to its code in an attempt to ward off similar lawsuits: "The code is intended not as a set of 'rules' but as a resource for ethical decision-making," the statement reads. "It is not—nor can it be under the First Amendment—legally enforceable."

It is unlikely, however, that the same judges who criticize journalism as the sort of profession that will "not give up the value of sensationalism and the profit of the hunt and the smear" and who compare journalists to snapping jackals, motivated by sensationalism and newspaper sales[40] will abide by the SPJ's self-serving legal advice.

The Blagojevich Decision and Beyond

What all of this shows—from the Hulk Hogan sex tape to teenagers' use of Facebook to push-the-envelope programming—is that we live in an age of over-exposure, at times bombarded with images and information once considered inappropriate for public consumption. Related changes in media— Gawker's decision to publish the tape, for example, or the *New York Times'* allowance of salacious comments after an appropriately ethical news story or *To Catch a Predator*'s close work with a vigilante group and police in arresting child sex predators—help fuel a sense that something must be done before all individual privacy is threatened and society as we know it crumbles. Now, journalists, whomever they are, seemingly cannot be trusted to make the right news decisions, and, in turn, the First Amendment and other journalistic legal tools are proving not to be as effective a shield or sword as they once were.

The chapters that follow chart this new age. They first explore the past, when media was at its peak and powerful protections followed. They then look to the present, a time when state and federal courts alike seem to be changing the course of constitutional and other legal protections, many times in the name of privacy. They examine the trouble with media, both mainstream journalism that pushes the envelope in a seeming effort to compete, and far-from-mainstream publications with little internal or external ethical restrictions. Later chapters argue that, because of these media practices, because of our over-exposure society, and because many legal arguments made by media are wrapped in a First Amendment framework despite appalling underlying media wrongs, traditional First Amendment protections vital to a robust press are in danger. Finally, the book ends with a call for change both in the law and in media practices—and argues that that is the only way we can prevent the burst of what has become a fragile First Amendment bubble.

At this book's heart, accordingly, is the backlash that Judge Mikva warned of in the mid-1990s: that irresponsible journalism was leading to a perceived need for changes in media-protective First Amendment doctrine. A related decision from Judge Mikva's home state of Illinois seems an appropriate full-circle end to this overview chapter.

The underlying case[41] was the criminal trial of former Illinois governor Rod Blagojevich, charged with attempting to gain personal benefit from the nomination to a vacant U.S. Senate seat. Breaking with tradition, the judge hearing the case, James Zagel, decided that no jurors' names or identifying information would be released to media until after the verdict. Mainstream media, including the *Chicago Tribune* and the *New York Times,* however, argued that they had a First Amendment right to access to a criminal trial and that the judge had no justification for keeping the names from them. But Judge Zagel disagreed in an opinion that tightens the reins of the press in the name of privacy.

First, Judge Zagel noted the difference in technology today and what he called astoundingly ubiquitous social networking websites that have great capacity to insult and could well lead to jurors' worry that their privacy had been invaded. "There is little precedent involving the unique circumstances surrounding this case," he wrote, "against a relatively new backdrop of public openness via blogs, electronic communication, and social networking sites." In doing so, he suggested that there would be a difference between the more controlled mainstream media that had filed the request and bloggers with different senses of ethics and decorum, including those who would use the trial simply "to be noticed." In response to assurances that the journalists would limit coverage of jurors if their names were released as requested, Judge Zagel explained that the mainstream journalists "do not speak for or represent all media" and suggested that some publishers would act differently.

Second, the judge had very real complaints about the mainstream press and about the "potential transformation" it had of turning jurors' personal lives into "public news." He grouped all media when he complained about modern, sometimes distasteful news judgment: "There is little emphasis today in media or entertainment on the notion of withholding judgment until all the facts are in," he wrote, pointing to a CNN poll from summer of 2010 of its viewers about how to stop the BP oil spill and a who-done-it poll from a so-called citizen journalism website regarding teenager Natalie Holloway's presumed murder. In contrast, the judge wrote, "[t]here seem to be few requests for public input on more obscure issues such as arms treaties and city parks," criticizing mainstream news judgment in a way that was utterly unnecessary to his underlying decision about the release of jurors' names.

Third, the press intervenors in the case attempted to cloak themselves with the First Amendment in a somewhat novel way that harkened back to journalism's golden age in which *Washington Post* reporters brought down a corrupt presidential administration. The press intervenors argued that if they were given the names of jurors in advance, they could then play a "watchdog" role in ferreting out wrongdoing by these jurors, presumably revealing conflicts of interest that the jurors had failed to identify to the court and serving almost as an investigative arm of the judiciary. The argument, a curious one given the judge's concerns about jurors' privacy, failed to impress the court.

Finally, it was clear that the judge's own sense of a loss of privacy contributed to his decision to protect the jurors. Throughout the opinion, Judge Zagel shared that his privacy had been invaded by phone calls, emails, and letters from the public springing from the case. "On one occasion," the judge wrote, "I was stopped on the street by a member of the public, who[m] I did not recognize, and advised" about what to consider in the underlying case. It is striking that the judge invoked his own experience of privacy loss in deciding to protect the jurors—this is surely happening in other media privacy cases today but often goes unstated. It is also striking because this judge suggested broadly that public figures in business, politics, sports, and entertainment "overwhelmingly . . . avoid the public," even shunning social media; the judge's own sense of privacy, therefore, may well be stronger than that of many in the public eye who actively trade on their celebrity.

According to one journalist mentioned in the case, then, for nearly the first time in his thirty five years of experience in journalism, a court had refused to give jurors' names to media—and all very much in the name of privacy.

In that one decision, we see the shift toward privacy in the courts, the fallibility of the First Amendment arguments today, the distrust judges have regarding media and technology, how some push-the-envelope media can potentially ruin access for all, and how judges' own senses of privacy help shape law in cases put before them. In other words, the *Blagojevich* case shows the limits on news and information that arise today in our age of over-exposure and that privacy is winning out over traditional First Amendment arguments.

It was not always this way.

2

Legal Protections for News and Truthful Information: The Past

The cover of the June 1940 edition of *Headquarters Detective: True Cases from the Police Blotter* magazine features a pale young woman bound to a chair. Her eyes are wide and her mouth is open as if terrified at what she sees off-cover. One of the straps of her tight, flimsy nightgown has fallen down her arm, making it seem as though her left breast will soon be exposed. The cover is mostly black and white, save for two red-highlighted articles: "Trailing the Tourist Camp Killers!" and "Slave to a Love Cult." Articles inside are head-lined "Murder in the AIR!," the story of what is alleged to be the first killing onboard an airplane, and "GIRLS' REFORMATORY," an exposé that reveals that even those girls who "came in there decent" left with "all the vices of the underworld." Many photographs inside the magazine feature scantily clad women-in-trouble but the most striking are those of the dead bodies of real-life crime victims, some in shockingly close-up detail.

Headquarters Detective was clearly one of the very first push-the-envelope publications, the precursor to today's reality crime efforts such as the television programs *Cops* and *The First 48* and the coverage one might find in tabloids like the *New York Post*. It is doubtful, however, that even the most strident of mainstream television programs, magazines, or newspapers today would publish the random bloodied dead body photos that appear to be a key part of *Headquarters Detective* magazine.

And yet, as the Supreme Court would decide in 1948, such sensationalism in news is perfectly fine in a constitutional sense.

That particular copy of *Headquarters Detective* had reached the Supreme Court after a bookseller in New York was convicted of a misdemeanor for selling it. Such a sale violated a New York statute that prohibited sales of any publication "principally made up of criminal news, police reports, or accounts of criminal deeds, or pictures, or stories of bloodshed, lust, or crime."[1] The June 1940 edition of the magazine was clearly that. A New York appeals court accurately described it as "a collection of stories that portray in vivid fashion tales of vice, murder, and intrigue . . . embellished with pictures of fiendish and gruesome crimes . . . besprinkled with lurid photographs of victims and perpetrators."

Though based on real-life crimes and related tales, the publication and sales of such magazines, a lower appellate court had decided, "tend to demoralize the minds of their more impressionable readers." For the betterment of society, its "general welfare" and "morals," the lower court held that the law forbidding sales of *Headquarters Detective* and its ilk was a perfectly constitutional use of the state's police power. To that court, freedom of the press was trumped by the state's interest in protecting its citizens from such mind-numbing licentiousness.

New York's highest court agreed.[2] Such magazines, filled with real-life "details of heinous wrongdoing," appealed to a certain segment of the public that needed guidance, the court decided, and the statute merely served to maintain public order and stop the corruption of their and others' public morals. The First Amendment, for its part, in the court's mind, did not protect the truthful lewdness that was *Headquarters Detective*.

With three strikes against it, the issue of the magazine featuring the bound woman with her mouth agape made its way to the U.S. Supreme Court. The Justices, however, saw things differently: they struck down the statute that had criminalized it.[3] In doing so, they both questioned and celebrated the *Headquarters Detective* family of publications. "Though we can see nothing of any possible value to society in these magazines," the Justices in the majority wrote, "they are as much entitled to the protection of free speech as the best of literature." Over the dissenting opinion of three Justices who argued that statutory prohibitions against mischief-making publications help solve societal problems, a majority of the Court decided that statutes like the one in New York were unconstitutional and that courts could not, in a constitutional sense, decide for all of society what is appropriate reading and what is not.

That decision from 1948 was one of the first indications that modern courts would look more favorably on truthful publications that push the envelope, even over arguments that public minds, public morals, and good taste were at stake. It marked what might be called a shift in the law, as up to that point, courts had more often condemned media for its immorality and bad influence. Now, even publications that arguably did not move society forward in any way and, in fact, reveled in its brutality, deserved the same level of protection as highbrow publications.

Headquarters Detective: True Cases From the Police Blotter would likely have received a far more skeptical look from the Court just fifty years before, when Justice Henry Brown sat on the bench.

Justice Brown and "The Right to Privacy"

In 1900, Justice Henry Brown, a former federal trial court judge from Michigan who had been appointed to the U.S. Supreme Court in 1890, gave a talk before the New York State Bar Association. In it, he railed against the press, its "ugly stories" and its sensationalism. Headlines about his lecture from the *Washington Post* read:

SCORES YELLOW PRESS

Justice Brown Denounces Sensational Papers

PUBLIC MEN ARE AT THEIR MERCY[4]

"[W]e are confronted by the fact that in this free country there has grown up a despotic, irresponsible power," Justice Brown maintained during his speech in front of the New York attorneys, "which holds our reputations completely at its mercy." That despotic power was the journalism of the day. His complaints about the press were many: that newspapers used sensational stories to drum up readership, that reporters seemed determined to investigate private domestic scandals, that they were especially inspired to report on politicians using unseemly undercover methods, and more. The *Post* seemed to want to distance itself from Justice Brown's criticism, suggesting that he had condemned not the *Post* but only those newspapers "of a certain class." Justice Brown's anti-media remarks appear not so limited.

Some of his complaints are surprising, especially those focused on what today we have come to accept as mundane. "The next step in [the newspapers'] downward career was the illustrations," he said, apparently in all seriousness, "and such illustrations!" He found troubling those newspapers that published "[p]ictures of current events" and "sudden deaths." Some of the worst offenders, however, were the publications he called "the weekly Sunday morning editions," bemoaning that, unlike the learned population, "the great mass of the American people are so imperfectly educated as to take pleasure in these abortions of the engravers' art." Indeed, a recent book filled with Sunday newspaper pages from the late 1800s shows how colorful the stories were, both literally and figuratively. One article published in color, "A Page of Eyes," asks the reader to match certain public figures' eyes with similar and personality-revealing animal eyes and another, captioned "Large Purses and Little Men," shows politicians being lifted by wings made of bags of money.[5]

But Justice Brown found what he called "assaults upon private character" the most egregious of the press's licentious ways at the turn of the century, labeling such assaults "cruelties, for no other word in the English language will adequately express the nature of these attacks."

It was obviously a time in which newspapers were growing and concerns about the press, especially among the elite in the United States like Justice Brown, were growing right along with them.

It is not clear what motivated Justice Brown to feel so strongly about newspapers that he would condemn them so completely in a public speech while a sitting Justice. He, like a majority of the other Justices, seemed to become of interest to the press only upon his nomination to the high court. Many newspapers covered his judicial work at least somewhat objectively, even though he wrote the majority opinion in *Plessy v. Ferguson*, one that upheld separate-but-equal accommodations. Newspapers may have overstepped their bounds on a few occasions, however, reporting that he had once killed a burglar who had entered his bedroom, or noting in a feature article that he and his wife were apparently unable to have children and that she was in declining health, or reporting that he had joked in a public forum when his wife was ill that riding with a mother-in-law at a wife's funeral would take the fun out of the occasion.[6] The newspapers of the day had also reported on the drinking and gambling habits of certain unnamed Justices and their wives, and this information surely would have implicated Brown even if his behavior were beyond reproach. Such coverage of the people of the Court could well have helped to spark Justice Brown's outrage.

But it is also possible that Justice Brown was inspired at least in part by a law review article titled "The Right to Privacy," a piece published in 1890 that parallels nearly exactly what Brown would argue ten years later. The article is, perhaps, the most famous law review article ever written in the United States—and its antipress rhetoric is just as strong as Justice Brown's. Its arguments were published as Brown ascended to the high bench and were gaining some traction in courtrooms when Brown spoke to the New York Bar ten years later.

Like Brown, the two authors of the Harvard Law Review piece, Boston lawyer Samuel Warren and his law partner, Louis Brandeis (who would later be appointed to the Supreme Court), had similar problems with "the evil of the invasion of privacy by the newspapers" and worried, like Brown, that the press was "overstepping in every direction the obvious bounds of propriety and of decency."[7]

Also like Brown, Samuel Warren, thought to be the article's primary author, had suffered the personal indignity of press coverage. He had married the daughter of a U.S. senator who would become secretary of state under Grover Cleveland, and Warren's wedding was covered in great detail by all major newspapers. Shortly after the wedding, Mrs. Warren's mother and sister had died within weeks of each other and precise details of the family's grief and blame for the daughter's illness was reported in newspapers such as the *Washington Post* and the *New York Times*.[8] Moreover, Mrs. Warren was friendly with Mrs. Grover Cleveland, the very young woman who had once been the president's "charge," and the press had reported on their scandalous relationship, wedding, and honeymoon in such detail that Cleveland himself complained of the "ghoulish glee" with which reporters desecrated "every sacred relation of private life." Surely, Warren, whose father-in-law was in the Cleveland administration and whose wife was a friend of the First Lady, felt first-hand and otherwise that the press had overstepped its bounds. In other words, there were many personal reasons for Samuel Warren to co-author "The Right to Privacy."

The law review article itself is filled with antipress rhetoric and many passages have become famous in their own right: "Gossip is no longer the resource of the idle and of the vicious, but has become a trade, which is pursued with industry as well as effrontery," the authors wrote, and "[t]o satisfy a prurient taste the details of sexual relations are spread broadcast in the columns of the daily papers" and "[t]o occupy the indolent, column upon column is filled with idle gossip, which can only be procured by intrusion upon the domestic circle" and "[e]ach crop of unseemly gossip, thus harvested, [belittles and perverts and] becomes the seed of more, and, in direct proportion to its circulation, results in a lowering of social standards and of morality." Such triviality, the authors argued, destroyed robustness of thought in ignorant and unsuspecting readers, crowding out items that the authors believed were ones "of real interest to the community." "No enthusiasm can flourish, no generous impulse can survive under its blighting influence," the authors maintained, in a world where "[i]nstantaneous photographs and newspaper enterprise have invaded the sacred precincts of private and domestic life; and numerous mechanical devices threaten to make good the prediction that 'what is whispered in the closet shall be proclaimed from the house-tops.'"

Their idea, one that was arguably not so novel in U.S. jurisprudence or elsewhere,[9] was that the law should embrace the so-called right to privacy, a tort that would allow those wronged to sue newspapers and others that had invaded their right to be let alone by publishing private information about them and their families. Like Justice Brown, "The Right to Privacy" authors worried about "the right to protect one's self from pen portraiture" and argued, perhaps based upon President Cleveland's real-life complaints, that even public figures should be able to keep their "private life, habits, acts, and relations" private.

The article reads as a condemnation of the press with a related conviction that the elite would be the best judges of what would be appropriate reading and news coverage for the masses, lest little minds go wasting. Ten years later, Justice Brown would refuse to go that far, but it was clear that the late 1800s and early 1900s was a time when journalism faced sharp criticism. And some of the sharpest and most influential barbs came from the bench and bar.

The Restatement and William Prosser

It is safe to say that the Warren/Brandeis/Brown ideal, in which the law would come down hard on scandal-mongering newspapers and protect privacy at nearly all costs, never really caught on that strongly in the United States. If one person were to thank for that, it would be William Prosser, the former dean of the law school at the University of California at Berkeley.

In 1960, Dean Prosser gathered all the privacy cases he could find that had been reported in the United States after the 1890 publication of "The Right to Privacy" and used them to write perhaps the second most important law review article ever published regarding privacy, titled simply "Privacy."[10] In it,

Prosser grouped the cases into four categories and argued that these were the four different privacy torts that had been recognized by then-modern courts: misappropriation (the use of someone's identity without permission, usually in advertising); intrusion (the peering in on someone in private or someone's private personal papers without permission); false light (the reporting of incorrect information about someone that both is offensive and portrays them in a false light); and publication of private facts (the offensive revelation in a newspaper or otherwise of private information regarding a person).

Publication of private facts is most like the tort suggested by Warren and Brandeis and Justice Brown: a right to sue a newspaper for invasion of privacy even though the information that was published was true. At last, even though such a legal idea had been around for decades, the wrong was an identified legal right, it had a scope, and it had a name.

A few years later, Prosser played another key role in the tort's history: defining in even greater detail and to a greater audience the publication-of-private-facts tort in a way that clearly limited the ability of plaintiffs to prevail in a cause of action against a publisher. Prosser was the reporter in charge of the second edition of the Restatement of Torts, a highly influential encyclopedia-like publication drafted by some of the nation's best legal minds, and used as highly persuasive authority by many courts. Prosser was skeptical about the constitutionality of the publication-of-private-facts tort and used language in the Restatement that limited its use. This language would later become law in many jurisdictions when courts generally adopted it and those of Prosser's three additional privacy torts verbatim.

The first Restatement, one drafted without Prosser's strong hand and published in 1939, had created a single "Interference with Privacy" tort and had suggested that a person who "unreasonably and seriously" interfered with another person's interest in "not having his affairs known" was liable for a privacy invasion, especially when the information involved intimate details or an embarrassing photograph taken without permission. "A distinction can be made for news items," was the conditional protective factor regarding journalism,[11] though the authors offered no real guidance beyond that.

The Second Restatement, in contrast, and very much in line with Prosser's "Privacy" article, offers much more explicit and significant protection for journalists who publish another's personal information. The tort is defined in a way that highlights the value of news:

One who gives publicity to a matter concerning the private life of another is subject to liability to the other for invasion of his privacy, if the matter publicized is of a kind that

    (a) would be highly offensive to a reasonable person, and

    (b) is not of legitimate concern to the public.[12]

In other words, a plaintiff who wishes to sue a publication for publishing private facts about her must show both that the revelation would be offensive to a reasonable person and that the revelation itself was not newsworthy.

The latter has proved to be a great burden to plaintiffs. Despite language within the tort's definition suggesting that only information "of legitimate concern to the public" is appropriate, the accompanying influential comments move decidedly away from a word like "concern" and replace it literally or figuratively with phrases like "public interest" and "popular appeal." Under the Restatement, then, news is not only information of public "concern" or information that the public "needs" to know, but it includes matters in which the public is merely interested and finds appealing.

Expanding the definition for newsworthiness even more, the current Restatement suggests that journalists themselves decide what is lawful news through their editorial decisions and that "a glance at any morning paper will confirm" what coverage is appropriate. More concrete Restatement examples of newsworthy stories include those regarding "homicide and other crimes, arrests, police raids, suicides, marriages and divorces, accidents, fires, catastrophes of nature, a death from the use of narcotics, a rare disease, the birth of a child to a twelve-year-old girl, the reappearance of one supposed to have been murdered years ago, [and] a report to the police concerning the escape of a wild animal." A story that includes photographs taken at the scene of an accident or a story that incorporates a report about a wife's witness to her husband's murder, while privacy-invading for those involved, is considered lawfully newsworthy under the Restatement. Such stories, the authors suggest, are of "more or less deplorable popular appeal," and, therefore, cannot be the basis for an invasion-of-privacy claim. According to the Restatement, valid news stops only at stories that involve "morbid and sensational prying for its own sake," a phrase that is given little definition.

Moreover, the Restatement gives journalists the right to report private information regarding voluntary and involuntary public figures with greater abandon, even when the information would otherwise be the basis for a successful privacy claim. "These persons are regarded as properly subject to the public interest, and publishers are permitted to satisfy the curiosity of the public as to its heroes, leaders, villains, and victims, and those who are closely associated with them," the Restatement reads. "Thus, the life history of one accused of murder, together with such heretofore private facts as may throw some light upon what kind of person he is, his possible guilt or innocence, or his reasons for committing the crime" are of legitimate public interest, as are "the home life and daily habits of a motion picture actress. . . ." Morbid and sensational prying under those circumstances, then, seems to be limited mostly to details about public figures' sex lives.

In other words, Prosser's Restatement, still in use in 2014, defines news extraordinarily broadly and in a way that has made it extremely difficult for a public figure or even a private figure to win a case against media.

The Supreme Court and Its Laudatory Language

As Prosser was helping to develop a highly influential version of the privacy torts, one that favored the press through a broad definition of what was news-worthy, the Supreme Court seemed to be unintentionally hammering away at the second point in "The Right to Privacy," that news media was out of control and needed to be stopped, preferably through law.

The period of the 1960s and 1970s was, of course, a golden age for journalism. The book and film *All the President's Men* glamorized the journalists who had uncovered Watergate misdeeds. Courageous news coverage of the Civil Rights Movement inspired many to take up the cause of equality. And the United States learned of the real costs of the war in Vietnam through the eyes and pens of the brave who reported from the front lines. When the Restatement authors wrote in 1977 that news "of more or less deplorable popular appeal" was appropriate, it was likely with that sort of journalism and those sorts of journalists in mind.

The Supreme Court, too, seemed perhaps at least somewhat inspired by courageous journalists and journalism in many cases in the years that followed the *Headquarters Detective* case. Privacy law scholar Neil Richards has called this the Supreme Court's "project of giving the First Amendment preemptive force over tort law."[13] In *New York Times v. Sullivan*,[14] the groundbreaking case from 1964 that decided that publishers could be protected from lawsuits stemming from inaccuracies, for example, the court wrote that there was a "profound national commitment to the principle that debate on public issues should be uninhibited, robust, and wide-open" and would necessarily include the press's "vehement, caustic, and sometimes unpleasantly sharp attacks on government and public officials." Without such protections, the Justices wrote, First Amendment freedoms would not have the necessary "breathing space" to survive, and a harsh decision would lead to a "pall of fear and timidity," "an atmosphere in which the First Amendment freedoms cannot survive." The "general proposition," the Court explained, is "that freedom of expression upon public questions is secured by the First Amendment" and that courts must protect some harmful inaccuracies to help grow the confident, robust newsrooms that are central to democracy.

That same year, the Justices held even more explicitly that news about public officials is of special importance and deserved protection: There is a "paramount public interest in a free flow of information to the people concerning public officials, their servants," the Court explained, "[and] [t]o this end, anything which might touch on an official's fitness for office [is] relevant" to public discourse, including "dishonesty, malfeasance, or improper motivation, even though these characteristics may also affect the official's private character."[15] (The *Conradt* court did not mention that decision when it upheld the intentional-infliction-of-emotional-distress claim involving the lawbreaking prosecutor.)

Three years later, in *Time v. Hill*,[16] the Court wrote that "[a] broadly defined freedom of the press assur[ed] the maintenance of our political system and an open society" and that journalists should not be saddled with verifying all information in stories lest it "create a grave risk of serious impairment of the indispensable service of a free press in a free society." Moreover, the Court lessened privacy's significance: "Exposure of the self to others in varying degrees is a concomitant of life in a civilized community," the Court wrote, and "[t]he risk of this exposure is an essential incident of life in a society which places a primary value on freedom of speech and press."

In 1971, the Court specifically opined that news meant many things and could "contain an almost infinite variety of shadings."[17] In 1974, it wrote that government should never exercise control over the choices of what goes into a newspaper because government regulation of the "crucial process" of editorial judgment could not be impeded "consistent with First Amendment guarantees of a free press."[18] "A responsible press is an undoubtedly desirable goal," the Justices noted, "but press responsibility is not mandated by the Constitution and like many other virtues it cannot be legislated."

The idea that courts could not control coverage extended into highly secretive, highly important, and highly private matters. In *New York Times v. United
States*,[19] the Pentagon Papers case, the Supreme Court held that the First
Amendment trumped government concerns about the publication of war documents. In *Nebraska Press Association v. Stuart*, the Justices refused to draft a
code of appropriate conduct for journalists, even in cases where the right to a
fair trial was at issue and even though they recognized media excessiveness in
cases involving scandal.[20] Even when a juvenile offender had been outed by
name and photograph, the Justices refused to step in,[21] later explaining that
the state interest in First Amendment free press protections trumped the right
of a juvenile offender to remain unnamed.[22] And in 1978, the Court overturned a newspaper's conviction for reporting on secret judicial proceedings,
finding that the public interest in the topic and related First Amendment
interests exceeded any state interest in keeping judicial affairs secret.[23] "State
action to punish the publication of truthful information seldom can satisfy
constitutional standards," the Court reminded in 1979.[24] As for liability based
upon violations of journalism ethics standards, the Court held that even an
extreme violation of such standards could not alone prove the actual malice
necessary in a defamation case.[25] The Court also held that plaintiffs could not
style their otherwise presumptively unconstitutional defamation cases as more
easily won intentional-infliction-of-emotional-distress cases consistent with
First Amendment free press protections.[26]

The Court may have made clearest its feelings regarding deference to journalists in *Gertz v. Robert Welch, Inc.*, a case it decided in 1974. Regarding the
question of "which publications address issues of 'general or public interest'
and which do not," the Justices wrote that they doubted "the wisdom of committing this task to the conscience of judges."[27] Ten years later, the Court
added legislators to the list of those it doubted could constitutionally decide
what news is appropriate.[28]

In terms of press access to public documents and trials, too, the Court
stressed the importance of an open government and the role of the press in
information dissemination to the public. "It is clear that the courts of this
country recognize a general right to inspect and copy public records and documents, including judicial records and documents," the Court wrote in 1978.[29]
Trials, meanwhile, the Justices noted, had always been open and such openness
was an "indispensable attribute" of court proceedings in the United States
based upon First Amendment guarantees, also stressing that the importance

that public discussion regarding court proceedings be informed.[30] Such access, they explained, allowed a concerned public to follow a shocking crime through the criminal process, providing an important outlet for understandable community concerns.

The two cases that perhaps best show the Court's First Amendment free press sensibilities involve crime coverage and were decided by the Court in 1975 and 1989. In *Cox v. Cohn*[31] and *Florida Star v. B.J.F.*,[32] the media defendants had published the names of crime victims—in *Cox*, the name of a rape and murder victim, and in *Florida Star*, the name of a living rape victim—in violation of newspaper ethics provisions and victim-protective state statutes. Nonetheless, in both, the Justices decided in favor of the media defendants over the privacy-related causes of action brought by the quite sympathetic plaintiffs. In both, the Court worried that press timidity and self-censorship would result from a too-restrictive law that prohibited the publication of truthful information, especially when the information was a part of official government records. "[W]here a newspaper publishes truthful information which it has lawfully obtained," the Court wrote in *Florida Star*, "punishment may lawfully be imposed, if at all, only when narrowly tailored to a state interest of the highest order." Protection of rape victims, like protection of juvenile offenders, then, seemingly failed to reach that extraordinary threshold.

It is important to note, however, that despite the protective and laudatory press language in many of those cases, the U.S. Supreme Court has never decided directly at what point personal privacy interests trump press freedoms. The closest it came was in *Cox* and *Florida Star*, but the Court both times expressly limited its holdings to the scenarios in front of it.

The fact that the Court's decisions regarding news value, then, were "narrow"—and that the Justices repeatedly stressed as much—would become important in later years.

The Result: The Press Trumps Privacy

Even before the *Florida Star* case was handed down by the Supreme Court, as a result of the Restatement language and the strongly press-supportive outcome in *Cox*, media law scholar Diane Zimmerman predicted the death of the publication-of-private-facts tort in a law review article she titled "Requiem for a Heavyweight: A Farewell to Warren and Brandeis's Privacy Tort,"[33] one that would be cited by multiple scholars in the years to come as some evidence of the tort's demise. It was indeed a time in which a strong press seemed strongly protected from liability, especially for publishing truthful information: the Supreme Court had repeatedly linked newspapers with doing important work, the Restatement had defined news in a very broad and accommodating way, and journalism itself had had a public relations boost from Watergate and other impressive news coverage.

This golden age for journalism and for media's lawyers is also shown by the extreme deference lower state and federal courts often showed news media throughout the period, sometimes in especially surprising cases. As a federal appeals court would put it in 1974, echoing language from the Supreme Court, "[t]he first amendment makes clear that it is beyond the competency of any government agency to determine . . . that any item of information is, for any news medium, not news."[34] News, therefore, meant for some courts whatever news media said it was, perfectly in line with what the Restatement suggested.

Four cases, two from each coast, help show just how broad the word "news" had become in a legal sense.

Example One: A Free Press and the Teen Model

The advice column in *YM* magazine, a publication for teenaged girls, was titled "Love Crisis" and, as one might imagine given its audience, the "love" modifier seemed exaggerated at times. The 1995 June/July edition, for example, featured a letter from someone who called herself "Mortified." She explained that she was just fourteen and had had sex with her eighteen-year-old boy-friend and two of his friends while drunk—or, as the pull quote from the advice column screamed in large typeface "I got trashed and had sex with three guys." The column's expert, an editor at *YM*, suggested that the young teen "face the facts" about her "pretty big mistake," get a pregnancy test, and refuse to hide even though the encounter had become the talk of the town.

Turns out that "Mortified" was not an anguished teen at all. The letter's author and the scenario itself were apparently figments of an editor's imagina-tion; the editor had come up with her own version of what a teen might ask and had published the question using a teen's voice.

And there was even more fiction published within the piece. The girl whose photographs were sprinkled within the column's copy was a fifteen-year-old model who would later explain to news reporters that, in a somewhat parallel turn of events, her classmates had found the column and, inspired by it, yelled profanities at her and posted at school the relevant magazine page with the word "whore" scrawled across it.[35] Those classmates apparently believed that she was "Mortified." She was: in the lowercase sense.

The images published as a part of the column were provocative. One featured the teenager hiding her face from a group of boys. A second pictured her looking anguished at herself in a mirror. In the third—the largest—she appears in a negligee, robe falling from her shoulder, hair and blankets tousled. She would later explain that she posed for the images because she had hoped that one of the photos might make the cover.

The teenage model sued *YM* under a New York statute that makes it a violation to use another's image without permission, a law that also made an exception for newsworthy items. The magazine, therefore, argued that the statute did not apply because the column and accompanying photographs concerned matters of public interest—teen sex and pregnancy—and had a reasonable relationship link to the news article itself. Skeptical jurors heard the case and awarded the teenager $100,000.[36]

The magazine appealed, once again suggesting that it was protected under New York law because the photographs and article themselves were newsworthy. The model argued that because the column was fictionalized and because it implied that she was "Mortified," the newsworthiness exception did not apply.

New York's highest court responded in a way that protected the newsworthiness of the piece despite its fictionalized nature.[37] Newsworthiness was to be "broadly construed," the court decided, newsworthy articles did not necessarily need to be "hard" news, and a publisher's interest in drumming up interest and sales of its magazine had no relevance to the underlying claim. Here, the column was newsworthy in that it was "informative and educational regarding teenage sex, alcohol abuse and pregnancy—plainly matters of public concern." "[T]he use of a photograph to illustrate a newsworthy article does not state a claim . . . regardless of any false impression created by the photograph," the court wrote, "so long as the article is not an advertisement and there is a real relationship between the photograph and the article." Such a decision, it explained, was consistent with the constitutional value of "uninhibited discussion of newsworthy topics even though a photograph may be seen as falsifying the plaintiff's relationship to the underlying article."

Even though the teenager pictured in the column, then, had testified that she had been harmed significantly by the use of the photographs to illustrate the column and even though the column itself seemed to be created out of whole cloth by editors at the magazine, New York's Court of Appeals deferred to the constitutional notion of a free press and the newsworthiness of the general topic at issue. "The [new] paradigm for editors is a 'newsworthy' homily to lovesick adolescents or any other audience," one judge wrote in dissent, "they then just have to use a journalistic conceit of tying the advice to a purported letter to the editor." The judge found that "not fair or right."

But journalists had persuaded New York's highest court that newsworthiness trumped individual privacy rights even when the news story at issue and its photographs were fictionalized.

Example Two: A Free Press and the Psychiatric Patient

In 1988, Pamela J. Howell was a patient at a private psychiatric facility in Westchester County, New York. Her stay there was secret—only her immediate family members knew—and her recovery, it was said, depended upon such secrecy. An unrelated fellow patient at the facility, Hedda Nussbaum, had become infamous for her alleged involvement in the death of a six-year-old child and the crime had attracted considerable press attention.

One day, Howell and Nussbaum took a walk on the grounds of the psychiatric facility. Nussbaum was well-coiffed and dressed in jeans and Howell wore clothing appropriate for tennis; both smiled as they walked. We know this because, unbeknownst to them, a photographer for the *New York Post* assigned the Nussbaum story had trespassed onto the facility's secluded grounds and had taken photographs of the two women using a telephoto lens. The facility found out about the enterprising press intruder and had asked that no photographs of patients be used. The *Post* nonetheless published a photograph of Howell and Nussbaum, pointing out some changes in Nussbaum's appearance and suggesting that "her face and mind are healing."

Howell's name was not mentioned in the photo's caption or within the accompanying story, but she was easily recognizable. As a patient who wished and needed for rehabilitative purposes to keep her hospitalization secret, she sued the newspaper on privacy and intentional-infliction-of-emotional-distress grounds. The *Post*, after all, had been warned by doctors not to publish photographs of private psychiatric patients.

New York's highest court, however, ruled that Howell could not prevail against the newspaper because First Amendment free press protections trumped whatever right to privacy she had in her treatment. Here, the court decided, despite the plaintiff's wishes for privacy, there was a real relationship between the news article about Hedda Nussbaum and the photograph of Nussbaum and Howell walking the grounds of the psychiatric facility. Therefore, the newsworthy photograph could not be the basis for any privacy claim.

As for the plaintiff's claims of intentional infliction of emotional distress, the court explained that the tort required outrageousness on the part of the newspaper, but held that the *Post's* behavior—trespassing onto a private psychiatric hospital's grounds and surreptitiously taking photographs of patients—did not even "remotely approach the required standard." The court did not explain why this was so even though medical treatment is generally one of the well-protected privacy areas, but noted that "the plaintiff was photographed outdoors and from a distance," which "diminish[ed] her claim even further."

In sum, the court explained that it was "reluctant to intrude upon reasonable editorial judgments" made by journalists. The case stands, then, as approving legally a reporter's trespass, photography, and publication of private medical information—all of which the *Post* defended successfully on newsworthiness grounds.[38]

Example Three: A Free Press and the Gay Hero

One of the most famous—or infamous—decisions showing courts' hesitation to second-guess media defendants is a 1984 California case brought by Oliver Sipple, a man who had saved President Gerald Ford from an assassination attempt.[39] Would-be assassin Sarah Jane Moore was in a crowd in San Francisco and aimed her gun at Ford, but Sipple acted quickly and knocked the gun away. News media at the time rightfully called him a hero.

After two days of coverage of the assassination attempt and Sipple's quick action, a columnist for the *San Francisco Chronicle* wrote that Sipple had since been "the center of attention" at the gay bar he favored and that Sipple was close with Harvey Milk and other gay activists. Additional newspapers picked up the story and reported more directly that Sipple was gay. The *Los Angeles Times*, for example, wrote that "[a] husky ex-marine who was a hero in the attempted assassination of President Ford emerged Wednesday as a prominent figure in the gay community." The newspapers also speculated that Sipple's sexual orientation was the reason that Ford had failed to thank him promptly.

Sipple, however, had not yet revealed his sexual orientation to many, and some family members were said to have abandoned him after reading the news reports. He sued the newspapers, arguing that they had published information regarding his private life and had caused him great mental anguish by doing so. The media responded that Sipple's sexual orientation was not private and, even if it were, that it was newsworthy that a gay man had saved President Ford in this way.

The California appeals court hearing the case on appeal after a trial court dismissal also ruled in favor of media. First it noted the "constitutional dimensions" of the case springing from First Amendment press freedoms and restated the Supreme Court warnings of the "chilling effect" an adverse decision would have on media. For those reasons, it found the trial court's decision to get rid of the case on a preliminary motion appropriate.

It also found the trial court's ultimate decision in the case appropriate. Sipple had frequented gay bars and gay areas of San Francisco; he was Harvey Milk's friend and their friendship had been reported in gay publications; he had marched in gay pride parades; and he would tell some people who asked that he was gay. Therefore, the court decided, Sipple's sexual orientation was not a private fact at all.

Given that decision, the court did not need to weigh the newsworthiness of the matter, but it did, and in a strikingly pro-media way. The newsworthiness of any article, the court wrote, hinged on the public's legitimate interest in the information and the current state of community mores. Here, the court found "legitimate public considerations" at stake, including questions about President Ford's potentially homophobic response and the work that the newspaper had done in "dispel[ling] the false public opinion that gays were timid, weak and unheroic figures." The court quoted with approval the way *Los Angeles Times* reporters had explained the news value of the story:

> First, since Sipple publicly performed a heroic act of national and international significance, reporting his connections to the gay community presented information contrary to the stereotype of homosexuals as lacking vigor—a concept apparently much desired to be reported by activist members of the San Francisco gay community. Second, the intimation that the President of the United States had refrained from expressing normal gratitude to an individual who perhaps had saved his life raised significant political and social issues as to whether the President entertained discriminatory attitudes toward a minority group, namely, homosexuals.

The court then reminded readers that when there is substantial legitimate public interest in a person, "a much greater intrusion into [his] private life will be sanctioned," even if the person is an involuntary public figure thrust onto the public stage by an act of bravery.

One man's privacy, then, the court decided, could be appropriately sacrificed for a growing of public knowledge: It was good for society that homophobes and others learned what Oliver Sipple considered private information—and society's interest was what mattered most.

Example Four: A Free Press and the Accident Victim

Involuntary public figures like Oliver Sipple are those who find themselves, through some trick of fate, involuntarily thrust onto a public stage. Ruth Shulman was also one of those persons, the unfortunate victim of a very serious automobile accident.

The California Supreme Court that would eventually decide Shulman's privacy case at first sounded understanding enough about her privacy concerns regarding push-the-envelope media.[40] "[T]oday's public discourse is particularly notable for its detailed and graphic discussion of intimate personal and family members," the court wrote after quoting "The Right to Privacy," "sometimes as simple titillation." But the court then immediately put itself in line with those courts that deferred to media: "The sense of an ever-increasing pressure on personal privacy notwithstanding," it wrote, "it has long been apparent that the desire for privacy must at many points give way before our right to know, and the news media's right to investigate and relate, facts about the events and individuals of our time."

Individuals like Ruth Shulman. Her serious accident in June 1990 would leave her with what a court described as permanent paralysis. Unfortunately for her, the medical helicopter team that arrived to treat her on scene and transport her to the hospital was working closely with reporters from *On Scene: Emergency Response,* a television program that tracked such treatment. The nurse at the crash site and in the rescue helicopter wore a small microphone; therefore, when Shulman told the nurse that the pain was so bad that she wanted to die, when she asked the nurse if she were dreaming, and when the nurse relayed Shulman's medical status to hospital personnel at the accident scene and inside the helicopter, it was all videotaped and recorded for potential use in the television program.

Shulman, in fact, was still in the hospital recuperating seven months later when a relative called to tell her that the accident was being featured that night on television. She would later say that she felt "shocked" and "exploited" by the program, one to which she said she had never consented and one that she did not want the public to see. She sued the producers for invasion of privacy.

The California Supreme Court put the issue this way: "At what point does the publishing or broadcasting of otherwise private words, expression and emotions cease to be protected by the press's constitutional and common law privilege—its right to report on matters of legitimate public interest—and become an unjustified, actionable invasion of the subject's private life?"

Not at Shulman's point, the court decided: The First Amendment's interest in newsworthiness trumped her right to privacy as a matter of law. A news item is newsworthy, the court wrote, "if some reasonable members of the community could entertain a legitimate interest in it." Here, it decided, there was an appropriate level of public interest in the accident scene itself and in the resulting rescue because others watching would someday be involved in similar accidents and would require the same sort of care.

The court also decided that Shulman's words were newsworthy as a matter of law, that her "confusion, pain and fear" made the nurse's measured actions all the more difficult and courageous and, therefore, of public interest. The standard was not whether the words themselves were necessary to the broadcast, the court explained, or whether the broadcast was distasteful to some, but whether there was a link to the news value at the heart of the story. "The challenged material," including video of Ruth's physical state and her disorientation and despair, the court decided, "was thus substantially related to the newsworthy subject matter of the broadcast and did not constitute a 'morbid and sensational prying into private lives for its own sake.'"

The *Shulman* court, like multiple others before it, explicitly worried not so much about Shulman's emotional harm, but about the chilling effect that second-guessing journalists' news judgment would have on newspersons' decisions as to what was appropriate news: "The courts do not, and constitutionally could not, sit as superior editors of the press," the California justices wrote. They could not become secondary news editors and "self-appointed guardians of public taste."

News, then, trumped privacy concerns, even in a situation in which a helpless and seriously injured accident victim was unknowingly speaking to the world when she thought she was speaking to her nurse alone.

A Free Press and Deferential Courts across the Nation

It wasn't just courts in New York and California that had decided that news value easily trumped privacy rights. A broad definition for newsworthiness— one that seemed to allow journalists to decide for themselves what was appropriate news—stretched across the United States, as did judicial opinions lauding expansive press freedoms.

The general idea was not new. Even in earlier years, before *New York Times v. Sullivan,* trial and appellate courts had frequently found, for example, that the news value in crime stories trumped privacy concerns. In Washington, D.C., a court held that those whose crimes had been previously reported by newspapers could not sue when those crimes were covered anew by the press or otherwise; "reasonable freedom of speech and press must be accorded and the fact of social intercourse must be recognized," the court held, worried that, otherwise, there could be no use of old newspapers for decorative or other purposes.[41] In Pennsylvania, a court held that coverage of a crime could not be the basis for a claim brought by surviving family members, even if the magazine made money off their plight through increased sales.[42] In South Carolina, a court rejected privacy implications in photos of arrestees; "[b]y the issuance of a warrant and the arrest of the plaintiffs, they became figures of public interest," the court held, and the public's right to know trumped any privacy concerns.[43] And in Connecticut, a court held that a surreptitious recording of a parole board hearing in a prison could not be the basis for a privacy claim because "prisoners are public figures in whose misadventures the community has a consuming interest" that trumps an inmate's right to privacy.[44]

In the 1970s, courts continued broad deference to news, even at times of individual vulnerability and otherwise. A Missouri court decided that a so-called "perp walk" wherein an arrestee was taken from a courthouse and recorded by television news reporters could not be the basis for a privacy claim; "complaints concerning crime and subsequent police action" are matters of appropriate public concern, the court decided, even though the arrestee was later released without being charged.[45] The surviving victims of a bridge collapse sued unsuccessfully in Ohio for invasion of privacy; "[o]nly in cases of flagrant breach of privacy . . . or obvious exploitation of public curiosity where no legitimate public interest exists should a court substitute its judgment for that of the publisher," the court wrote, finding that the historic review of the bridge collapse was not such a case.[46] And a federal appeals court hearing a case from New Jersey in which a regulation prevented lottery numbers from being broadcast wrote that "[t]he first amendment makes clear that it is beyond the competency of any governmental agency to determine . . . that any item of information is, for any news medium, not news."[47]

Around that same time, *Sports Illustrated* published a photograph of a male fan at a football game whose pants were unzipped. Even though the court noted that the journalists should have known that the photo would be offensive and embarrassing, it held that "courts are not concerned with establishing canons of good taste for the press or the public" and protected the photograph as constitutionally newsworthy.[48] And the Iowa Supreme Court decided that there was no privacy violation when a newspaper outed a woman who had undergone involuntary sterilization; the story was "investigative journalism," the court explained, refusing to impose its own views about appropriate community interest and finding that the newspaper had a "right" to name the young woman:

> In the sense of serving an appropriate news function, the disclosure contributed constructively to the impact of the article. It offered a personalized frame of reference to which the reader could relate, fostering perception and understanding. Moreover, it lent specificity and credibility to the report. In this way, the disclosure served as an effective means of accomplishing the intended news function. It had positive news value in attracting the reader's attention to the article's subject matter and in supporting expression of the underlying theme.[49]

The pro-media cases continued into the 1980s. A federal court in Washington, D.C., dismissed a privacy case brought by a surviving witness to a murder over the argument that it was too old to qualify as "news"; the court worried that First Amendment values would be threatened otherwise, suggested that news included "interesting phases of human activity," and wrote that "[f]reedom of speech would be crippled if discussion of matters of public interest were narrowly circumscribed."[50] In Colorado, a court found no valid privacy claim after a doctor facing a malpractice action was revealed by a newspaper as allegedly having psychological, marital, and other personal problems; "[i]f the press is to have the generous breathing space that courts have accorded it thus far, editors must have freedom to make reasonable judgments" the court wrote, calling it the newspaper's "editorial discretion." A Georgia soldier photographed in his underwear in an embarrassing way could not bring a privacy claim because prisoner-of-war training was newsworthy and the press required "breathing space."[51] In Florida, a woman pictured only wearing a dishtowel as she ran from a hostage situation had no privacy claim either; the photograph may have been in bad taste, the court decided, but it was "newsworthy" and "in the public interest" as "a typical exciting, emotion-packed drama to which newspeople, and others, are attracted."[52] A Louisiana court held that brothers who had lived upstanding lives despite an arrest twenty-five years before could not sue when a newspaper republished articles about their arrests as part of a history section.[53] "The compass of the First Amendment covers a vast spectrum of tastes, views, ideas and expressions," a court wrote in a newsworthiness case out of New York in which a celebrity brought a claim against a magazine that had published a misidentified nude photograph, and "[t]o hold otherwise would draw a tight noose around the throat of public discussion" on a topic of public interest, albeit a vulgar one.[54] Another New York court agreed: "Determining what editorial content is of legitimate public interest and concern is a function for editors," it wrote in a case involving coverage of a suicide, and "[t]he press, acting responsibly, and not the courts must make the ad hoc decisions as to what are matters of genuine public concern."[55] And the federal appeals court for Texas found that a rape victim whose name and home were used in a television news story had no valid privacy claim; "judges, acting with the benefit of hindsight," the court wrote, "must resist the temptation to edit journalists aggressively," suggesting that "[e]xuberant judicial blue-penciling after-the-fact would blunt the quills of even the most honorable journalists."[56]

That same decade, the Supreme Court of Oregon decided that a television news station could use videotape of an accident scene as part of an advertisement for news programming. The court wrote that a review of cases since 1967 had shown "no reported case in which a plaintiff successfully recovered damages for truthful disclosure by the press."[57]

In the 1990s, the decade in which tables seemed to start to turn against some media, some courts still routinely rejected plaintiffs' claims. A news report about a private police investigation, for example, could not be the basis for a privacy claim, a court in Pennsylvania decided in 1990.[58] "Were this court one of manners or ethics," the judge wrote, "it might well reprove the defendants; because it is one of law, it cannot." It did, however, suggest in dicta that a hypothetical newspaper that would publish a list of persons who were HIV-positive would not have a valid First Amendment newsworthiness defense. Around the same time, the federal appeals court for Illinois decided that an investigation into an eye doctor's practices could not be the basis for a valid privacy claim even though the reporters went undercover to do the story; "[t]oday's 'tabloid' style investigative television reportage, conducted by networks desperate for viewers in an increasingly competitive market," the court wrote, despite being "shrill, one-sided, and offensive," was entitled to the same level of protection as other, more mainstream media.[59] The federal appeals court for Arkansas meantime decided that an auditor's expunged criminal record was valid news because the underlying charges and trials themselves were public events;[60] the federal appeals court for Michigan similarly decided that mug shots of arrestees were of public interest.[61]

As for news media's use of one person's story to illustrate a larger issue of importance, known as the "personalization" of a news story, a New York court held that not only would it refuse to second-guess an editorial decision, it found that the media was generally legally permitted to use such a familiar journalistic technique.[62]

Despite such broadly favorable holdings, however, there were signs that the days of strong deference to media to decide for itself what was newsworthy were ending. The *Shulman* case involving the accident victim in California is a good example. There, even though the court had found the accident and the medical response newsworthy and, therefore, insufficient for a publication-of-private-facts claim, it found the plaintiff's intrusion tort claim valid. The justices of California's highest court reasoned that the reporters had intruded into the plaintiff's seclusion by placing a microphone on the flight nurse at the scene and, later, by accompanying and recording the plaintiff on her emergency helicopter ride to the hospital. In other words, while what was ultimately broadcast was protected under the First Amendment, the actions that gathered the medical information for the broadcast were not.

There were signs that the U.S. Supreme Court, too, was pulling back a bit.

Bartnicki's Shift

There is no precise moment at which the tables began to turn for media, of course. And clearly, given such strong pro-press history and language, many courts continue to decide cases in the media's favor. It seems, however, that the turn of the century—perhaps not coincidentally also the time in which the Internet became significant—is when courts more routinely began to second-guess news judgments and when many began to drop the use of language that was excessively deferential to media.

The U.S. Supreme Court expressed its own concerns during that period in a roundabout way in *Bartnicki v. Vopper*.[63] The case was a win for media, but hinted of a significant forthcoming loss.

The *Bartnicki* facts were slightly different from those in which journalists had reported information gleaned from a police source: a news-talk radio station in Pennsylvania had played a tape of a cellular telephone conversation that had been recorded surreptitiously. The tape of the phone call had been placed anonymously in a local citizens group leader's mailbox and was then passed on to the radio station. The recorded call, between the chief negotiator for a teacher's union and the president of that union, suggested that violence might be appropriate should negotiations break down. The president was said to have said:

> If they're not going to move for three percent, we're gonna have to go to their, their homes . . . To blow off their front porches, we'll have to do some work on some of those guys. Really, uh, really and truthfully, because this is, you know, this is bad news. . . .

After the radio station aired the conversation, the union negotiator and union president sued it and others for statutory violations related to wiretapping. The radio station defended on First Amendment grounds, arguing that the news value of the tape in which a union leader seemed to threaten violence trumped whatever privacy concerns existed in the conversation itself. When the case reached the Supreme Court, the Justices put the issue this way: "[W]hat degree of protection, if any, [does] the First Amendment provide[] to speech that discloses the contents of an illegally intercepted communication?" It explained that the conflict was one between interests of the highest order: the value of public information versus the value of individual privacy.

In the end, the news media and the value of public information won out. Six of the Justices joined a majority opinion stating that they were "firmly convinced" that the radio station that played the tape was protected in doing so by the First Amendment, given the news value of the conversation. "In this case," the Justices wrote, "privacy concerns give way when balanced against the interest in publishing matters of public importance." They explained that the surreptitiously recorded conversation involved a matter of unquestionable public concern—the months-long negotiation over a teachers' contract—and therefore trumped any privacy for those whose conversation had been recorded. The Justices noted in particular that the broadcasters themselves had not done anything unlawful and stressed that their lack of involvement in the underlying illegal activity was key to finding that their behavior in airing the tape was protected constitutionally.

The three dissenting Justices, however, valued privacy more strongly than the news value within the taped conversation and voted against the media defendants. "Surely 'the interest in individual privacy' at its narrowest must embrace the right to be free from surreptitious eavesdropping on, and involuntary broadcast of, our cellular telephone conversations," the dissenters wrote, noting that those involved in the conversation had only intended to have a private telephone conversation and had not intended to contribute to a public debate about anything.

What makes *Bartnicki* such a close decision despite its six-three outcome, however, is that two of the Justices who signed onto the majority opinion wrote a separate concurring opinion that warned that an end to expansive media freedoms in the area of news judgment was on the horizon. "[T]he Court's holding does not imply a significantly broader constitutional immunity for the media," the Justices explained, restating that the *Bartnicki* decision was a narrow one and suggesting that in a situation involving the publication of "truly private matters," the Court would have decided it differently. The two Justices then wrote that new encroachments upon privacy had created a need for strong pro-privacy legislation, harkening back to Warren and Brandeis's sensibilities in "The Right to Privacy":

> Clandestine and pervasive invasions of privacy . . . are genuine possibilities as a result of continuously advancing technologies. Eavesdropping on ordinary cellular phone conversations in the street (which many callers seem to tolerate) is a very different matter from eavesdropping on encrypted cellular phone conversations or those carried on in the bedroom. But the technologies that allow the former may come to permit the latter.

"Legislatures," the Justices explicitly advised, may therefore draft "better tailored provisions designed to encourage, for example, more effective privacy-protecting techniques" without constitutional worry because the interests in protecting "basic personal privacy" were so strong.

It is possible, then, to read *Bartnicki* as a five-to-four decision *against* media, one in which five Justices, a majority, ruled that personal privacy did, in fact, trump newsworthiness at certain times—just not under these unique facts of a teachers' contract and threats of potential violence.

Moreover, and as if foreseeing the Hulk Hogan sex tape scenario, the two concurring Justices suggested that even public figures had the right to private communication and private matters, explaining that, to them, a sex tape featuring a "famous actress and a rock star" would not be a matter of legitimate public concern.[64] Of great relevance to Hulk Hogan's plight, if three justices would have found a privacy violation in the broadcast of a surreptitiously recorded phone call regarding union activities, they certainly would have found a privacy violation in a surreptitiously recorded bedroom encounter. Added to the two concurring votes, then, this makes a five-four majority in favor of privacy over news specifically involving a sex tape.

It seems, then, that the death notice and celebratory funeral for the Warren and Brandeis privacy tort had come too soon and that, perhaps, Gawker's First Amendment calls and claims were more self-righteous than right. Despite its near death in the 1970s and 1980s, at the dawn of the twenty-first century, a majority of the Justices on the U.S. Supreme Court had explicitly found privacy viable, even in a case involving a public figure.

3

Legal Protections for News and Truthful Information: The Present

In *Florida Star*, one of the Supreme Court cases involving media identification of a rape victim, there was one horrifying fact on which the Supreme Court majority did not dwell: after publication of the article that had named the victim, a man had menacingly called her home to warn that she would soon be raped again. The newspaper's release of the victim's identity, therefore, had presumably caused her to be doubly victimized.

Justice Byron White, no fan of journalism since his college and professional football days when eager sports writers had dubbed him "Whizzer White," held fast to that fact in his dissent. How dare a news reporter, who had admittedly violated ethics rules, publish the identity of someone sure to be a target for harassers or for the rapist himself? Surely, this sort of publication had crossed a line when society and journalism itself so strongly protects these victims in particular.

But no, the modern trend in the courts, he complained (sarcastically placing quotation marks around "modern"), had been to constitutionally sanction any truthful information that the press wanted to publish, which necessarily meant that any individual privacy rights would be eclipsed by press freedoms.

"Today," he wrote in reference to the *Florida Star* majority, "we hit the bottom of the slippery slope."

Justice White may well have been at least partially right, if rock bottom meant a privacy plaintiff's lowest low. Since about the time of *Florida Star*, courts in many cases have turned away from press protections and have moved more frequently to protect privacy in cases with far less horrendous facts than those in *Florida Star.* At least four states, for example, have accepted publication of private facts as a tort for the first time since *Florida Star* was decided, despite *Florida Star*'s broad definition for news and its notable protection for the editorial decisions of journalists.[1]

A 2007 decision from Ohio's highest court indicates the reasons for those changes: today's publishers go far beyond what Justice Brown in 1900, or even Justice White in 1989, could have imagined and their push-the-envelope behavior has elevated privacy concerns to new levels.

This chapter begins with that Ohio decision and follows it with tens of cases in which courts have ruled against media today, examples that mostly involve truthful reporting or investigative work. They show a judiciary sometimes out of touch with what the public might consider newsworthy, one willing to protect public entities from press inquiries, one pushing back against media's excesses, and one seemingly at ease with finding privacy rights even for public figures. The cases include those springing from publication of private facts, infliction of emotional distress, intellectual property rights, neutral and fair reportage, and Freedom of Information Act arguments.

Many of these cases come from trial courts or intermediate-level appellate courts and, because attorneys may feel pressure to settle after an unfavorable decision, often no higher court opinion follows. But even trial-level cases that involve preliminary motions have significance for media as they contemplate whether to challenge or settle a newly filed lawsuit. If a federal trial court in New York City, for example, has decided that a claim for intentional infliction of emotional distress could well be valid when journalists fail to abide by lofty and aspirational professional standards, as did the court in *Conradt*, that decision could well have the same strong effect—a pressure to settle quickly under similar facts—as would an appellate court decision. In other words, despite an often Supreme Court-centric focus to First Amendment-related jurisprudence, it is also important to recognize what is happening below, where even trial courts can have significant impact. The many cases that follow, therefore, be they trial or appellate level, help provide support for at least the beginning of a pro-privacy, anti-media trend.

False Light, FOIA, and Protection of the Innocent

When William Prosser in effect created the privacy torts, false light was one of them. He defined the tort as the publication of information about another person that places that person in a false and offensive light before the public. Because false light is very similar to defamation, however, it seemed to many to be an end-run around defamation's First Amendment protections.

Multiple courts, therefore, initially refused to accept false light; many explicitly worried that an incorrect news report that merely offended the plaintiff's sensibilities could be the basis for liability even though defamation would require much more. In a 2002 case from Colorado, for example, the state's highest court wrote that false light "risks inflicting an unacceptable chill on those in the media seeking to avoid liability," and was "too amorphous a tort" that would "invariably chill open and robust reporting."[2]

By 2007, however, an inspired Ohio Supreme Court saw things differently.[3] It accepted false light for the very first time in the state—and for precisely the same reasons that the Colorado court had rejected it: perceptions about media. What is remarkable about the decision is that the underlying facts did not involve media at all; the defendants were business owners who had printed flyers in search of the culprit who had thrown a rock through their window. The plaintiffs had argued that a targeted distribution of such flyers had falsely implicated their son.

It was a simple neighborhood dispute, and yet the justices criticized not overzealous amateur sleuths, but media offenders.

The privacy torts themselves, the court wrote, had been suggested by Warren and Brandeis during a "period of the excesses of yellow journalism" and had lost legal favor over the years once "formal training in journalism and ethics" became common. Such a change for the better in journalism, the court noted, had ameliorated concerns about "the damage that could be done to individuals by the press." Earlier courts that had rejected false light as unnecessarily duplicative, therefore, were correct in doing so at that time, because journalism's ethics and training were strong.

In today's world, however, the justices continued, "the ethical standards regarding the acceptability of certain discourse have been lowered," creating a need for additional legal ammunition for wronged plaintiffs. "Today, thanks to the accessibility of the Internet," they wrote, "the barriers to generating publicity are slight," and such an information explosion, with a related profound decrease in publishers' moral and ethics codes, required legal action that had been unnecessary just twenty years before.

"As the ability to do harm has grown," in Ohio and elsewhere, "so must the law's ability to protect the innocent," the justices ruled. And with that, false light became one of the privacy causes of action that plaintiffs in Ohio can bring against media and others who have offended them.

Since 2007, multiple courts have latched onto the Ohio court's reasoning, finding explicitly that publishing is different today and that courts must bolster privacy and other related causes of action in response. In Kansas, for example, one court held that the same mindset applied in the state's publication-of-private-fact cases:

> Cognizant of the purpose behind recognizing the tort of publicity of private facts, the trend in sister jurisdictions, the prevalence of the Internet, and the relative ease in which information can be published over the Internet, the Court concludes that Kansas does not, as a matter of law, preclude a privacy claim simply because the defendant communicated the private fact to a small group of people. Courts must look to the context of the communication—e.g., its medium and content—before makings its determination.[4]

And in Missouri, a court relied upon the Ohio Supreme Court's language about the Internet, a decline in ethical standards, and the need to protect the innocent in its opinion also embracing false light.[5]

The Ohio Supreme Court had put crisply and significantly what other courts had been suggesting since at least the 1990s: that media had changed, that media could be trusted less, and that the law needed to change in response to media's shortcomings.

The U.S. Supreme Court had opened the door to such reasoning in a case involving the Freedom of Information Act decided three years after *Bartnicki* and three years before Ohio's acceptance of false light. The case, *National Archives v. Favish*, involved photographs of a public official's suicide.[6] Vince Foster, a White House deputy counsel, had shot himself in a Washington, D.C.-area park and the act generated much news coverage and conspiracy speculation. Despite significant public interest in the subject, the Court sided with Foster's family and decided that family members' privacy interests trumped the public's right to know more about the death scene.

It would be the first time that the Court would hold that family privacy interests trumped the Freedom of Information Act promise of access to government records and that relatives who wished to "secure their own refuge from a sensation-seeking culture" should be protected. When Foster's sister expressed her horror and devastation at the press's use of a leaked photograph of the suicide scene, the Justices quoted her with compassion: "I fear," she had written, "that the release of [additional] photographs certainly would set off another round of intense scrutiny by the media." She had described additional worry that "[u]ndoubtedly, the photographs would be placed on the Internet for world consumption [and] [o]nce again my family would be the focus of conceivably unsavory and distasteful media coverage."

Acknowledging those concerns, the Court wrote that it "had little difficulty" in finding "the right of family members to . . . limit attempts to exploit pictures of the deceased family member's remains for public purposes." Even though, here, the deceased was a public official and even though his suicide had generated tremendous news coverage, the Court ruled that the family's privacy interests trumped. The outcome, of course, affected not only the attorney who had asked for the photographs, but all media and other entities and individuals that would make similar requests for government-held evidence in the future. Suddenly the privacy interests of others—here, specifically family members—could affect public access to government information about the deceased.

At around the same time, a California court ruled that the spread of "horrific" and "graphic" death photographs of an eighteen-year-old accident victim could be the basis for a privacy claim by her surviving relatives.[7] Police officers had emailed the photos to friends on Halloween in what the court called an "unthinkable exploitation" of her death and they caused "a malignant firestorm" to spread across the Internet. Such use of the photographs was one "of pure morbidity and sensationalism without legitimate public interest," the court wrote, upholding privacy and intentional-infliction-of-emotional-distress claims. A concurring justice wrote specifically that there was a "lack of newsworthiness" in the precise facts of what had led to the young woman's death— the "gore revealed in photographs," where and how she had landed after the crash, and how her face appeared. Here, the justice wrote, those gruesome details lacked news value and, therefore, would be an adequate basis for a survivor's privacy claim as well.

All three main cases just mentioned—the Ohio Supreme Court's false light case, the U.S. Supreme Court's FOIA case, and the California appellate court's decision in the viral death photos case—contain critical language affecting all media. In Ohio, journalists, quasi-journalists, and others will now face false light claims in response to what the court called the unethical free-for-all on the Internet; in federal FOIA cases, media and all others will not have access to crime-scene and other images of decedents because survivors' families need protection from sensational internet dissemination; and in California, media must be cautious to describe a fatal accident scene, lest surviving relatives have a valid privacy claim arising from the information.

Suddenly, protection of the innocent seems to have much greater weight than ever before—and journalism's news decisions are directly affected.

A Nascent Trend against News

While the First Amendment remains a significant protective force for media, the highly subjective way privacy and some other laws are written, media's broad decline, and a growing sense that privacy needs strong protection have led some courts, even in non-media cases like those just mentioned, to second-guess media's news choices or investigations. While impossible to measure precisely, significant numbers of reported cases seem to show this nascent trend of favoring privacy over press rights.[8]

In the 1980s, fewer than a dozen or so cases in the United States seemed to rein in media's news judgment. The North Carolina Supreme Court, for one, noted that those were journalism's golden years: "Most modern journalists employed in print, television or radio journalism now receive formal training in ethics and journalism entirely unheard of" at the turn of the century, the court wrote in 1984, crediting the journalists of the time with being "more responsible and professional . . . than history tells us they were in [the Warren and Brandeis] era."[9] Because the North Carolina justices were so confident in journalism's practices, they summarily rejected false light as a viable claim in the state.

But there were hints of cracks in journalism's façade even then. A justice on the Supreme Court of Louisiana, for example, wrote a strong dissent in a case in which the majority favored media: "Irresponsible columnists sometimes sail upon a sea of yellow ink, submerging in their wake the privacy and sensibilities of persons not possessed of the power and means of the Third Estate."[10] Courts at the time with similar worries decided that a news story concerning an underage teenage father was not of public interest,[11] ruled that a witness who was named in a story about a murder had a valid privacy claim,[12] and decided that an accurate story about a mock "unwedding" ceremony held outside but covered without permission by a Connecticut paper could be the basis for a publication-of-private-facts lawsuit.[13]

In the 1990s, the number of cases in which the courts decided against media's news judgment grew:

- a couple videotaped at a hospital's celebration for in vitro fertilization births could sue on privacy grounds;[14]
- a family could sue for outrage after a station aired video of a child murder victim's skull;[15]
- a band featured in a "funniest video" television program after a stage collapse could sue the broadcaster for making them the subjects of ridicule;[16]
- a rape victim could sue the television station that aired an interview with a police officer who hinted that he doubted her story;[17]
- those featured in a reality crime program had a privacy claim because they had no idea that broadcasters, not police, had wielded the cameras that had entered their home;[18]
- an AIDS patient's $500,000 verdict was upheld against a television station that had promised him that it would obscure his face but did not;[19]
- a newspaper story on a woman's life as a swinger could be the basis for a privacy claim;[20]
- a broadcaster could be sued by a man featured in news teases as part of a sleep experiment;[21]
- a television reporter could be liable in negligence after she broadcast an interview with a man who promptly killed himself;[22]
- a website that had threatened to publish a celebrity sex tape could be liable for a privacy invasion for doing so;[23]
- a woman who wanted to keep her facelift surgery private could sue a television station for failing to protect her identity;[24]
- so-called psychics who had been videotaped by undercover journalists at their workplace could sue for privacy invasion;[25]
- and, by 1999, a privacy-supportive California federal court wrote that, while celebrities might be public figures, celebrity-watching and related matters would not be of public interest.[26]

Perhaps based upon those cases and others like them, at the turn of the century, constitutional law scholar David Anderson warned that, though both socially and politically risky, the protection of the press as a legally favored class was disappearing.[27] A few months later, Barry McDonald, another constitutional law scholar, suggested that newsgathering was being protected only in a "fragmented and inconsistent" way.[28] And, by 2014, David Pozen, the Columbia law professor, suggested that *New York Times v. Sullivan* was an "interesting cultural artifact" but did not reflect how current courts view journalists.[29]

The numbers provide strong evidence of those observations. In the 2000s, cases questioning media's news judgments in some way grew to more than eighty. And as of the mid-2010s, the number of decisions that have reined in news reporting in some way appears to be at a record level. Consider this: In 2013, a court that had previously defined news as "any issue in which the public is interested" backtracked and found that a public tiff between a celebrity and her celebrity stylist regarding loaned designer clothing was of absolutely no public interest. This, despite significant older coverage of the women's friendship and multiple newer news stories about the dispute and the resulting court case.[30]

Recent court decisions like that one, in which courts have written in dicta or otherwise that there is no newsworthiness in certain information, can be grouped into five main categories, included here as an overview before a closer look at specific causes of action: (1) those in which the disputed information shows, to this author's mind, clear newsworthiness; (2) relatedly, those involving information concerning public wrongs; (3) those that seem a response to push-the-envelope media; (4) those involving celebrities in some way; and (5) those involving nudity.

First, some courts seem to disagree with what would likely be a broad swath of the public about news value in certain cases. Recent courts have written, for example, that software data-mining capabilities were not of significant current public interest[31] and that FBI terrorism-related activities were not of widespread and significant concern.[32] (Data breaches, like one at Target stores in 2013, and terrorism-related information, including terrorism worries at the 2014 Winter Olympics in Sochi, Russia, are often the lead and most-read stories on news websites.) The disconnect occurs in similar, "hard news" cases: A federal court in Washington, D.C., once suggested that aircraft mishaps involving Marine helicopters in Iraq would not be newsworthy and that "corrective action taken by the Marine Corps" would have minimal public interest.[33] A court in Texas decided that no public controversy existed in "rural health care" and that a Foreign Service blog's coverage of retaliation for whistleblowers in the Foreign Service was "not even close" to proving "robust public discussion" of the subject.[34] One court shut the lid on news regarding Princess Diana's death and alleged National Security Administration taping of her phone calls, finding that two years after her death, it was not the "subject of a currently unfolding story."[35] The best example of this, however, may be the federal trial court in Pennsylvania that opined that the national trauma of September 11, 2001, "was no longer timely and had been extensively chronicled" and

suggested in an intellectual property-related case that there was "no significant newsworthiness" in a photograph of the plane that had crashed into a
Pennsylvania field during the 9/11 terrorist attacks.[36]

Second, and relatedly, some courts have questioned the validity of press
investigations into public and government entities and have valued privacy
interests even more strongly than the public's interest in those cases. A
Connecticut court, for example, refused to give the Associated Press prison
records regarding a wrongfully incarcerated inmate, finding that such information would not be of public interest because he did not commit the crime,
even though an administrative body had found such records to be logically
related to the newsworthy story of his release from prison.[37] A federal trial
court in Idaho similarly ruled that any "personal information contained in
inmates' criminal, institutional, and medical files" should be kept from media
on privacy grounds even though the underlying lawsuit alleged that there was
violence against inmates and that the prison had used gangs to facilitate order-
liness and inflict punishment within the facility.[38] Another Connecticut court
decided that the person involved in a sexual relationship with a police officer
had privacy interests strong enough to trump news interest in her identity,[39]
and a court in Florida kept media and others from certain court records in an
investigation it described as "a highly publicized phone-sex scandal" involving
the State Attorney's Office and an incarcerated felon, because allegations in
the records were of a "highly personal and inflammatory nature" that warranted shielding people from "potentially embarrassing publicity."[40]

Also in connection with media's attempted investigations into public entities, a court in New Mexico found that there would be no public interest in
how particular government workers spent tax dollars and, therefore, that the
public would have no interest in a person alleged to have purchased a car with
a government credit card.[41] A different court found that a romantic relationship between two police officers was of no public interest whatsoever because
such information gave publicity to a "private aspect of the plaintiff's life that
would be highly offensive to a reasonable person."[42] Another ruled that media
had not proved public interest in a disputed story involving a police chief's
alleged mistreatment of officers who were said to have detained his sons.[43]
And, finally, a Texas court wrote in upholding a publication-of-private-facts
privacy claim against a newspaper that "[w]hile underlying facts reflecting
criminal activity can certainly be of legitimate public interest," it could find no

authority "holding that the public has a legitimate interest in the mere fact that an individual has been accused of a crime."[44]

As part of the third category, there continues a pushback against what the courts perceive as push-the-envelope programming. In another claim stemming from NBC's *To Catch a Predator*, for example, a federal court in California found that a man arraigned on a felony charge and eventually convicted on a misdemeanor could bring an intentional-infliction-of-emotional-distress claim against NBC because "the alleged sensationalization of the news could be deemed outrageous—beyond the common bounds of decency—by a reasonable jury."[45] ABC suffered a similar setback after it aired an investigative report into casting workshops in which aspiring actors had apparently paid to meet a casting director; the plaintiff convinced the court that the subject was not truly newsworthy because ABC itself had not covered public hearings regarding related issues.[46] On the local level, a television station in Michigan that had revealed an accident victim's first name, her address, her x-rays, and that she was on an antidepressant was forced to defend a publication-of-private-facts claim;[47] and there were similar preliminary decisions based on various privacy grounds in cases brought against a network television series titled *Trauma: Life in the E.R.* in which the cameras entered emergency rooms to film patients suffering from various afflictions, criticized by one plaintiff as "shock TV."[48] Finally, a California federal court upheld a police officer's right to prevent a newspaper photographer from photographing an accident scene on a public highway. The journalist had arrived at the scene well in advance of police and had felt that the lack of an immediate police response itself was newsworthy, but officers grabbed his camera when they arrived and arrested him. "Plaintiff," the federal judge wrote after the reporter filed suit, "does not offer any evidence that suggests that the general public had a right to exit their vehicles on the freeway and stand in the freeway to take photographs"[49] despite clear public interest in accident scenes.

Fourth, there are some recent examples of courts deciding that celebrity news has little news value. One court maintained that a story regarding movie star Ben Affleck's alleged relationship with a nude dancer was a "trivial affair[]" and "far from the sort of important matters debate about which the First Amendment is intended to protect" and that "mere curiosity" about their alleged relationship did not mean that it was the subject of public interest.[50] Another court wrote that the newsworthiness in magazine coverage of a famous quirky surfer in a feature-like story was "suspect."[51] And finally a

California appeals court ruled that actor Eddie Murphy's son and former girl-friend had a valid publication-of-private-facts claim against a tabloid that had reported the amount in the child's trust fund.[52]

Fifth, and least surprising except perhaps to Gawker, in the opinion of many judges, nudity published against the person's wishes often lacks news-worthiness. Examples include pictures published in *Hustler* magazine without the woman's consent,[53] women who "flash" their breasts in public (as discussed more completely in Chapter 5),[54] and those who appear only in body paint at a well-attended party.[55] All those plaintiffs had valid privacy claims despite First Amendment-based arguments by the defendants.

Not all courts today are so ready to rule against media's news judgments, of course. In 2008, a federal judge in Texas, echoing the Supreme Court in the *Headquarters Detective* case, worried that that some on the bench had "some-times mix[ed] Victorian concepts of what is acceptable with elitist disdain for the stuff other people read."[56] "The idea that a court decides what is of public interest is the antithesis of free expression," the judge wrote, "its central idea is that the reader, listener, and watcher is free to decide for himself what inter-ests him."

But in a world of push-the-envelope media, allowing the watcher to watch what he likes is often at the peril—and the privacy invasion—of the watched.

Despite the Texas judge's warning, then, about second-guessing media's choices and judging critically information in which some of the public is inter-ested, many courts today have sharpened their editing pencils. Of special interest here are the times judges have done so in particular cause-of-action or defense-related categories in which media have traditionally been at least somewhat protected or bolstered. These include: (1) publication of private facts, especially determinations of newsworthiness, (2) intentional and negli-gent infliction of emotional distress, a tort sometimes known as outrage, (3) intellectual property, (4) neutral reportage, and (5) access to information. What follows is an overview of each of these five categories with short high-lighted case examples that help show significant discord.

Law's Pushback against Media:
Publication and Newsworthiness

In 2013, a California appeals court quoted a warning from 1890's "The Right to Privacy": that advances in photography and a proliferation of newspapers had invaded sacred precincts of domestic life and threatened to proclaim from rooftops what is whispered in closets.[57]

"Evidentially not much has changed in more than a century," the court added critically and promptly extended the publication-of-private-facts tort in the state to include the spoken word. Since the tort's inception, the court reasoned, it had existed "to allow a person to control the kind of information about himself made available to the public—in essence, to define his public persona." With such a focus on the person wronged and his rights, the court found that there was no reason not to include oral privacy invasions as the basis for publication claims. The judges blamed talk radio and confessional television as forcing the extension.

That case shows how the dynamics of the publication tort are becoming more plaintiff-friendly, based significantly upon perceived changes in media and the disdain some courts have for certain publishers. The decision also indicates that some courts hope increased liability will change what they perceive as media's privacy-invading behavior. Finally, it shows the way some courts have started to give the plaintiff some control over what the public knows about him, as opposed to deferring to media and its news judgment.

Despite earlier courts' concerns about the chilling effect that blue-penciling would have upon journalism, therefore, some judges have jumped in to condemn news in the name of privacy in ways that may have surprised even Warren and Brandeis:

- A court in 2007 wrote that there was no newsworthiness in a priest's relationship with a woman even though he had left the priesthood and, presumably, a large congregation: it was "a truly private matter in which we can discern no legitimate public interest," the court wrote[58] at a time when the Catholic Church continued to face significant criticism for its insistence that priests be unmarried and celibate and when parishioners, at the very least, would be quite interested.
- A Georgia appeals court in 2009 questioned *AdWeek*'s news coverage of an advertising executive's move to another firm. The story may have appealed to readers' morbid curiosity, the court wrote, but there was no evidence that it had significance for anyone other than the ad executive's family,[59] even though trade magazines routinely report on such moves.
- And a New Hampshire court decided that a man's admitted criminal history was of no public concern because the burglaries at issue affected

only those whose homes were burglarized and had not received much news coverage.[60]

As one frustrated-with-media federal judge would write regarding news-worthiness and the need he felt to limit its journalistic definition, we live in a world of "news reports [that] run the gamut of celebrity marriages and divorces, waterskiing squirrels, exploding whales, and national anthem singing tryouts."[61] If the court were to accept the media defendants' definition for newsworthiness, the court complained, there would be "no subject, comment or action that would ever be beyond the public interest."

Today's expanded judicial editing is in direct conflict with the Supreme Court's warning from the heyday of journalism: that journalism needed "breathing space" even when it acted wrongly lest a "pall of fear and timidity" develop in newsrooms, that to second-guess news editors would be inconsistent with First Amendment principles, and that state action to punish truthful information should rarely, if ever, be constitutional. But those concerns proved of little worry in the four cases that follow in which judges were forced to delve more deeply into what sorts of stories, in their opinions, should be considered valid news.

Child Sex Abuse and a Team Photo

In 1999, *Sports Illustrated* published a standard team photograph of a California Little League team. The photo takes up three-quarters of a two-page spread and features two posed rows of young teenaged boys, about a dozen in total, most of them in various stages of a smile, and most wearing yellow-and-black Little League uniforms. In the back row center stands the team coach and manager in the same sort of uniform. He appears to be in his fifties, graying, and of average height and weight. He is not smiling. Shortly after the photo was taken, he would plead guilty to having molested five children he had coached in Little League over a five-year period, four boys and a girl.

Sports Illustrated used the photograph, one given to them by a Little League parent, to illustrate an article it titled "Every Parent's Nightmare."[62] "The child molester has found a home in the world of youth sports, where as a coach he can gain the trust and loyalty of kids—and then prey on them," is the article's subhead.

It is not clear how many of the boys pictured in the team photograph had, in fact, been molested by the coach, but ten of them sued the magazine for publishing the photo, claiming both invasion of privacy and infliction of emotional distress. They also sued HBO for broadcasting "a fleeting shot" of the team photo.[63]

Sports Illustrated and HBO both argued that the photograph itself, taken outside on a baseball field and given to all team members, was not private. Moreover, they argued, other news outlets had reported the fact that unnamed players on the team had been molested by the coach and that, given the community knowledge of who played on what team, team membership could not be a private fact. The defendants also argued that the "offensiveness" element of the tort could not be met by those whose sole basis for the lawsuit was that they were members of the Little League team in question.

As for newsworthiness, the two media defendants argued strongly that, based upon prior California precedent, the court could not act as a superior editor over their decision to publish the team photograph. The defendants maintained that the subject of sex abuse by those with power over children was newsworthy and that the photo helped both to establish the hard truth of the story and to show parents that anyone, even a responsible community leader, could potentially be a pedophile. The photograph, they argued, personified the story in a key way that prose alone could not.

But the court rejected those arguments and found that the plaintiffs' privacy-based claims were valid. First, it wrote that the defendants had somehow mixed up privacy and secrecy, finding that the teens' membership on the team may not have been a secret but could still, somehow, be private. As regarding newsworthiness, the court found that this was one of those "extreme" cases in which it could, in fact, second-guess media, because the Little League case involved more personal and intimate matters than had previous cases, including *Shulman*, the case that found news value in an accident victim's medical treatment.

As for the photograph itself, the court decided, it was not editorially necessary to the magazine article and, at the least, could have been manipulated to obscure the players' faces. For support, the court looked primarily to public policy, finding that some state laws prevented the naming of minors in sex abuse cases as did journalism's ethics codes.

Ultimately, the court decided, "the private fact of their membership on [the coach's] team was not newsworthy," and the privacy invasion based upon the publication of the photograph far outweighed "the values of journalistic impact and credibility."

There are additional reasons beyond the lack of deference why the holding was surprising. First, only four of the dozen or so team members photographed could have been the victims of sexual abuse by the coach who had confessed in the underlying case, yet the court seems to suggest that all players had a valid privacy claim. Second, the court seemed intent upon finding a way around strong case precedent in the state, writing, for example, that there was a distinction between the Little League case and Ruth Shulman's case, but then suggesting without explanation that the photograph itself was not newsworthy and that Shulman's intimate medical information was. Moreover, the court gave short shrift to the value of news story personalization, the common journalistic technique for making news stories more accessible, relevant, and interesting, and a key reason that earlier decisions including *Shulman* had rejected privacy claims.

In the end, the California court had decided that publication of a matter-of-fact team photograph taken outside and given to all team members could be the basis for a privacy claim because some pictured had been molested by the coach.

A Mother's Grief

Courts have also ruled in favor of less obvious plaintiffs in newsworthiness determinations, including a mother who lovingly spoke words over the body of her dead son and was then surprised to learn that she was quoted the following day on the front page of the *Chicago Tribune*.[64]

Tribune reporters had received permission to be at a hospital during the final days of 1992, working on a series on gun and gang violence in Chicago. The assignment makes journalistic sense: the hospital was in a dangerous neighborhood and the series would likely culminate in a story based upon one of the final deaths of the year. Sure enough, on the evening of December 30, a sixteen-year-old boy was brought to the hospital suffering from a bullet wound. His parents were called and he died in the hospital shortly thereafter on December 31. Reporters asked the mother for a statement and she refused. When she moved to her son's body, she told him how much she loved him, that she had warned him about "this street thing," and said that her "baby" was now with the Lord.

Each of those statements became a part of the *Tribune* reporters' article titled "Deadly End To Deadly Year: 934th Victim Part Of Record Homicide Rate"; it was published the next day on the front page beside a large photograph of the youth's body laying on a gurney.[65] In addition to the mother's words, the article included a description of the hospital's attempts to keep the boy alive: "For 15 minutes the team worked feverishly to revive the young man, finally opening his chest and massaging his heart," it read.

The mother, who had never agreed to speak with the reporters and who had apparently refused to give them a statement, sued the *Chicago Tribune* for invasion of privacy and other related causes of action.

A trial court granted the newspaper's motion to dismiss, refusing to find the scenario a private one. When the plaintiff appealed, the *Tribune* again argued on appeal that the mother's words, spoken in front of others in a public hospital room, were not private. That strong argument combined powerfully with the *Tribune*'s First Amendment claim: that the article, about the alarming increase in gun and gang violence among young people, was newsworthy and that the young man's death helped show in a gentle, yet graphic and powerful way, how families are devastated by it.

The court rejected both arguments. A hospital room could well be a private space, the court ruled, and, therefore, so too could the mother's words be private. Moreover, it decided, a jury could find her words not newsworthy. "[T]he publication concerned an extraordinarily painful incident in the plaintiff's life," the court wrote, "when she first set eyes on her minor son after he had been shot to death." A reasonable jury could well find that the journalists did not need to include in their article the mother's pained words to her son or the photograph of his body or the description of life-saving attempts at the hospital. Tracking the language in the Restatement, the two-judge majority held ultimately that "[a] jury could find that a reasonable member of the public has no concern with the statements a grieving mother makes to her dead son, or with what he looked like lying dead in the hospital, even though he died as the result of a gang shooting."

The appellate judges also allowed the plaintiff's intentional-infliction-of-emotional-distress claim to continue to trial, writing that the *Tribune*'s actions "suggest an alarming lack of sensitivity and civility" and had potentially gone far enough to constitute outrageous conduct.

The single dissenting judge wrote with alarm that the First Amendment should have protected the *Tribune*; he found strong news value in the mother's words, the photograph, and the article itself. Importantly, he ended his dissent with language that closely echoed Judge Mikva's warning of a coming backlash in First Amendment jurisprudence:

> There are, no doubt, cases in the pipeline where the phenomena of "info-mercials," "info-tainment," "docu-dramas," and "reenactments" blur the differences between legitimate news and pulp fiction. The shield of the First Amendment may develop cracks as courts respond to this trend and the insensitive aggressiveness of legitimate news gatherers who must compete with the purveyors of soft core "information" to supply market demands. This case is not one of them.

The majority had found precisely that insensitive aggressiveness on the part of the reporters, however. Despite strong First Amendment protections, those judges recognized not only the potential for a valid privacy claim based upon the mother's words, but also a claim for the publication of a photo of her son's body and the description of the attempts to save his life. Here, too, the court seemed determined to take the *Tribune* to task for what it obviously saw as an affront, even though past courts and the Restatement seem not to recognize privacy interests arising from such descriptions.

The case settled shortly thereafter.

Privacy, Quasi-Celebrities, and Dating

Warren and Brandeis warned in 1890 that gossip had become a trade. A federal court in Washington, D.C., many years later did something about it.

The case involved a woman who worked as a CNN assignment editor. She was single and had apparently dated a number of high-profile men, including a prominent business owner, a lawyer and political player, and the University of Maryland basketball coach. A newspaper gossip column noted as much in a report headlined "Controversial Love for CNN Producer" that included defamatory information and derogatory innuendo apparently fed to the paper by the producer's disgruntled ex-boyfriend. The column suggested that the producer had used her position "to meet all the 'right' people" and it named the men. It also used the slang "hooked up" at one point, which can mean sexual intercourse.

In addition to multiple defamation-related claims, the producer sued the newspaper for publication of private facts, based upon the truthful report that she had dated the men she had, in fact, dated. In response, the newspaper argued that the facts it had revealed were not private, given that few would find dating an "offensive" subject and given that most dates happen in public. But the federal trial court ruled in favor of the CNN producer. It found, apparently as a matter of law, that the plaintiff's "personal, romantic life [was] not a matter of public concern." In upholding her publication-of-private-facts claim, the court determined whether the disclosure would be actionable by looking not to what the public would be interested in, but to what the CNN producer would prefer that they not know:

> The court is persuaded that it is unlikely that an unmarried, professional woman in her 30s would want her private life about whom she had dated and had sexual relations revealed in the gossip column of a widely distributed newspaper, particularly in the context in which the information was revealed.[66]

Such a publication, the court noted, was unwanted and would cause an average person "suffering, shame or humiliation." Therefore, the plaintiff's claim based on publication of private facts was valid, even though most celebrity magazines routinely include similar articles within their pages.

It is true that the plaintiff's other causes of action, defamation among them, appeared far stronger and that the publication-of-private-facts claim against the newspaper seemed almost an afterthought. But the court could have easily stricken that particular part of the plaintiff's complaint and allowed the rest to continue to trial. Instead, it changed the publication privacy tort's definition to include what truthful facts the plaintiff herself would like published . . . or not.

A Private Business Transaction

A Louisville television station, like many across the country, has as a part of its newscast a "Troubleshooter" segment in which it helps consumers solve problems. In 2004, Troubleshooter journalists focused on a home purchase made by a woman who was blind. Her police officer co-worker had contacted the station alleging that the sellers had "taken advantage" of the blind buyer by selling her a house that was "in pretty bad shape."[67] The plaintiff sellers strongly disagreed with that assessment and sued the television station for defamation and false light. The court, then, was forced to decide whether the topic of the Troubleshooter segment was a matter of public concern. If so, the plaintiffs would be held to a higher standard of proof and a successful claim would be less likely. If not, they would need to show only that the television station was negligent and any burden to prove the truth of the broadcast would fall upon the defendants' shoulders.

The television station argued that, indeed, the segments were of public concern: they were "primarily directed toward educating viewers about general problems confronted in the community, and that the individual transaction [involving the house sale] was merely used to illustrate [such] problems."

But the court rejected the station's argument, ruling that the television news segment was instead "an exposé about a private transaction between two people" and found its focus not on generalized public lessons but on the precise transaction itself. Therefore, it decided that the news segment was not a matter of public concern and that additional First Amendment protections should not kick in for the defendants.

An interesting aspect about the case is that the court seemed certain in its assessment of the lack of news value within the consumer segment, even though many television and newspapers have such investigative consumer-based units and even though most of them focus on helping individuals in an attempt to personalize common consumer problems.

Law's Pushback against Media: Editorial Outrage

Some of the plaintiffs just discussed brought intentional-infliction-of-emotional-distress claims in addition to their publication-of-private-facts privacy claims. So-called IIED claims offer additional examples of courts' attempts to limit media.

Intentional infliction of emotional distress, also known as the tort of outrage, can be dauntingly difficult to prove. First, the plaintiff's emotional injury must be truly severe; in some jurisdictions that means that the plaintiff must provide evidence of a doctor's care. Proving outrageousness, defined in many jurisdictions as an act that is utterly intolerable in a civilized community, is an even greater burden. First Amendment issues abound in such cases because the act causing the distress is the written word, speech, or some other means of expression.

For a while, journalists had relied on a key Supreme Court case, *Hustler v. Falwell*, to protect them from IIED claims. There, *Hustler*, a magazine that features photographs of nude women, successfully defended an IIED claim brought by the Reverend Jerry Falwell after it had published a mock advertisement suggesting that Falwell had had sexual relations with his mother. The Supreme Court held that the First Amendment protects even embarrassing, outrageous, and offensive speech—and decided that public figures need prove both falsity and actual malice before an IIED claim could be supported. The case has been considered a particularly significant one because it extends First Amendment protection for speech precisely in a context where it is most likely to offend and outrage. "'Outrageousness,'" the Court wrote in *Falwell*, "is a highly malleable standard with an inherent subjectiveness about it which would allow a jury to impose liability on the basis of the jurors' tastes or views, or perhaps on the basis of their dislike of a particular expression." But the case can be read more narrowly to protect media only when public figures or public officials bring claims based upon some sort of satirical expression.

In 2011, the U.S. Supreme Court again entered the IIED fray in *Snyder v. Phelps*, the case in which the Westboro Baptist Church picketed a military funeral carrying highly offensive signs.[68] The Court upheld church members' right to protest in a public place over a distraught father's emotional distress claims, a significant First Amendment victory for freedom of expression. But the Justices also seemed to suggest that the published word aimed at a particular individual may not be protected in the same way: the court wrote in a footnote regarding the organization's more targeted-at-individuals website that "an internet posting may raise distinct issues in [the IIED] context." Therefore, the opinion is potentially a narrow one that did not necessarily address claims based upon more directed, emotionally harmful speech.

That footnote means that the following cases and others in which the media has been found liable for intentional infliction of emotional distress could well be constitutional despite *Snyder*'s otherwise broad protections for expression.

An Allegedly Taunting Tabloid

Natalee Holloway disappeared during her high school senior trip to Aruba and the crime instantly became the focus of mainstream media, television talk shows, and tabloids. The *National Enquirer*, for example, published multiple stories about what is thought to be her murder (her body was never found). As a court would later explain:

> The articles described a map that purported to show where Natalee's body was located, a "secret graveyard" where Natalee had been "buried alive," and other details about her "murder" and the treatment of her "corpse,"

including that it had been secreted temporarily in a coffin with another corpse before being moved to a final location.[69]

Natalee's mother, Elizabeth Ann Holloway, sued the publication for IIED, alleging that the articles, which were apparently false, along with photographs and sensational headlines, had caused her severe emotional distress.

The *National Enquirer* defended on First Amendment grounds, and argued, among other things, that both the *Falwell* and *Snyder* cases applied to protect the articles' publication, but the court sided with Holloway's mother. *Falwell* did not apply, the court ruled, because, among other things, parody was at issue in the *Falwell* case and was not an issue here. *Snyder* did not apply because, in Holloway's case, "the newspaper articles at issue were 'intended' to cause [Holloway] distress" unlike the more generalized picketing at military funerals that was not targeted at a particulate person. "*Snyder* implies that knowingly false speech motivated by a specific intent to cause emotional harm to a particular person" may fall outside First Amendment protections, the court wrote. In upholding the claim under Alabama law as well, the court noted that some successful IIED cases had been based upon the conduct of funeral homes in caring for relatives' corpses, that some courts had ruled that relatives had a privacy interest in autopsy records, and that still other successful claims had been based upon words alone.

In summary, the court wrote that it had decided that "the publication of gruesome, false descriptions of a daughter's death can be 'outrageous'" to parents despite an obvious public interest in the story and, therefore, can be a sufficient basis for a successful IIED claim. The court added that it was indeed at least arguable "that a parent's personal privacy interest is invaded also when private, personal information about his or her minor child is involved."

Years of First Amendment doctrine, then, had not protected the *National Enquirer* from an action based upon its sensationalistic articles regarding not the plaintiff herself, but her daughter. And, based upon the court's language, additional lawsuits brought on privacy grounds appear just as promising.

The two parties settled, so the case will never go to trial or be heard by a higher court.

A Teen Takes on Gawker

Gawker, the website that published the Hulk Hogan sex tape and defended its publication on First Amendment grounds by arguing that it has the right to publish what it wants, also used a First Amendment defense against a claim of negligent infliction of emotional distress (NIED) brought by an eighteen-year-old teenager who had just graduated from high school. The Gawker headline for the relevant story read "Female High School Student Accused of Flashing Vagina in Yearbook."

The court that would hear the case at trial reproduced the Gawker story in full in its opinion,[70] including a line that suggested that she had lifted "her graduation gown and expos[ed] her hooha." A photograph that accompanied the Gawker article showed a high school student "in her cap and gown—her face and pelvic area . . . obscured by black bars," though the article itself noted that the other photograph, the one at issue in the case, could well have been one of a "girl's" thighs "bunched together" instead of anything more private.

In defending its article on First Amendment grounds, Gawker argued that *New York Times v. Sullivan* and other related Supreme Court decisions protected the publication because the information published was of public concern. "[D]ebate on public issues," Gawker argued familiarly, must include "vehement, caustic, and sometimes sharp attacks" for the sake of the "breathing space" that freedom of expression needs to survive in a democracy.

As one might imagine, given the case's adversaries—a tabloid-like website known for pushing the envelope and a recent high school graduate suffering because a high school yearbook snafu had suddenly been propelled onto the national scene—the court wrote that it had had little difficulty in ruling for the eighteen-year-old on her NIED claim:

> The article lured readers to the website with a sensational headline focused on "Flashing Vagina[s]" and leads off with two entries: (1) a blacked out picture altered to suggest a partially nude teenager and (2) a description of the picture as being that "of a girl lifting her graduation gown and exposing her hooha." The article itself scoffs at the social value of the controversy, calling it a "manufactured moral panic" and suggests that there would have been no controversy had not school officials blown it out of proportion. Repeated references to teenage genitalia, "hoohas," "crotchbooks," and "upskirting pedophiles," coupled with a censored photograph of a young female, all tend to suggest a comedic and "voyeuristic" journalistic approach lacking in substance on the pressing policy issues of the day.

Therefore, the court decided, First Amendment protections did not apply and simple North Carolina NIED did. "Because of the age of the Plaintiff [and] the widespread nature of the Defendant's media reach," the court wrote, and the embarrassing nature of the article, the plaintiff had met her burden.

The court added language of special importance here: "[T]he vulnerability of private individuals in the press," it wrote, was another important reason to uphold the plaintiff's NIED tort claim.

Here, then, precisely because of what the court called the press's power over vulnerable individuals, the court upheld the NIED claim, even though some would argue that Gawker is not "the press" in any traditional sense, and even though what Gawker reported was at least substantially true.

Law's Pushback against Media: Intellectual Property Rights

In the fall of 2012, actor and musician Justin Timberlake married actress Jessica Biel in what was described as a multimillion dollar wedding in Italy.[71] As a part of the reception celebration, some friends created a video titled "Greetings from Your Hollywood Friends Who Just Couldn't Make It," in which ten street people were interviewed about the pending nuptials.[72] Gawker posted part of the eight-minute video that included well-wishers who appeared to be intoxicated, homeless, and/or mentally ill.[73] When Gawker approached the attorney for one of the creators for comment, the attorney threatened a copyright claim. The wedding guest had created the video "to be used and exhibited privately at Justin Timberlake's wedding as a private joke" the attorney suggested, and had not authorized anyone to use any portion of the copyrighted tape.

In response, Gawker took the video down. Given its argument in the Hulk Hogan case that it had the right to publish what it wanted, that might seem surprising, but Hogan's request, one founded in privacy, was more subjective and involved abstract concepts like newsworthiness. A copyright claim is far more objective: If the intellectual property rights (or "IP" rights) belong to someone else, the infringing material must be removed or the internet publisher can be held liable.

Intellectual property law in some cases, therefore, holds more power to protect privacy interests than do the privacy torts. Under copyright law, there are certain so-called "fair use" exceptions that include, by name, "news reporting," but the copyright statute does not give media or anyone blanket immunity. Instead, the court considers: "(1) the purpose and character of the [allegedly infringing] use, including whether such use is of a commercial nature or is for nonprofit educational purposes; (2) the nature of the copyrighted work; (3) the amount and substantiality of the portion used [by the alleged infringer] in relation to the copyrighted work as a whole; and (4) the effect of the [allegedly infringing] use upon the potential market for or value of the copyrighted work."[74]

Given that balance, the Supreme Court has held that "verbatim excerpts from [an] unpublished manuscript" cannot be protected fair use even in news reporting and that there exists "no warrant for expanding the doctrine of fair use to create what amounts to a public figure exception to copyright."[75] Therefore, in a case involving a Human Cannonball that is discussed more fully in Chapter 8, it found no First Amendment journalistic right to broadcast video of a newsworthy but only seconds-long performance.

The attorney for the Timberlake-Biel wedding guest argued that Gawker, therefore, had infringed on his copyright in the tape and, given the strength of copyright law, Gawker was apparently sufficiently concerned that he was correct, even though the video was so sufficiently newsworthy that it had sparked tabloid, celebrity magazine, and significant mainstream newspaper coverage of what appeared to be Hollywood's tone-deafness to the plight of the homeless.

Justin Timberlake, though not apparently directly involved with the production, would later explain in a *People* article about the video that he is "a pretty private person." In this instance, favorable copyright laws helped him maintain at least some of that privacy, more generously than would have been available to him through traditional privacy tort protections. In any event, a seemingly newsworthy story was, in the end, affected.

There are other examples.

A Victim's Nude Pictures

Nancy Benoit was a professional wrestler who had married another professional wrestler. After several years of marriage, Christopher Benoit killed Nancy Benoit and then killed himself. The murder-suicide attracted much attention in the media.

That included *Hustler* magazine. Its March 2008 issue included a short story about the crime along with ten photographs taken of Benoit during a nude photo session many years before. Its cover headlines included "Wrestler Chris Benoit's Murdered Wife Nude."

A distressed Maureen Toffoloni, Nancy Benoit's mother, sued. Because Benoit was dead, she could not claim a privacy tort violation for her daughter because oftentimes the right to sue for a privacy invasion dies with the one whose privacy has been invaded. However, a separate but similar tort, the right to publicity, nearly identical to privacy's misappropriation tort, gives some heirs the right to sue on a deceased's behalf. It arises when someone has used another's name or likeness without permission, giving individuals the right to control their images so that others do not profit from them.

Like copyright, however, the right to publicity has a newsworthiness exception. This ensures that magazines or websites are not sued each time they report Hollywood gossip or publish a celebrity photograph. Courts have held that "where an incident is a matter of public interest, or the subject matter of a public investigation, a publication in connection therewith can be a violation of no one's legal right of privacy" and that "where the publication is newsworthy, the right of publicity gives way to freedom of the press."[76]

Hustler magazine argued that its use of the Nancy Benoit photographs was in connection with a newsworthy story, her murder, and that the photos helped show the modest start to her career. Publisher Larry Flynt would later testify that he believed that the photographs were newsworthy based upon First Amendment press freedoms and the considerable mainstream coverage of her murder.[77]

The court hearing the right-to-publicity claim put the issue it had to decide this way: "whether a brief biographical piece can ratchet otherwise protected, personal photographs into the newsworthiness exception."

The court decided that the answer was no. In doing so, it rejected *Hustler*'s claim that the photographs had news value—and in a surprisingly broad way. First, it noted that most people are nude at some point daily and yet news media do not report on such mundane occurrences. Second, it noted that it had the right to draw lines between newsworthiness and morbid prying, even though the cases it used as precedent had pro-media outcomes. Third, it based part of its determination on the way the story was laid out: "The heart of the article was the publication of nude photographs—not the corresponding biography," the court wrote, finding the short biographical sketch merely "incidental" to the publication of the photographs, and not the other way around.

Ultimately, the court held that the photographs had absolutely no news value, no relevance to anything of legitimate public concern, and in "no conceivable way" were related to the appropriately newsworthy story of Benoit's death. *Hustler* "may not make public private, nude images of Benoit that she, allegedly, expressly did not wish made public, simply because she once wished to be a model and was then murdered," it wrote.

The court's surprisingly strong rejection of any newsworthiness could well have a lasting effect on future cases for reasons in addition to its anti-media holding. A jury had awarded Nancy Benoit's mother $125,000 in compensatory damages and $19,603,600 in punitive damages in the case, though later court decisions reduced those numbers considerably, based upon other, proof-related grounds.

A Copyrighted Secret Marriage

Noelia Lorenzo Monge is a pop singer and Jorge Reynoso is her manager. For several months, there were rumors that the two had been married in a secret ceremony, but both denied it, even to their families. In 2009, Reynoso's mother called to confront him because this time she had proof: their wedding photos, taken two years before, had been published in the Spanish-language gossip magazine *TVNotas*. The wedding was touted on the cover as "The Secret Wedding of Noelia and Jorge Reynoso in Las Vegas" with a subhead promising "We even have photos of their first night as a married couple!"

The magazine had purchased the photographs from the couple's occasional driver who, somewhat implausibly, had a parallel career as a sometime-paparazzo. He had given Reynoso the use of his car and he claimed that he had found the photographs on a USB drive left behind. He sold the photos to *TVNotas* for $1500.

Monge and Reynoso were outraged. They had purposely kept their wedding secret from everyone because, as the federal court hearing an appeal in their case against the magazine put it, they "[v]alu[ed] their privacy, and Monge's image as a young, single pop singer."[78]

Any privacy claim brought against the magazine, of course, would fail because it is newsworthy when a celebrity weds, even if that celebrity would rather the information remain private. But because intellectual property law is significantly less protective of revelation journalism, Monge and Reynoso brought their claims under copyright, arguing that they had intellectual property rights in the photographs that they had taken of themselves during their wedding.

The federal trial court hearing the case decided against the celebrity couple, finding that the news value in their wedding and the newsworthiness of the photos gave the magazine "fair use" rights to publish them. A two-judge majority on appeal, however, sent the case back to the trial court in an opinion that clearly sided with the celebrities and their privacy, even though the court was quick to point out that "the protection of privacy is not a function of copyright law."

First, the appeals court judges called the wedding photos "sensational" and criticized the magazine for its commercial nature, for manufacturing newsworthiness, and for attempting to scoop the story. Second, they suggested editorially the ways in which the magazine could have covered the matter without, in their opinion, violating copyright:

> While we do not discredit [the magazine's] legitimate role as a news gatherer, its reporting purpose could have been served through publication of the couple's marriage certificate or other sources rather than copyrighted photos. Even absent official documentation, one clear portrait depicting the newly married couple in wedding garb with the priest would certainly have sufficed to verify the clandestine wedding. Maya used far more than was necessary to corroborate its story—all three wedding images and three post-wedding photos.

In working through the fair use newsworthiness test, the court found that all four parts of the analysis seemed to favor the couple's copyright claim: first, the publication was decidedly a commercial endeavor; second, the photographs were creative and had not yet been published; third, the magazine had used multiple photos of the wedding, "much more than was necessary to corroborate the story"; and, fourth, such use had left the couple unable to sell their wedding photos for a profit.

The court's focus, then, was decidedly not on the news value of the photographs but on their value as property. "Waiving the news reporting flag," it wrote, "is not a get out of jail free card in the copyright arena." In favoring copyright, the court helped any celebrity who, like Monge, wished "to protect her image of being a single singer to appeal to young people" despite the truth that she was married.

The dissent worried about implications of the decision far beyond a celebrity wedding:

> The majority's fair use analysis in this case is inconsistent with Supreme Court precedent, and thwarts the public interests of copyright by allowing newsworthy public figures to control their images in the press. The majority

contends that the public interest in a free press cannot trump a celebrity's right to control his image and works in the media—even if that celebrity has publicly controverted the very subject matter of the works at issue. Under the majority's analysis, public figures could invoke copyright protection to prevent the media's disclosure of any embarrassing or incriminating works by claiming that such images were intended only for private use. The implications of this analysis undermine the free press and eviscerate the principles upon which copyright was founded. Although newsworthiness alone is insufficient to invoke fair use, public figures should not be able to hide behind the cloak of copyright to prevent the news media from exposing their fallacies.

The dissenting judge used as two examples Tiger Woods and Anthony Weiner, arguing that intellectual property rights in Woods' texts and Weiner's sexts would have prevented media from reporting fully on their missteps.

"The majority's proposed test," the dissenting judge warned, and its decision that the photographs were "unnecessary" to the news story, "would effectively vest in the courts the power to circumscribe news stories and the sources upon which the media may rely"—even in a case in which traditional privacy law would not apply.

Law's Pushback against Media: Neutral Reportage

When a person is accused of or is arrested for a crime, media generally receives notice in the form of a press release from law enforcement authorities. The strong public interest in crime news means that reporters will often communicate with police several times a day to find out about or update criminal investigations. Reporters then use the information gleaned from police sources to write news stories. Many times, they will add information from outside sources, including interviews with witnesses or even the accused himself.

Sometimes, the person accused or arrested is later found to be unconnected with the crime. For him, however, the stain of the accusation remains in the pages of newspapers and, today, on webpages. The information about the arrest remains true, but its gist is no longer completely accurate because the person was absolved.

To prevent the numerous arrested and once-accused from bringing hundreds of thousands of claims against journalists, therefore, the law has traditionally protected media through privileges, including those known as neutral reportage and fair reportage.

In order for such privileges to apply, "the accusation must concern a matter of public interest" and "a media defendant must have accurately and disinterestedly republished the defamatory accusation" or the now-defamatory accusation that was released by police or another government source. The idea is that journalists should be free to report newsworthy information when it is released and not be forced to wait until a trial is completed to report that someone had been arrested for a particular crime.

But, as in the other examples within this chapter and otherwise, legal protection for media based on neutral reportage is waning. Media law scholar Kyu Ho Youm suggests that in recent years it has "suffered a series of significant setbacks in the United States."[79] Two examples follow.

Reporting on a Press Release

The Catholic Diocese of Steubenville, Ohio, issued a press release regarding a high school teacher and head football coach in 2011. Diocese officials reported that their initial investigation had found a student's claim of physical abuse to have "a semblance of truth" and that, as part of the Archdiocese's "Decree on Child Protection" mandating certain procedures in the event of such an accusation, the authorities had been contacted and the teacher had been placed on paid leave.

The next day, the Steubenville *Herald Star* newspaper wrote an article based in large part upon the press release. The article also contained the teacher's biographical information and detailed the procedures mandated in the Decree on Child Protection. Finally, it contained a "statement" from the Survivors Network of Those Abused by Priests suggesting that anyone who had been harmed by the accused teacher come forward to police, who were "the proper officials to be investigating crimes against kids."

At the time, of course, people in the United States continued to read about very serious allegations of child sexual abuse brought against multiple Catholic priests, and several leading figures in the Roman Catholic Church had been reprimanded for keeping claims quiet. The Decree on Child Protection was designed in response, both to prevent abuse and to prevent the suppression of information on an alleged child abuser. "There is benefit to a forthright and honest presentation of the Church's attempt to provide a suitable response to incidents and allegations of child abuse within the Church," the Decree read in 2013.[80]

After the teacher/coach was cleared by the Diocese, he brought an action against the newspaper for IIED, NIED, and defamation for publication of the article regarding his paid leave and the investigation. He argued that, because he had ultimately been cleared, the article contained false statements and that anyone who had read the article would have concluded that he had physically abused a student. The journalists defended against the claim on neutral reportage grounds, arguing that the article accurately described the press release, and that at the time the article was written, the information within it was substantially true.

The trial court sided with the journalists, finding that the information revealed in the release and news story was "a matter of public record" and that the statement at the end concerned a matter of public interest and had come from a prominent and responsible source. Moreover, the court concluded, the journalists had reported it in a "disinterested" way. Therefore, the neutral reportage privilege applied.

The appellate court, however, reversed and praised the teacher's arguments as "meritorious." First, it noted that while several intermediate level appellate courts in Ohio had adopted the principle of neutral reportage, its own appellate jurisdiction had never decided a neutral reportage case and, therefore, had never adopted it. Second, the Ohio Supreme Court had never explicitly adopted the privilege and, therefore, there was no mandatory authority from a higher court. Because the appeals court found neutral reportage unavailable as a defense within the jurisdiction, it sent the case back to the trial court to hear all of the teacher's claims.[81]

The decision, of course, has far-reaching effects within that jurisdiction and beyond. If claims of emotional distress and defamation claims can be brought based upon an article regarding an official news release about an official investigation, reporting on similar pending matters with appended comments from interested parties creates a minefield for journalists.

It is also worth noting that the Ohio appellate jurisdictions that had accepted the neutral reportage privilege had done so in the 1980s heyday of journalism. This court, in 2013, flatly rejected it.

A Failure to Attribute and Fairness

Like the neutral reporting privilege, the fair reporting privilege serves to protect journalists who report on judicial and other proceedings of public concern, including related documents. The idea is that such protection allows "the press [to] freely serve as a kind of 'government watchdog'" and to report on matters springing from the courtroom and beyond.[82] Kentucky, of relevance here, codified fair reporting in 1936.

In 2004, a newspaper in Kentucky reported that various state offices, including the Kentucky Board of Medical Licensure, had been investigating a radiologist based upon a letter from another doctor accusing the radiologist of failing to perform his job; the letter was said to have criticized the radiologist's "quality of medical care" and "professionalism,"[83] and requested that he be fired. An Office of the Inspector General investigation concluded that the allegations in the letter were substantiated.[84] An additional complaint led to an additional investigation and those allegations were said to have been substantiated as well. The findings led to threats that the medical center where the doctor worked would lose its Medicare and Medicaid funding. After the facility instituted a "Plan of Correction," that did not happen.

At the same time, as the trial court hearing a related case explained, the hospital had launched its own internal investigation and had temporarily suspended the radiologist's clinical privileges to interpret imaging. A committee interviewed others at the hospital and discovered what was said to be a "general lack of confidence" in the radiologist's practice. Committee members recommended that the hospital revoke the privileges. In the meantime, several patients had brought civil claims against the radiologist, claiming that he had misread their x-rays.

Ultimately, the hospital's board terminated the doctor's contract but explained that it was not a for-cause termination. The state initially suspended him from practicing medicine in the state but later reinstated his medical license with "certain restrictions and conditions."[85]

At the time of the state investigations, a Kentucky newspaper had published a series of articles about the proceedings and had included some of the allegations that had been made in the original letter critical of the radiologist. The newspaper's editor would later testify that those in the newsroom had "published the article without regard to the truthfulness of the allegations," as the fair reporting privilege allowed, "being only concerned with reporting the [letter's] allegations accurately." Meantime, a local television station had received a letter containing allegations against the doctor that had reportedly been sent to the state and similarly reported on the alleged wrongdoing.

The doctor eventually sued the newspaper for torts that included false light and IIED. As the court hearing the case would explain, "[s]everal of the articles began on the front page of the newspaper and continued to interior pages [and] Plaintiff alleges that the articles were maliciously false" by accusing him of gross negligence and placing patients in danger.[86] The media defendants, meantime, argued that they were protected by the statutory fair reporting privilege based upon the original critical letter that had become part of the public investigations.

The trial court, however, strongly rejected the newspaper's defense. First, even though it was a federal court and thereby mandated to apply state law, it decided that the state's fair reporting privilege did not apply under the circumstances: "The Court does not believe . . . that Kentucky courts would hand news reporters a carte blanche privilege," it wrote, and that "[t]o exercise the watchdog role legitimately, the publisher must have knowledge that he or she is reporting on a relevant proceeding." That had not been shown to the court's satisfaction.

In the relevant articles, the court decided, there was no mention of the letter being connected to any state investigation. Even though the letter ultimately was, in fact, connected and had been filed as a part of the investigative proceeding, in the court's mind, the newspaper's failure to mention the connection meant that it could not use the fair reporting privilege as a defense. As the court explained, "[T]he public's interest is only served if the reader understands [that] the article describes government proceedings." Put succinctly, then, no attribution meant no privilege, because there was no "substantially accurate account"—even though the articles themselves had apparently fairly and impartially described the letter itself.

Because the fair reporting privilege failed to apply, the plaintiff needed only to prove that the media defendants had been negligent, the court reasoned, and then suggested that, in its opinion, the defendants had behaved negligently.

Law's Pushback against Media:
FOIA and Other Limits on Access

The U.S. Supreme Court decided in the *Favish* case that family privacy could trump freedom of information, thereby keeping certain government records in the files of government and out of the hands of media and other interested parties. Other courts have similarly restricted public information on privacy-related grounds, perhaps the most interesting of which involve traditionally newsworthy events: the arrest of a public figure or certain coverage of a high-profile trial. While it is true that FOIA and FOIA-like state statutes give everyone the right of access to certain public documents and therefore are not journalism-specific, many journalists use such laws in their reporting and some state freedom-of-information statutes offer news media some procedural protections. Hence, any new restrictions are especially relevant to journalism.

Mug Shots and Privacy

Edward J. DeBartolo, Jr., owned the San Francisco 49ers football team for five of its National Football League world championships. He had "guided the [team] to greatness," the New Orleans *Times-Picayune* reported in 2013, naming him as one on the short list for induction into the NFL's Hall of Fame. The newspaper suggested that DeBartolo had experienced some of his highest highs and lowest lows in Louisiana: he had both won a Super Bowl there and had been arrested there on federal charges related to his involvement with corruption-plagued Louisiana governor Edwin Edwards. As the *Times-Picayune* put it, "Edwards tried to extort $400,000 from DeBartolo Jr. so that [DeBartolo] would be awarded a Louisiana casino license" and, later, DeBartolo "pled guilty in federal court in Louisiana to failing to report an extortion attempt by a public official."[87]

A 2013 story on the *Times-Picayune* website featured a close-up photograph of DeBartolo from the newspaper's archives, eyes down, lips pursed, taken outside the federal courthouse in Baton Rouge. That may have been where a mug shot of DeBartolo would have illustrated the story had the *Times-Picayune* had access to DeBartolo's mug shot.

When someone as high-profile as DeBartolo is arrested, news organizations will oftentimes use such a photo when possible to illustrate a story on the arrest. Mug shots, booking photographs taken by a police agency shortly after someone is arrested, are government records generally made available to the public through police department press offices. Many police departments routinely release mug shots within hours of booking. When actress Reese Witherspoon was arrested in 2013, for example, multiple mainstream newspapers and multiple celebrity blogs published her mug shot as part of their news stories on her arrest.[88]

The reason media and others have access is because federal FOIA and state laws like it embody "a general philosophy of full agency disclosure"[89] and an exception to that openness on privacy grounds exists only when the information "could reasonably be expected to constitute an *unwarranted* invasion of personal privacy."[90] Traditionally, then, any privacy claim regarding mug shots would be quashed in light of strong presumptive disclosure language and strong, longstanding public interest in arrests and criminal charges. The Chicago Police Department, for example, releases all mug shots of those who have been arrested for prostitution in a sort of virtual shaming on its website.[91]

One court explained that the release of mug shots more generally helps "subject the government to public oversight,"[92] including evidence of police brutality or, for public figures and officials who are arrested, indications of special treatment. When Witherspoon was photographed for her mug shot, for example, her eyes were closed and her head was tilted downward; it is difficult to imagine that police would allow a non-celebrity to take a mug shot so demurely.[93]

When DeBartolo was arrested in conjunction with the corruption trial of a Louisiana governor, as a matter of course, the *Times-Picayune* asked the government to release his booking photo. The newspaper explained that, among other reasons, it wanted the photograph to help show that DeBartolo's "wealth and status ha[d] not exempted him from the procedures utilized in connection with all individuals charged with federal crimes."[94]

But the U.S. Marshals Office, the keeper of the photo, refused to release it to media—and a federal court backed that decision, mainly on privacy grounds. The court explained that a mug shot deserved protection because it was different from a regular photograph, both in terms of negativity and in terms of quality:

> Mug shots in general are notorious for their visual association of the person with criminal activity. Whether because of the unpleasant circumstances of the event or because of the equipment used, mug shots generally disclose unflattering facial expressions . . . and, arguably most humiliating of all, a sign under the accused's face with a unique Marshals Service criminal identification number.

Sure, DeBartolo was a "celebrity and a public figure," the court explained, but suggested that that was simply another good reason to keep the mug shot within the government's watchful hands. "Rival businessmen" might reason-ably be expected to use the mug shot, the court reasoned using surprisingly far-reaching speculation, "to perpetuate [DeBartolo's] criminal association," which would then trigger additional media coverage that would necessitate renewed use of his mug shot. To release this particular mug shot now, the court wrote, would be setting a public figure up for a domino-like effect of future uses by scheming rivals and eager media.

Moreover, the court extended its reasoning far beyond the case at bar to all mug shots ever taken, calling them all so "unique" and "visually powerful" that even those who had been convicted and sentenced would have grounds based on personal privacy to keep their government-taken mug shots out of the hands of media forever. "[A] mug shot's stigmatizing effect," the court explained, "can last well beyond the actual criminal proceedings" and can contribute to no legitimate interests, proved, it reasoned, by continued news coverage of DeBartolo's arrest despite the lack of a booking photograph.

But the court hinted that another reason had caused it to rule against the *Times-Picayune*. This case, it suggested, ultimately had had at its heart the fact that "printing the mug shot would invariably help sell newspapers"; in the court's mind, a for-profit news media publisher could not be trusted.

Meantime, the close-to-the-vest U.S. Marshals would just a few years later agree to participate in a reality television program titled *Manhunters: Fugitive Task Force*, in which cameras would follow them around as they pursued sus-pects in criminal activity and attempted to capture fugitives from justice. As the cable channel that aired *Manhunters* explained on its website, the program

> continues to have unparalleled and unprecedented access, granted by the Department of Justice and the U.S. Marshals, to ride along with the agents of the NY/NJ Task Force, the busiest in the country, as they track down violent criminals on the run. Audiences see these real-life Marshals in a way rarely seen in unscripted television. And audiences get much more than just great action, they get inside the minds of the fugitives as the Marshals anticipate their next moves.[95]

Mug shots of fugitive suspects featured prominently in two randomly selected segments of the program uploaded to YouTube.

But the Louisiana mug shot decision stands and in 2012, the U.S. Court of Appeals for the Tenth Circuit used it in part as support for its holding that "the privacy interest in [mug shots] outweighs the public interest in disclosure."[96]

High-Profile Privacy

In 2011, Apple Incorporated sued Samsung Electronics Company for patent and design infringements. The lawsuit attracted strong media attention; nearly 25,000 news items mentioned it from the time of filing through the appeal. As the U.S. Court of Appeals for the Federal Circuit, the court that heard the appeal, would explain, it was called by many "The Patent Trial of the Century."[97]

Because of considerable media interest, the federal trial court judge in California who had been assigned the case decided that the news media would be given "extraordinary access" to the proceedings and told the parties that "the whole trial is going to be open." Most motions and exhibits and other trial materials were shared with the press the day they were introduced. Only "exceptionally sensitive information" would be sealed, the trial court decided, given the jurisdiction's "strong presumption in favor of access to court records."

The dueling companies, however, complained that some of the items that the court had ordered unsealed needed to be kept confidential for business reasons; company officials explained that the files contained financial information, source code, market research, and licensing information. The trial judge withheld some of the files in response to those concerns but ordered that "documents disclosing the parties' product-specific profits, profit margins, unit sales, revenues and costs," market research, customer surveys, and some licensing information be unsealed because the information would be of public interest and because of the strong presumption in favor of release.

Ultimately, the matter reached the federal appeals court. Both litigants, of course, asked that the documents at issue be kept out of public and news media hands. Multiple news organizations and companies joined the appeal, arguing that the material should be unsealed as the trial judge had ordered because "the public has a strong interest in the financial information in question," including "financial risks for shareholders," "strategic impact on the companies," and consumer interests in pricing and manufacturing.

Despite the jurisdiction's mandate that court records are presumptively open, the Federal Circuit overturned the California federal trial judge's decision to unseal the documents. The appeals court noted that the companies had an interest in keeping financial information private, given the "competitive harm" that they could suffer.

In addition, directly contradicting what the trial court had held, the appellate court wrote that the public interest in such information was minimal and "not necessary to the public's understanding of the case." The media had argued that if the material were released, the public would benefit from knowing of financial risks and marketing decisions and that such information would help underscore the potential harm that the companies could face. But the court wrote flat out that such information would be "irrelevant to the public's understanding of the judicial proceedings" and that what it called "mere curiosity" would not be enough to outweigh the companies' privacy interests.

Finally, in a part of the decision sure to have far-reaching consequences, the court relied on the fact that "the material [at issue had been] stamped confidential, and [that, therefore,] only certain individuals" on a need-to-know basis had been allowed to see it. Today, it would be foolish for any company that wished to keep certain documents out of press and public hands not to indicate explicitly in-house that such documents are confidential.

The public interest in "the Patent Trial of the Century," then, was not strong enough public interest to defeat the litigant companies' privacy.

The Result

In Chapter 2, one that focused on the past, news media had it fairly good. Courts, including the Supreme Court, often lauded journalism's work and they protected speech and press from plaintiffs' privacy, intentional-infliction-of-emotional-distress, and related claims. Congress and legislators passed laws in part so that information would be accessible to media so that they could be the eyes and ears of the public. For the most part, it seemed, judges trusted journalists.

In this chapter, one focused on the present, things are not so easy. In many of the cases discussed, someone's privacy or a privacy-related right trumped what media would consider its right to know or to report or to gain access.

In some of the cases, certainly, the media overstepped an ethics line. Gawker's humiliation of the high school student is one example. But in many—the dating gossip case or the married celebrities' case or the mug shot case—such overstepping is far from clear.

These cases and their impact, as the Supreme Court warned decades ago, have the potential to change journalism. If it is possible that publishing a description of an accident scene will invade the privacy of surviving relatives, for example, or if covering a prosecutor's arrest will cause him emotional distress, or if an acquired celebrity wedding photograph could well be considered a copyright violation, a seasoned editor or media attorney may well advise a journalist not to publish, especially when mainstream media continues to hurt financially and have limited financial resources to defend lawsuits.

That could be a good thing in part, of course. Perhaps mainstream journalism has gone too far in reporting from accident scenes or in covering arrests of those later proved innocent or in violating intellectual property rights. As the next chapter shows, it has clearly overstepped some bounds.

But it can also be a very bad thing. Many journalists would likely agree with the Court that a timid press is one not likely to investigate and explode Watergate, National Security Agency wiretapping, and the use of performance-enhancing drugs among top athletes. If we don't know such things, the argument goes, we don't truly understand what is happening with our government and in our world.

The four chapters that follow explore in greater detail the reasons for this constriction in laws that once favored journalism. Today, journalism's practices, quasi-journalism's practices, a push for privacy, and a pushed-to-the-limit First Amendment have all contributed to this legal legacy.

Once, the Supreme Court worried about a chilling effect on media. Today, some courts are eager to put it on ice.

4

The Devolution of Mainstream Journalism

If indeed the tide is turning against all media, mainstream media itself is in part to blame. One example to start this chapter: the growing use of mug shot galleries within mainstream news publications.

A small number of photo galleries, for example, are always a part of the *Chicago Tribune*'s website's main page.[1] Three of the four photo galleries, or five of the six, change regularly to reflect interesting news stories of the day, upcoming events, or sports-related matters. The final is a fixture. It is titled "Mugs in the news" and it is a rogues gallery of unfortunates who were arrested in the city of Chicago in the days and weeks before.

These are not your grandmother's mug shots; they are not booking photos of the most-wanted bank robbers or hijackers or serial murderers that once graced corkboards at post offices across the nation.

Instead, they are photographs of everyday people who have been arrested, often for quite unremarkable crimes. One day in 2013, for example, the *Tribune*'s "Mugs in the news" featured people arrested for theft, for reckless driving, and for trespassing on state land. There were ninety-nine arrestees profiled that day, each identified by full name and photograph and pending charge, and each looking with a different degree of hardness, shock, or despair into the police camera. An interested viewer had to click through to each additional photograph after looking at the first; the gallery was designed to require a separate click for each mug shot.

A paragraph at the top of each photograph read, "Arrest and booking photos are provided by law enforcement officials. Arrest does not imply guilt, and criminal charges are merely accusations. A defendant is presumed innocent unless proven guilty and convicted." In order to see the full charge facing each person, however, one had to scroll down so that part of the reminder disappeared. On some laptops, the boilerplate disclaimer, then, was shortened to read simply "proven guilty and convicted."

The purpose behind the gallery of mug shots appears to be something other than public safety. As one clicked through, ads on the pages changed from car dealer to carpet cleaner to insurer to department store. Rayvon, arrested on a weapons charge, had a Sports Authority ad displayed near his photo, while Sheldon, also a weapons arrestee, had one for Macy's. The real beneficiary seems to be the *Chicago Tribune*; it receives some ad revenue, or the potential for increased ad revenue, for each ad brought up by each click.

This chapter could be titled Mainstream Media Behaving Badly for its focus on times that mainstream news media outlets have crossed or nearly crossed an ethics lines in their everyday coverage. The examples that follow are intentionally mostly routine and ordinary, as opposed to the extraordinary ethics lapses that might be discounted as anomalies.[2] Here, ordinariness helps prove an overall ethics shift that could well decrease both public and judicial reverence for news media. The mug shot parade on the *Chicago Tribune*'s website, published daily, is one such example.

The *Tribune* is not alone in its use of booking photographs. That same day in 2013, the website for a New Orleans television station featured a slideshow titled "Best of the worst: Mug shot hall of shame."[3] (One mug shot was of a blond young man with a swollen eye and a bloody cheek who had apparently climbed naked into someone's bed in West Palm Beach, Florida; these were not local mug shots.) The *Tampa Bay Times* website, meantime, featured what it boasted were the "342 people who were booked in the last 24 hours in Pinellas, Hillsborough, Manatee and Pasco counties," a gallery that obviously included many people arrested for minor offenses.[4] And the *New York Daily News* website featured eighty-six of what it called "The World's Most Hilarious Mug Shots," including the lead photograph of a 425-pound man arrested for false imprisonment—and, given his considerable girth, looking very much like a cartoon character.[5]

The explosion of such coverage—people arrested for big crimes and small and identified by name, photograph, charge, and, at times, other identifying information like height and weight—comes at the precise moment that courts are beginning to find some level of privacy in booking photographs, even, as was noted in Chapter 3, for those who later plead guilty or later are actually convicted of a crime.

Meantime, long-standing journalism ethics code provisions suggest that the publication of such mug shots could well be an ethics violation. An adherence to such ethics standards often differentiates mainstream journalism from quasi-journalism and other publications, and yet, at times it seems that the two are not so very far apart.

The Ethics Codes

The Society of Professional Journalists, with a national membership that includes news reporters and editors who work in print, web, television, and radio, adopted its current code of ethics in 1996, but similar codes have influenced the profession since at least 1926.[6] Many newsrooms and journalism organizations have their own ethics codes, but the SPJ code is overarching. It might be considered the most-relied-upon ethics code within journalism today.

The SPJ code has at its heart four main points of guidance: "Seek Truth and Report It," "Minimize Harm," "Act Independently," and "Be Accountable." Each of these sweeping measures contains several more specific provisions that are meant to help guide journalists' behavior. The code is slated for some revision in late 2014, but early proposed changes appear to be in line with the 1996 code: the four points of guidance remain, for example, as does much of the original language.

The quick descriptive sentence following "Seek Truth and Report It" suggests that "journalists should be honest, fair and courageous in gathering, reporting and interpreting information." Provisions that follow highlight the importance of accuracy in reporting and urge that journalists test the truthfulness of their stories, encourage story subjects to respond to allegations, be certain that headlines or news teases do not misrepresent the news that follows, and avoid undercover or surreptitious reporting unless "traditional open methods will not yield information vital to the public." These provisions, then, encourage courageous reporting built upon good, fair journalism.

The description for "Minimize Harm" reads, "Ethical journalists treat sources, subjects and colleagues as human beings deserving of respect." The provisions that follow in the 1996 code suggest that journalists think deeply before publishing any story that might cause someone emotional distress: "Show compassion for those who may be affected adversely by news coverage" especially children and the inexperienced, "[b]e sensitive when seeking or using interviews or photographs of those affected by tragedy or grief," "[s]how good taste," and "[r]ecognize that gathering and reporting information may cause harm or discomfort." One provision especially relevant here reads, "Only an overriding public need can justify intrusion into anyone's privacy" (though that sole mention of privacy could well be removed from any new version). The "Minimize Harm" provisions are meant to remind journalists of the harm that their stories can do and to urge them to use their publishing powers to invade privacy, to humiliate, and to embarrass only when necessary.

The "Act Independently" category suggests that "[j]ournalists should be free of obligation to any interest other than the public's right to know." Provisions that follow caution journalists to avoid real or perceived conflicts of interest, to refuse gifts and favors and special treatment, to be "vigilant and courageous about holding those with power accountable," and to deny advertisers any special treatment such as good story placement or news choices. Public relations professionals often attempt to persuade journalists to cover their clients' stories or to focus stories in a particular way and, at times, offer journalists free trips and other coverage incentives. This category urges journalists to reject those advances.

Finally, "Be Accountable" suggests that "[j]ournalists are accountable to their readers, listeners, viewers and each other." Here, the code encourages journalists to admit and to correct mistakes, to invite dialogue with the public about news coverage, to expose others' unethical practices, and to "[a]bide by the same high standards to which they hold others." Such provisions remind journalists that their own and others' mistakes must be corrected to encourage public trust in journalistic publications.

Given those ideals, a journalist who abides by the SPJ code should seemingly hesitate to publish a parade of mug shots. Several provisions put such a practice directly in conflict with ethics choices: journalists are supposed to give story subjects the opportunity to respond to stories in which they are featured; they are supposed to "give voice to the voiceless"; they are supposed to be compassionate with inexperienced subjects who find themselves suddenly a part of the news; they are supposed to recognize the harm that a public revelation such as an arrest can cause; they are supposed to give private people more power to control information about themselves than public figures; and they are supposed to use a standard of "need" as the only means to justify a privacy invasion. More directly, journalists are supposed to both "[b]e

judicious about naming criminal suspects before the formal filing of charges"
and "[b]alance a criminal suspect's fair trial rights with the public's right to be
informed." At least eight separate provisions, then, should cause a journalist
who follows the SPJ code to hesitate to publish mug shots in this manner.

The provisions within the code, however, are not meant to be hard-and-fast
rules for journalists; they are far from the mandatory ethics provisions that
lawyers and judges must follow, for example. As the SPJ explains, its code is
simply "a resource guide for ethical decision-making." Several of the current
provisions, in fact, conflict directly or indirectly: it would be impossible to
"seek truth and report it" courageously and yet minimize the certain harm
that such a story could cause someone, or to use public "need" as the standard
for invading privacy and then report a story involving a murder-suicide or a
celebrity divorce, because it is debatable whether anyone aside from relatives
really needs to know about such an event.

Seasoned, responsible journalists must therefore navigate these occasionally conflicting directives in shaping news judgment from case to case, always
sensitive to the particular context. In some rural communities, it is not unheard
of for newspapers or local radio stations to broadcast a list of the day's ambu-
lance calls, for example. The disclosure of reported medical emergencies could
be considered highly invasive, yet in the context of a community in which
neighbors wish to rally to those in need, such information could be considered
newsworthy.

Along the same lines, some newspapers, both rural and urban, publish
regular listings of all people arrested for drunk driving. The public interest
in featuring these arrestees may be less in the specific lapse or incident leading
to their arrest, than in the broader public desire to use notoriety to curb a
social ill. Whether publishing mug shots is justified may similarly depend on
the context. Few, it seems, would doubt the public's legitimate interest in a
wanted notorious criminal suspect, or in seeing photographic images of his
arrest.

This may not mean, however, that every use of a name or of a mug shot is
categorically justified by an ethically responsible sense of news judgment.
Publicizing, as does the *Chicago Tribune*, the forlorn images of random citizens who are said by police to have run afoul of a lesser criminal statute is
harder to square with the SPJ code. The difficulty stems not solely from the
humiliation of the news subject but also from the weakness of the public
interest on the particular facts.

Yet lawyers and judges, though no strangers to tensions and gray areas in the ethical rules governing their own profession, may be less attuned to the nuances and shadings of news judgment and more drawn to using high-sounding principles in the codes to condemn journalistic choice.

As noted in Chapter 1, in one of the cases brought against NBC's *To Catch a Predator*, for example, the court used what it perceived as a violation of SPJ ethics standards to support a claim of intentional infliction of emotional distress; in the court's mind, NBC had failed to recognize the harmful effect that its reporting would have on the prosecutor who had solicited a child online. Since then, plaintiffs' attorneys in other *To Catch a Predator* cases have at times wielded the code provisions in a similar fashion.

In response, as noted earlier, drafters hastened to add the disclaimer that the SPJ code "is not—nor can it be under the First Amendment—legally enforceable." Drafters note instead that the provisions are merely "voluntary" and simply "a framework" to give the public and other journalists the ability to evaluate ethical behavior and to hold news reports up to ethical scrutiny based upon professional standards. Besides, the SPJ website further explains, the organization's mission is not only ethical journalism but also the preservation of First Amendment rights. "[W]e don't want the pursuit of one," the explanation reads, "to have a negative effect on the other."

But such provisions are tantalizingly appealing to some judges, especially when they seem to be increasingly broken by news media. As a federal court in Ohio put it in a case involving coverage of a suicide and a claim by the plaintiff survivors for intentional infliction of emotional distress, "the degree of 'newsworthiness' of suicides is exemplified in [the journalists'] own policy regarding the reporting of suicides . . . [a] policy [that] provides: 'We do not report suicides unless they are part of an unusual story. . . .'"[7] How better to gauge a story's newsworthiness than by using the news organization's own newsworthiness standards, self-interested First Amendment warnings or not? A jolt to media brought through an adverse courtroom decision may, in fact, have the deterring effect that some disgusted judges have been searching for.

And yet it is important to remember that mainstream journalism remains distinctly separate from other news media—what I call quasi-journalism here—for the simple reason that it often *does* follow those provisions and others like them. In *Deciding What's News*, an overview of the news decisions of several leading journalistic publications, Herbert Gans described the ethics process in story selection this way: journalists "work within organizations

which provide them with only a limited amount of leeway in selection decisions, which is further reduced by their allegiance to professionally shared
values."[8] In other words, in a mainstream news organization, individuals must
write and report within an ethics framework based upon core values and those
values arise within the journalist herself, within her newsroom, and within
her profession.

And sometimes that ethics framework leads to surprisingly deferential
news-related decisions, even on the national level.

In 2013, for example, the U.S. government closed embassies and consulates
around the world in response to worries of a terrorist attack; a CNN story
about the move linked it to an intercepted al Qaeda message but the second
paragraph of the story read, "CNN has agreed to a request from an Obama
administration official not to publish or broadcast additional details because of
the sensitivity of the information."[9] That same year, the *Washington Post*
reported on The Smoking Gun tabloid website's publication of hacked emails
from former President George W. Bush that contained photographs of his art-
work, but it refused to publish the emails or the photographs themselves, citing
privacy concerns.[10] The *New York Times* was said to have ignored the story
altogether aside from a quick online mention.[11] In a lawsuit brought against a
former CIA agent accused of disclosing classified information to a *New York
Times* reporter, the court noted in its written opinion that the *Times* had agreed
not to publish information about the secret program in question, known as
"Classified Program No. 1."[12] And, in a decision that likely surprised many
nonjournalists, the Associated Press ended its relationship with a Pulitzer
Prize-winning photographer because it claimed that he had benignly altered a
photograph to remove a camera captured accidentally in the frame.[13]

On a more local level, in Detroit, the *Detroit News* refused to name the
suspect in the 2013 high-profile shooting death of a woman who was knocking
on his door for help; it explained that he was not being identified because no
charges had then been filed.[14] And a television station in New Orleans in 2014
decided not to use videotape of a major fire that had occurred years before in
which people had jumped to their deaths: "Television cameras captured the
horrifying moment," the station explained, "[but] Eyewitness News has
chosen not to replay it, out of respect for the victims."[15]

Every journalist has additional, more mundane examples involving politicians' alleged affairs or recreational drug use, public figures' personal lives, or
similar somewhat sensational stories, all unpublished because, ethically, in a

reporter's or editor's opinion, the individual's privacy interests or that of his family outweigh the news value of the story.[16] An ethics text used routinely in journalism classrooms across the nation puts it this way in its materials on privacy: the public perception that "journalists will do anything to get a story [is] at odds with reality."[17]

Even when mainstream publications do publish something that they fear will raise ethics concerns, they often address the matter directly. When the *Los Angeles Times,* for example, published a photograph of the body of Ambassador Christopher Stevens being dragged from the U.S. consulate in Benghazi, Libya, after a terrorist attack there—his ashen, bloody face clearly the focus of the photograph—an editor, in line with the SPJ code of ethics, explained the paper's decision:

> What makes the photograph disturbing to some readers is also what makes it newsworthy. An assault on a U.S. diplomatic mission, resulting in the death of an ambassador, is a very rare and significant event. The circumstances here made it particularly newsworthy: U.S. military action helped Libyans topple a dictator a year ago, and Stevens was well known to Libyans and admired by many.
>
> The image of the stricken ambassador, apparently being tended to by Libyan civilians, vividly captured this important event. *Times* editors, after careful consideration and discussion, selected the least grisly of the available images. Our job is to present an unvarnished picture of the news, without carelessly offending our readers. That is the balance we tried to strike with the Stevens photo.[18]

That delicate balance between newsworthiness and publication of intimate details and a refusal to publish something simply because the public would be titillated by it is why courts traditionally deferred to journalism and its news judgments. But such a subjective balance, and the shocking-to-some choices made by newspapers like the *L.A. Times,* is also why, today, some courts have started to weigh the considerations differently, increasingly siding with family privacy interests over any public right to know.

Overstepping Bounds

At the same time the *Los Angeles Times* was struggling with whether to use a photograph of Ambassador Stevens' body, a CNN reporter had found the ambassador's personal diary in the rubble of the consulate, took it, opened it, read it, transcribed it, shared it with multiple people within the news organization, and then, according to CNN news anchor Anderson Cooper, "reported what [CNN] found newsworthy." The network said that it needed to report the information to contradict the government's initial claims that the attack did not appear to be terrorism;[19] in other words, it used information from the diary that it believed had news value, specifically Stevens' worries about a terrorist attack at the consulate. That does not explain its decision to pick up the diary in the first place and read through it, however.

In response to that behavior and the newsroom decisions that followed, the State Department issued a blistering criticism of the network's conduct:

> Given the truth of how this was handled, CNN patting themselves on the back is disgusting.
>
> What they're not owning up to is reading and transcribing Chris's diary well before bothering to tell the family or anyone else that they took it from the site of the attack. Or that when they finally did tell them, they completely ignored the wishes of the family, and ultimately broke their pledge made to them only hours after they witnessed the return to the United States of Chris's remains.
>
> Whose first instinct is to remove from a crime scene the diary of a man killed along with three other Americans serving our country, read it, transcribe it, email it around your newsroom for others to read, and only when their curiosity is fully satisfied thinks to call the family or notify the authorities?
>
> When a junior person at CNN called, they didn't say, 'Hello, I know this is a terrible time, but I'm sure you want your son's diary, where do you want it sent?' They instead took the opportunity to ask the family if CNN could report on its contents. Contents known only to Chris Stevens, and those at CNN who had already invaded his privacy.[20]

In a legal sense, of course, CNN hadn't invaded Stevens' privacy at all because, traditionally, the right to sue for a privacy invasion dies with the person. But the episode in Benghazi provided more evidence in the minds of some that journalists no longer have boundaries of their own.

As CNN's use of the diary came to light, some viewers and readers accused the network's reporters of being opportunistic[21] and of using the personal diary in stories for the media giant's own economic gain.[22] The charges are common ones after publication of many sensational stories, and, given mainstream media's economic interests and the news choices that can result, they have at least some basis in reality. CNN itself provides a fine example. One day in late

2012, at least thirteen of the nearly forty stories highlighted on CNN's important "This Just In" list on its main webpage had no significant news value, at least in a traditional sense. They included "Would you use this glass restroom?" and "Dad pranks tot with sour candy." One of the admittedly newsworthy but also titillating stories, "Bisexual congresswoman elected," had been placed between "Most-watched YouTube video ever is . . ." and "Apes have mid-life crisis too," and had been linked on the website for well more than a day. Such headlines, such an overall news scheme, and such extended use of stories point to economic concerns rather than news-based choices.

Thoughts that economic pressures drive many of today's news decisions make sense when a historically significant newspaper like the New Orleans *Times-Picayune* in 2012 fired nearly half its seasoned reporters, including prize winners, replacing some with younger, less experienced journalists hired at a lower wage, and moved to a three-day-per-week publishing schedule for the traditional newspaper.[23] A local city paper described the firings as "newsroom carnage," a "Katrina"-like event that would surely also kill local coverage.[24] The story tracked the journalists' fate with an initial focus on an individual reporter:

> He was just one of more than 200 *Times-Picayune* employees who were told that day that their services would no longer be required after Sept. 30[, 2012]. Eighty-four of the cuts came from the newsroom staff that previously numbered 175—a 48 percent reduction. . . . [T]he paper's entire marketing department was fired save one person. All special sections employees, the library staff and human resources employees were presented with severance papers. The pressroom was cut by nearly 40 percent.

Shortly thereafter, one of the experienced and involuntarily let go journalists sent an email to newspaper executives. She explained that she had just worked a Saturday night because, apparently for economic reasons, there was no Saturday night reporter and she felt responsible for a breaking murder story. The next day, she had attempted to write an overview story on the day's crimes, but found an article about a second killing buried online at the bottom of the "river" of less significant stories that had been more recently filed. With obvious frustration, she mourned the end of the type of journalism she cared deeply about:

> I am writing you because I care about our product and I care about being the best reporter—sorry—content provider—I can be until I no longer have

a job. But our product is suffering. Big time. And you all should be aware of that because it means losing respect in the community and losing readers and I'm not sure ya'll want to be risking that right now. I talk to the community. A lot. I'm not sure if any of you are on the streets getting the opinions of our readers, you should be—during this time of transition. But if you aren't—I can tell you that everyone hates our website and is losing respect for us as a hard news leader. And this morning—despite the hard work I do to provide the story—I can see why.[25]

Meantime, at the *Chicago Sun-Times,* newspaper executives in 2013 announced that the paper's entire photography staff would be laid off in favor of freelancers.[26] Writing about the layoffs, a *Chicago Magazine* writer mused that "it's little wonder that 'demoralized,' 'depressed,' and 'disrespected' are the words [he had] hear[d] most from *Sun-Times* staffers to describe the mood in the newsroom."[27] The Poynter Institute, the journalism ethics think tank, explained in an interview with a journalist why those feelings would be increasingly universal, based in part on the new journalistic pressure to "feed the beast." Consider the following description of the standard operating procedure at one publication and the resulting potential legal implications:

> We don't hold information anymore. The station bought us iPhones about a year ago. As soon as you get on the scene of a story, you snap a couple of pictures and you get it on the website. You're streaming video on the Web if you're not going to be live on TV. This constant flow of information starts the moment you get somewhere. You may sometimes hold back if you don't see another crew somewhere, but most of the time that ends up blowing up in your face, so most of the time we instantly put it on air or online.[28]

The Poynter writer explained that such reports were not reviewed by an editor in advance of publication and, therefore, had led to proliferating "typos, factual errors and single-source stories."

The Pew Research Center's Project for Excellence in Journalism in its 2013 Annual Report on American Journalism also highlighted the problem when it identified "[t]he effects of a decade of newsroom cutbacks" as the first of six major trends of 2013.[29] It warned that "a continued erosion of news reporting resources" had led to "a news industry that is more undermanned and unprepared to uncover stories, dig deep into emerging ones or to question information put into its hands."

Therefore, CNN, obviously, is not alone in its quest for readers. Other bottom-line–conscious mainstream publications seem to focus on the sensational or the unusual for the sake of clicks. In 2012, the *Washington Post* sent out two "breaking news" emails when the CIA director resigned. The first, which one reader received at 2:30 p.m., had a subject line that read simply, "CIA Director David Petraeus resigns." The information in the body of the email reported only that the four-star general had submitted his resignation, along with a link to a story. The *Post*'s second breaking news email, presumably written for additional clicks, arrived three minutes later and was more sensational. Its subject line read "CIA Director Petraeus steps down, citing extramarital affair"; the body of the email repeated the information about the affair, naming the Director of National Intelligence as the source and provided a different link.[30] The information about the affair was significant, of course, but perhaps not so much that it warranted its own follow-up "breaking news" alert three minutes after some readers had already been invited to link through to the story of his resignation.

The way in which the pursuit of clicks is reshaping featured content is also shown by mainstream journalism's increasing use of slideshows. As one expert explained, "[s]lideshows result in a ton of pageviews, which increases banner ad impressions, which, in turn, makes advertisers feel like they got more eyeballs than they really did."[31] Those slideshows would include, presumably, the *Chicago Tribune*'s gallery of ninety-nine mug shots that requires ninety-nine clicks, and, among many others, the *San Francisco Chronicle*'s "Top Ten Cannabis Strains of 2012"[32] and the *Washington Post*'s "Top ten most-stolen vehicles,"[33] both of which required ten clicks and both of which featured stock photos. The latter list caused a commenter to complain:

> The Washington Post used to be a real newspaper. A slide show of cars? Wow, color me unimpressed. Why not an article on why these are the most stolen. Is it ease of stealing? Availability? "Chop-Shop" potential? Do parts fit multiple models? Do they have good use in other criminal activities ([a]re they [favorites] of drug runners, etc.)? This isn't journalism—it is reprinting a list from an agency.[34]

Also for financial reasons, newspapers like New Orleans' *Times-Picayune* have abandoned or curtailed printing daily newspapers and have shifted significantly to online platforms. The newspaper's website, Nola.com, is now a river of stories in which the latest story to post pushes the story below it down and, eventually, off the homepage. This is said to somehow encourage more clicks through Google searches but it can leave hometown readers confused about the location of, the importance of, and even the truthfulness of news stories they have heard from others. On Nola.com's homepage, a very small number of "top" stories are posted above the stories posted chronologically, but no other layout helps guide readers toward the top stories of the day. On most days, at least one of the highlighted few is sports related and, within the river itself, often an important crime story is pushed off the main page by a flood of sport-related snippets.

The Horrifying, the Provocative, the Embarrassing

As journalism ethics texts suggest, the news choices that seem to leave the strongest negative impression on readers are those that seem more clearly to violate ethics and also seem to have been made more precisely with an eye toward an economic bottom line. These news choices range from the horrifying to the provocative to the embarrassing-for-some; they are sometimes based on what journalists would call enterprise reporting, or a reporter's own story-generating sense, and sometimes based on what others have reported.

Three examples follow.

First, the horrifying. Just after Thanksgiving in 2012, fifty-eight-year-old Ki Suk Han waited for a subway train at the Times Square station in Manhattan. An apparently homeless man confronted him and, after the two exchanged words, the man pushed Han onto the tracks in front of an approaching subway train. Han knew that he was about to be hit. He grabbed the side of the platform with his left arm and faced the subway train's two front lights. Seconds later, the train would crush him to death.

We know Han's precise posture as he faced his demise because the *New York Post* tabloid published a full-page photograph of him, mere seconds before impact, on its cover on December 4, 2012. "DOOMED," the headline read just below the photograph of Han as he struggled to hang on to the side of the platform. Just above Han's head, the subhead read, "Pushed on the subway track, this man is about to die."[35] Even in the world of tabloid journalism, admittedly very close to the quasi-journalism line, such a photograph with two such horrific headlines was shocking. On the paper's website, the same photo of Han facing death appeared, with an inset photograph of Han's face, presumably from his driver's license.[36] The photograph's cutline read, "Ki Suk Han, 58, of Queens frantically tries to climb to safety yesterday as a train bears down on him in Midtown. He was fatally struck seconds later."

The photographer, described as a freelancer for the *Post,* suggested that he had had no time to try to save the man and that, on autopilot, he had attempted to use his camera's flash to alert the train. "Critics Are Unfair to Condemn Me," the headline for the *Post*'s story about the photographer's actions read.[37] Aside from a general ethics discussion regarding whether anyone should get involved in a public fight,[38] there is no evidence online that the *Post* ever explained its choice to publish the man's final seconds on the tabloid's front page where it would be seen on newsstands and in newspaper boxes across New York City. The focus of that general ethics discussion was very much on what had happened on the platform—the taking of the photograph by a photographer who explained that he was on autopilot—and not on what had happened in the newsroom—the decision to publish such a photograph, sure to emotionally injure Han's already devastated family members and in a way that they would be most certain to see it.

In covering the *Post*'s story, CNN's focus, in contrast, was on the decisions made in the *Post* newsroom. "This is what tabloids do," then-CNN media critic Howard Kurtz wrote with disgust, "milk tragedy for every ounce of emotional impact." He theorized with at least some hyperbole that the *Post* had known that "everyone in New York would be gripped by the image."[39] In CNN's video report about the death, it obscured Han's face both in a video of him standing in front of the man who would soon push him onto the tracks and in a still photograph taken from that video. CNN did not use an image of the *Post*'s cover in its story.

The *Chicago Tribune,* however, published a photograph of the *Post*'s "DOOMED" cover, as part of a story it described rather matter-of-factly as "reviv[ing] a journalistic dilemma that now has a 21st Century twist." The *Tribune*'s focus was on whether the photographer had done the right thing: "Do you risk your own life to save the man? Are you too stunned to react at all? Do you take pictures?" the lead *Tribune* paragraph asked in a series of what some might consider tone-deaf questions because, even if you do, you can choose not to publish those images, as can a re-publisher such as the *Tribune* itself. The *New York Times,* too, published online a picture of the tabloid's cover.

The Poynter Institute addressed the coverage from an ethics perspective. "All journalists," a columnist reported on the website, who were "talking about [the decision] online [had] concluded [that] the *Post* was wrong to use the photo, especially on its front-page."[40] Presumably, then, at least two nontabloid publications were wrong to use it in their coverage as well. The *New York Post* is owned by the notorious tabloid titan Rupert Murdoch. But the *Chicago Tribune* and the *New York Times* are not.

A second example, one of the provocative, comes from the *Chicago Tribune*. As a part of its "Watchdog" series, in 2009, the newspaper published several articles subheaded "Clout goes to college," a multi-part exposé of a University of Illinois practice that gave some well-connected applicants a preference for admittance into various undergraduate and graduate programs despite at times lower grade point averages and standardized test scores.[41] "The records chronicle a shadow admissions system in which some students won spots at the state's most prestigious public university over the protests of admissions officers," the *Tribune* reported, "while others had their rejections reversed during an unadvertised appeal process." *Tribune* reporters had confirmed the story through redacted-for-student-privacy emails from and to university leaders, which had been made available to them through freedom-of-information laws.

Throughout its series, the *Tribune* did not name the students themselves, though at times the hints were strong enough so that anyone who knew them would have been able to recognize them. Not naming them seems ethically correct: it was not clear that any of the students, many of whom were still teenagers and some of whom were undoubtedly minors, had known that well-placed others had gone to bat for them in their quest to be admitted to the university.

As a part of the series, the *Tribune* published copies of several of the emails in question, including one in which, presumably through university error, a student's last name was not redacted. That student's full name and his email address were scrawled at the bottom of the reproduced email, presumably by a reporter who had attempted to contact the student. Shortly thereafter, the email was taken down. Ethically, that protected the student's privacy at least in part; the image of the email itself had alleged that his test scores and GPA were "well below" the twenty-fifth percentile of the incoming class. "There is no track record of success," the email as it was initially published read, and its author, an admissions officer in the university's law school, suggested that the university was setting the student up to fail, that there was absolutely no reason to expect anything other than failure, and that the student would both struggle with classes and with the bar exam. When the email was reposted, it did not contain that information or any student identifiers.

That much of the story is not so remarkable; the email publication appeared to be a momentary, accidental lapse. What is remarkable, however, is the *Tribune*'s use of public comments after many of the "Clout Goes to College" stories, including one it titled "Squeeze on Law School."[42] With ample hints throughout the story about the students in question, it required no great leap to recognize that some would wish to posit about just who these students were.

One comment, posted by a person who called himself or herself "Not messing around," reprinted a job description that one of the allegedly "clouted" students had posted online several months before. "Not messing around" also named the student. Another poster, "Observer," responded that the so-called "clouted" student—a person "Observer" described as low-scoring and unqualified—currently worked at a government job in Chicago. Poster "Morse L Stop is Awful" joined the fray to inform others that the student had become an attorney after passing the February bar exam; he or she asked if anyone knew whether the student had taken the test earlier. A poster who called himself or herself "okay" reported, potentially with no basis in fact, that the student had in fact failed the previous July's bar exam. "Okay" posted a new message just a few minutes later, noting that the University of Illinois bar passage rate was over 90 percent at the time the student was alleged by commenters to have taken the bar exam and failed.[43]

In other words, even though the *Tribune* had been careful not to name students directly within the text of its stories, it had allowed commenters to do so freely, uniting strangers' either defamatory or privacy-invading missives with its own reporting. Certainly, those who decided to open the story to comments knew that commenters would disparage those individuals at whom the stories hinted. Today, the *Tribune* closes some news stories and features, including "Mugs in the News," to public comments.

Third is an example that involves the publication of deeply embarrassing information. There are, of course, a vast number of embarrassing vignettes published online, but many of them are posted by quasi-journalists or other publishers. Take the video apparently surreptitiously recorded and later posted to YouTube of a woman inside a vehicle driven by her husband. The woman appeared to be in her twenties and would have been recognizable to anyone who knew her. As the video continued, she got increasingly frustrated because her husband would not take her to "the lake," and eventually kicked her legs up within the vehicle, screaming repeatedly in a sort of temper tantrum. At various points in the video, the husband chuckled audibly, knowing that he was recording her. At the video's end, the wife admitted that she would soon text her friends to complain about her husband's decision to spend time with his truck instead of her. In response, he turns the camera on himself and says with a smile, "When they see this video, they'll understand."

Her friends presumably did see the video because it eventually found its way to CNN. Though it is not clear precisely when the husband posted the video, posters on the internet-sharing website Reddit apparently first discovered it and began discussing it on July 21, 2013, though the original comment string has since been disabled. The very next day, the tabloid website Gawker linked the video in a story it titled, "Man Records Final Fight with Soon-to-Be-Ex-Wife, Uploads It to YouTube," one in which it named the couple.[44] As Gawker reported, apparently based upon an interview with the husband (and presumably one-sided information that could very well not be accurate and, therefore, potentially defamatory):

> After dealing with her drinking problems ("she is on probation for a DUI"), trying to patch things up through marriage counseling ("she showed up 10 minutes late and left"), and suffering in silence while she repeatedly tried "to convince all of her friends that I was always yelling and cussing," [the husband] decided to call it a day.

That Gawker post and the copy of the tantrum video that accompanied it received nearly 800,000 views. On July 23, the day after Gawker had published its first story, the video landed on the tabloid *New York Daily News* website, among others. The day after that, Gawker suggested that the video was "the temper tantrum heard round the world" and began a follow-up story this way: "By now you've no doubt seen the video of [the husband] . . . and his wife of 15 months . . . engaging in a lovers' spat over a cancelled trip to the lake."

Finally, on July 25, presumably less than one week after the husband had posted the video, CNN covered the story. It blurred the wife's face in its report but aired her screaming complaints. The line at the bottom of CNN's video read, "Husband: Social Media Ruined Marriage," though the story noted that the husband was the one who had originally posted the video "for the whole world to see."

Indeed, the world had seen it; news websites in Great Britain and New Zealand reported on the videotaped tantrum, and the *Daily Mail* interviewed the wife's mother, who reported that her daughter, a nurse, was "humiliated," "blindsided," and had had no idea that she was being filmed.[45] By summer's end, YouTube had removed the original post "as a violation of YouTube's policy prohibiting material designed to harass, bully, or threaten," but the video remained on many media websites, including the portions that aired on CNN.

Within a matter of just a few days, then, a woman's private meltdown inside a private vehicle in front of just one other person had become worldwide mainstream news with a video record of her actions seen by millions.

Each of those examples of mainstream media pushing an ethics envelope—the horrifying, the sensational, the embarrassing—is far from unique. In 2012, a Fox cable channel aired live video of a man who ended a chase with police by exiting his car and shooting himself in the head.[46] In 2011, the *Chicago Tribune* reported the story of a teen who had murdered his four-year-old sister and included in highly graphic, gut-wrenching, and horrifying detail information about the way the girl looked, what she was wearing and doing as her brother attacked her with a knife, and precisely what she said when she pleaded with him to stop stabbing her.[47] In 2013, the *New York Daily News* included actual video taken from a cell phone of a woman's suicide jump it titled "Terminally ill woman jumps to her death from Argentina's Iguazu Falls in front of horrified tourists."[48] The *New York Post* tabloid published an article quoting the husband of a woman injured by teens who had thrown a shopping cart from a walkway above; the article showed the husband running in Central Park and included the happy news that she was recovering, based upon a reporter's interview with the husband.[49] In the first comment after the story, however, a commenter who identified himself as the husband wrote that he had been hounded by the reporter: "I did not 'speak out,'" he explained in his comment, "I was chased into central park while walking my dogs. The reporter ran to catch me. Stood in front of me and asked me a few questions. It is not my intention to be rude. But I have not sought press and would appreciate having the surveillance of our house suspended. . . ." Finally, in 2013, a Detroit newspaper published the story of a fifteen-year-old girl who had run away with a thirty-seven-year-old man. She had required "days in a hospital psychiatric ward" and was "ashamed" and "humiliated" by her decision to leave home with him, the paper reported, feelings likely exacerbated by the invasive and seemingly ethics-violating newspaper coverage of her mental state.[50]

Those are all more horrifying examples of mainstream journalism overstepping an ethics line. Some examples of provocative mainstream reporting with the same outcome include a series of articles written by mainstream news outlets presumably in response to news releases sent by "the world's largest Sugar Daddy web site."[51] The press releases and the resulting news stories suggested that there had been a tremendous increase in college women who had signed up to search for "sugar daddies," men they hoped would help pay their tuition in exchange for sex; there had been a "113% growth" in such hopefuls, one breathless mainstream newspaper reported.[52] Numerous print media, including the *Detroit Free Press*,[53] the *Philadelphia Inquirer*,[54] and Memphis' *Commercial Appeal*[55] reported that college girls were on such a hunt, but in doing so the newspapers were forced to use numbers given them by the website itself because, presumably, there could be no other proof. That month, the "Sugar Daddy" website had cleverly released its "list of the 20 fastest growing Sugar Baby schools" and it seems that journalists had responded in the way that the website had hoped they would.

A second example of provocative coverage that straddles an ethics line is a photograph that accompanied a *Times-Picayune* story about a local pastor, an outspoken critic against homosexuality, convicted of obscenity for masturbating in a public park. The photograph featured the man walking arm and arm with his wife, who was identified by name.[56] Commenters after the story rated her looks and her embarrassing predicament. And, finally, in a provocative example of newsgathering, a paparazzo called Suri Cruise, the young daughter of actors Tom Cruise and Katie Holmes, "a little brat" and another foul word while shooting photographs of the little girl as she emerged from a hotel.[57]

Some representative examples of more embarrassing (and, at times, potentially defamatory) coverage include initial coverage of a peripheral figure in the David Petraeus affair, reporting that described her as having "a thin resume, a troubled family, shaky finances" and explained that her unofficial nickname around town was "Tampa Kardashian."[58] (The woman, whom one paper later described as a presumably newfound "apostle for privacy," has filed a privacy-based lawsuit against the government for outing her.[59]) A number of news outlets in 2012 reported that reality television star June Shannon, mother of Honey Boo Boo, had been arrested in 2008 for "theft and contempt of court" and at least one published her four-year-old mug shot.[60] And, in a particularly sad example, a woman who had been featured in a *Tampa Bay Times* story regarding her very rare sexual disorder, something the paper called persistent genital arousal disorder, killed herself just a day or two after the story, including her photos, ran. The presumably guilt-ridden newspaper explained in a follow-up story that the woman had seen a copy in advance and had thanked them for the coverage.[61]

In many of those examples, privacy interests, broadly speaking, seemingly came second to the conveyance of unimportant but titillating, sensational subject matter.

Four Ethics-Eroding Trends: Comments, Sources, Archives, and Citizen Journalists

As seen in the story examples just described and others sprinkled throughout this book, there are at least four main trends in mainstream journalism that can be seen as helping to push the conviction that ethics and privacy concerns are becoming less important today; these news decisions may raise readership but have the potential to lower respect for journalism and make courts less inclined toward deference. The first and the most ubiquitous is the inclusion of comments after news stories and the second is mainstream journalism's own tabloidization through its coverage of tabloids' coverage and its reliance on other nontraditional sources. The third concerns unique issues that arise within internet publishing and access to past events, and the fourth is the blurring in multiple ways of "real" news with that which many would say is not.

Comments, such as those seen in the preceding example involving the *Chicago Tribune* and admissions policies at the University of Illinois, often include information, true or false, that could not be a part of a news story because of ethics or liability concerns. An example would be an ethics restriction against naming a crime victim, one that would lead a news website to omit such a name in a story about the crime—but then to allow public comments after the news story that do just that.

The ethical dilemma of user-generated comments hurtled onto the scene in the late-2000s. In 2007, only 33 percent of the top one hundred newspaper websites in the United States allowed readers to comment on news stories. Just one year later, by 2008, that number had risen to 75 percent.[62] Though some publications suggest that their interest is in promoting free speech, the interest is at least in part financial. A 2007 report by the Bivings Group,[63] a media consulting firm, noted that newspapers, facing increasing competition from internet-only publications, could "expand their reach and revenue" by "develop[ing] new business plans" that included user participation such as online comments.[64] As readers click through comments, the number of page views increases and additional web traffic is generated as readers return to the site to read follow-up comments. Moreover, readers drawn to comments sections will be drawn to newspaper websites instead of community discussion boards.

In an effort in part to keep online discussion more civil, some news websites have moved away from anonymous comments and require that commenters identify themselves in some way, usually through Facebook. But Facebook-linked comments, while sure to be fewer or at least generally less offensive in number, offer mainstream news websites a different sort of financial advantage: "In addition to raising the quality of discourse, Facebook comments help sites attract more visitors," Poynter Institute experts have noted, because "[e]ach time a reader leaves a comment, it can be cross-posted to her Facebook news feed, with a link to [the news] story [and any] replies posted on the user's Facebook wall also are synced to the article page."[65] In other words, the fact that the commenter commented on a newspaper story will be sent to the commenter's multiple contacts and a link will be included. The commenter, then, in a sense has advertised the news website to friends.

A newspaper editor in Texas who announced his paper's move to Facebook commenting in 2013 explained that it was a means to end the "cesspool" that anonymous comments often created.[66] But he also noted that it was meant to help stop comments that cross a legal line, like those that defame, invade privacy, or seem intentionally to inflict emotional distress. There are likely hundreds if not thousands of examples of such comments from mainstream news websites across the country. There was a comment left after a story on a Grand Rapids television station's website about a missing woman, for example, literally naming a man who, the commenter believed, fit the description of the sketched perpetrator, and including information regarding his employer, his vehicle, and the fact that he was on vacation the week the woman disappeared.[67] On the *Houston Chronicle*'s website, too, an accusatory comment appeared following a story about a missing twelve-year-old boy; it suggested that his body was in a ditch and that his parents would be executed for his murder.[68] An unrelated woman would later be charged with the crime.

Sleuthing commenters in 2013 literally identified their suspect in articles on the grand jury investigation into the death of JonBenét Ramsey.[69] On the *Washington Post* website a number of comments blamed a murder victim for his own death, criticizing him for spending time with friends and not his wife; they also named people they believed were the culprits.[70] A 2013 article in the *Detroit News* that covered a University of Michigan freshman's death was followed by a comment from a reader suggesting that the student was gay and that his death, therefore, was karma.[71] A *Times-Picayune* website's story about a teacher who had pleaded guilty to "lewd and lascivious" contact with her teenaged student—a story in which the reporter had specifically noted the fragile mental condition of the student-victim and had also specifically mentioned the victim's thoughts of suicide—was followed by comments criticizing the student-victim, suggesting that she had come forward only when she began to feel guilty about the relationship and that she was "wrong," "knew d[—] well what was going on," and, like the teacher, should also be held "accountable."[72]

Of note here, online news organizations that publish such comments for financial benefit or otherwise are able to defend themselves from lawsuits springing from such comments because, for the moment at least, a federal law generally protects websites from liability for comments left by others.[73] That law is beginning to become less protective, however, in response to comments encouraged and published by quasi-journalists, a phenomenon explored in the next chapter.

Aside from comments, the use of nontraditional sources in mainstream journalism also provides evidence of its seeming shift away from ethics concerns, especially with regard to privacy. The example of the viral video of the woman filmed by her husband shows how some stories migrate from an internet site like YouTube to the tabloid press to the mainstream media in days.

This happened with even greater significance in 2011 when Gawker published a story it titled "Married GOP Congressman Sent Sexy Pictures to Craigslist Babe," about New York Congressman Christopher Lee's exploits.[74] He resigned just three hours after Gawker posted his shirtless photos, supplied by a woman he had attempted to woo, and both the *Washington Post* and the *New York Times* sent breaking news emails that credited the line-pushing website. The same photo that appeared on Gawker illustrated the lead story on both the *Times'* and CNN's websites that day.

And in 2014, the *New York Daily News* published an article about a teacher who had been arrested for filing a false police report about a missing cell phone.[75] The police report allegedly had suggested that those who took the cell phone had thereafter posted nude photographs of the woman on a revenge porn website, information that the police later said was not true. The news-paper story about the teacher's arrest was supplemented with a strategically edited photograph and comments about the teacher taken directly from the revenge porn website. The newspaper story explained that the commenters "appeared to know" the woman and that those commenters had posted that rumors had been swirling about her, that she was "not innocent," and that she had had inappropriate behavior with students. The paper presumably, there-fore, had relied upon anonymous commenters on a revenge porn website as sources for its own story.

A reliance on others' material like that, especially on user-generated mate-rial, can be dangerous. "Hundreds" of news organizations recognized as much in 2013 after they posted and broadcast a YouTube video of a young woman moving her body provocatively in a dance move known as "twerking." As she did a handstand against her apartment door, continuing to twerk, her room-mate entered, causing the twerking woman to fall upon several burning can-dles. In multiple examples of coverage of the "humorous" accident—one that ends as the woman's yoga pants catch fire—the hundreds of mainstream news organizations called it a "twerking fail" and suggested light-heartedly that this might signal an end to what they considered a culturally reprehensible twerking trend.

The prominent play given to the "Twerking Fail" by news outlets across the country unfolded during a week in which Congress was feverishly debating President Obama's request for authorization to launch a military attack on Syria. Yet even in one of the busiest news weeks of the year, mainstream media found ample air time and website space to devote to the uncorroborated story of a girl who had seemingly set her pants on fire while doing a sexy dance.

Unbeknownst to any of these news organizations, however, Jimmy Kimmel, the late night television talk show host, had engineered the YouTube video and had cast a Hollywood stuntwoman, who used a fake name, as its star. Kimmel would maintain later, after mainstream coverage that included CNN, The View, and the Today Show, that he had done nothing to promote the video itself but that social networking and mainstream news coverage had brought nearly nine-million viewers to the YouTube page in less than one week. As he later suggested, he had simply posted the video to YouTube and "let the magic happen." This means, presumably, that the news organizations that had made the video "news" had done so without confirmation from anyone involved that the event was as it appeared to be. CNN, one of the news outlets that had initially eagerly featured the supposed twerking fail on its website and television broadcasts, sheepishly and blame-shiftingly began its later coverage on Kimmel's role this way: "Ok, people, let's say it all together again: If it looks too good to be true, it probably is."[76]

Surveying the viral media coverage, Kimmel quipped, "Good thing nothing is happening in Syria right now."

A second example of user-generated material that ultimately backfired occurred when mainstream media, again including CNN, reported that the New York Stock Exchange had flooded during Hurricane Sandy, all based upon an apparently intentionally false social media tweet.[77] As a third example, a number of media outlets, including the Associated Press, apparently relied upon a fake posting on a press release distribution site by an apparent hacker, falsely reporting that Google had purchased a certain Wi-Fi provider for $400 million dollars. Later news reports described the quality of the release itself as "pretty crappy" and suggested that it was one that should have raised "red flags" for mainstream journalists.[78]

There are ethics concerns even when stories with internet-based sources appear to have some basis in truth. In 2013, when a nine-year-old girl hanged herself apparently in response to her mother's new pregnancy, the *New York Daily News* quoted the mother's online blog suggesting that the soon-to-be parents were happy until the little girl expressed her sadness about the expected baby. The mother, the newspaper reported, had "talked openly" on the blog that the nine-year-old liked being an only child.[79] Like the mother who had expressed herself freely in the hospital room with *Chicago Tribune* reporters present, one suspects that this mother never thought that her blog posts, surely ones of quite limited interest prior to the suicide, would one day become part of a mainstream news story in a major tabloid newspaper. Moreover, comments after the story implicated family members in the girl's death and criticized her mother's insensitivity.[80]

The openness of the Internet presents another threat to privacy: the ceaseless availability of old news. Once, news stories had a short shelf life and yesterday's news could be dredged up, if at all, only with considerable effort in the dusty archives of a research library or microfilm room. Today, news stories remain online long after the facts have changed and, key for those once accused of crimes, long after charges have been dropped. In mid-May 2014, for example, a story originally published in early May 2013 and titled "Dark Picture of Castro Family Emerges" named the man suspected of holding three women captive in his Cleveland home for ten years.[81] But it also reported that his two brothers had been arrested as suspects and included mug shots of all three men. Police had released the two brothers in mid-May 2013, one year earlier, finding no evidence of their involvement.

Finally, some mainstream media organizations, especially, it seems, CNN, have welcomed so-called "citizen journalists" into their journalistic fold, filling news holes with eager on-the-scene members of the public willing to share their stories or cell-phone videos for little or no compensation. CNN calls its citizen journalists iReporters and, on its iReport website, invites anyone interested to join. "Everything you see on iReport starts with someone in the CNN audience," the "About" section explains. There is apparently minimal editorial control for those who choose to post stories: "The stories here are not edited, fact-checked or screened before they post," an iReport webpage reads almost boastfully. In other words, the stories are presumably uploaded directly to the iReport website by the iReporter and then made available for people around the world to read under the auspices of CNN's website. It is only when CNN chooses to put the information on the main part of the website that producers vet and fact-check an iReport story.[82] As long as "it's yours," "it's true," and "it's new and interesting," the story is "welcome," guidelines explain.[83] They do suggest that iReporters post a warning, however, for "difficult to stomach" stories: "Sometimes a story that has news value can be hard to stomach. If you're posting material you think may be difficult for sensitive audiences, mark the 'discretion advised' checkbox and the CNN iReport tools will add a warning to its page," the "Community Guidelines" portion of the website reads. CNN is probably more understanding of its iReporters and their gaffes than of those it pays a salary; the rules suggest that only when someone posts three guideline-violating reports will CNN deactivate that iReporter's account.[84]

There are indications that some have used the iReport part of the CNN website to report things other than pure news. In 2013, for example, a California court wrote in a defamation case arising from a child custody dispute that one of the parents had posted to CNN's iReport website disparaging remarks about a counselor in the case:

> One of these statements, posted on CNN's iReport Web site, accused [the doctor] of "criminal fraud and modern day slavery using Parental Alienation SCAM, enslavement of children for $$$$$$ in California." The posting continued: "Corrupt Criminals like [the doctor] and their good-ol-network

are today's 'modern slave traders' trading 'children' with vindictive retribution and for money." The posting also accused [the doctor] of "child abuse" and "financial extortion."[85]

The iReport was marked later that year as "not available." "This iReport has been removed," the page explained, "because it was flagged by the community and found to be in violation of the iReport Community Guidelines and Terms of Use." The court, meantime, found that the doctor had a valid defamation claim against the iReporter.

One iReport story was published in 2012 but likely never would have been reported by a mainstream journalist who followed a professional ethics code. It was headlined "Halloween Scares from Texas!"[86] and, as the iReporter explained, it was "[a] fun little experiment" he and some family and friends had put together. "We packed up a few camera's [*sic*], a scary monster outfit, some stilts," he reported, "and headed towards the Alamo in San Antonio to see what kind of reactions we would get." The video features an extra tall and extra scary monster with skeleton hands and long flowing hair as he makes his way down the street scaring people. A CNN producer would later describe the man who made the video as a "filmmaker by night [who] says he loves prank shows on TV and wanted to see if he could pull off something similar." The iReporter suggested that they had ventured out both to scare people and that "[b]y the end of the night [he] had a large crowd waiting and watching for the next 'victim' to walk by."

The video production is remarkable because its scare tactics approach, certainly tame for YouTube, is at least arguably unethical in a journalistic sense, and, for those left too frightened by the unexpected scary monster, potentially tortious. Even more remarkable, however, is that the iReport was given CNN's official blessing and was featured on CNN's main page, marked "Approved for CNN."

In an example of similarly outside-generated content, this time content that apparently backfired, in 2013, CNN was forced to remove a post on its "photo blogs" section that focused on what the photo blogger called an Israeli sexual therapy center. "Healing through sex with a stranger" was its titillating title. "Contrary to information provided to CNN by the freelance photographer," a post that replaced the violating post read, "we later learned that the photos did not show one of the center's clients, but instead were staged."[87]

CNN is not alone in its use of reader-generated content, of course. A 2008 Bivings report showed that nearly 60 percent of the top one hundred newspapers in the United States allowed user-generated photos on their web-sites. Fewer accepted user-generated video (18 percent) and still fewer news articles (15 percent), but, overall, more than half of newspaper websites allowed readers to post their own material, even though it seems that news organizations' reputations are potentially on the line with each post.[88]

Quite apart from the use of iReporters, it might be said that the most inter-esting examples of news line blurring also occur at CNN. In 2014, CNN anchor Wolf Blitzer's entry on the Internet Movie Database listed his multiple media appearances.[89] Most are CNN-related, but IMDb includes Blitzer's roles in *The Campaign*, a 2012 fictional comedy starring Will Ferrell, and in *Skyfall*, a 2012 James Bond film. In both Hollywood movies, he delivers news reports that are completely fictionalized.

Moreover, in late 2013, Blitzer and colleague Anderson Cooper both did mock interviews in which they talked about their relationships with Ron Burgundy, the fictional television news journalist featured in the Hollywood film *Anchorman 2*, and played by Ferrell. A link to those interviews appeared on the main CNN webpage headlined "CNN Anchors Talk Ron Burgundy." Beneath the link, it read "SPONSORED BY ANCHORMAN 2."[90] Of note, fifteen years before, Blitzer was said to have had turned down a movie role that had required him to report fake news because he reportedly considered it not the right thing to do. Apparently sparked by similar ads it finds poten-tially misleading, the Federal Trade Commission has warned that it will more stridently enforce its rules because of "a growing wave of digital advertising that is intended to look like the news articles and features of the publications where they appear."[91]

And finally, also in 2013, CNN featured a series it called "Distraction," one it subtitled "[It's Not News]." One "not-news" story featured a "Baby feeds dog" video described as "The family bulldog gets a special treat."[92]

Any court expecting today's news coverage to mimic that of the 1980s important but dry *MacNeil/Lehrer NewsHour* on PBS is sure to be disap-pointed.

Pushback from Courts and Community against Push-the-Envelope Behavior

Given the multiple cringe-worthy examples in mainstream media just dis-cussed, some involving highly sympathetic individuals and ethics-questionable behavior by journalists, it is not surprising that some people claiming push-the-envelope behavior by mainstream news media have found their way into sympathetic courtrooms. And it is also not surprising that despite significant First Amendment protections for media generally, some courts have ruled against mainstream media defendants. Many of these cases are reported in Chapter 3 and elsewhere in this book.

Two cases are worth special mention here, however. If the media behavior alleged by the plaintiffs in these two cases were, in fact, true, both would involve clear journalism ethics violations. Either way, both also help show courts' increasing impatience with all of journalism as it pushes against the bubble of First Amendment protection for what counts as news.

The first case example involves a murder-suicide near Sacramento, California, of a mother and her two young children, aged six and three. Friends of the victims, also young children, lived next door.

After the crime, a cameraman from a local television station came to the neighbors' door. No adults were home, only children aged eleven, seven, and five. After telling the children to "let me just open the door," the cameraman allegedly opened the door himself. For two minutes thereafter, he interviewed the children, first asking if they knew the children next door. The children confirmed that the youngsters next door were, indeed, playmates and friends.

In the language of the court that would hear a claim brought against the journalist and his station, "[a]t this point defendant state[d]: 'Well, the mom has killed the two little kids and herself.'"[93] After hearing the shocking news, one of the children exclaimed, "Oh my God!" The cameraman then continued to question the children about the family next door. The plaintiffs alleged in their IIED lawsuit that he had conveyed the information about the deaths "in such a manner as to cause the children emotional distress so that their visible emotional distress would be demonstrative to the TV audience."

The defendant-journalists argued in response that the cameraman's behavior was not extreme and was not outrageous enough to support IIED liability. Though the court agreed that the cameraman had spoken to the children in a nonthreatening way and did not reveal any specifically gruesome information about the deaths, it allowed the children's IIED claims to continue. The judge noted that the children were of "tender years" and that it was reasonable to infer that the questioning, though possibly innocent at first, changed "in the hope it would elicit a reaction that would be 'newsworthy,' e.g., suitable to redeem a promise of 'film at eleven.'" Outrageousness, the court ruled, could be shown through a deliberate attempt "to manipulate the emotions of young children for some perceived journalistic advantage."

"If indeed defendant sought to elicit an emotional reaction from the minors for the voyeuristic titillation of [the station's] viewing audience," the court wrote in explanation, "this is shameless exploitation of defenseless children, pure and simple" and "not the gathering of news which the public has a right to know." Moreover, the court concluded, a free press would not be threatened by basic rules of decency.

The second case also involves minors. In it, journalists who worked for a television station in Utah were accused of asking high school students to chew tobacco for a news story.[94] The students alleged that the journalists had told them that they would not be punished for their tobacco use and that the images of them chewing tobacco would be "for the camera" and only as background video for a news story on the dangers of such a practice. The journalists disagreed with that depiction of their behavior and explained that they had simply told the students gathered outside the school to do "what they would ordinarily do."

Prosecutors charged the journalists with contributing to the delinquency of minors but the journalists argued that "their only intention was to cover a legitimate news story" and not to encourage delinquency. Moreover, they argued, their activities were protected under the First Amendment's promise of a free press, an argument supported in an amicus brief by the Utah Chapter of the Society of Professional Journalists. The video, they maintained as a part of their case, was "essential to television journalism."

The court, however, differentiated between story coverage itself—coming upon children already chewing tobacco, it explained—and allegedly "setting up the visual images to illustrate the story." Because there was evidence that the children had been asked to chew tobacco, the court ruled, First Amendment protections did not apply. "[R]epresentatives of the press may not encourage crime so that they may record it and report on it, and then claim that the prosecution amounts to an attempt by the government to restrain or abridge the freedom of the press," the court explained as it ordered the case to a criminal trial. "As important as a free and unfettered press is to the survival and prosperity of a free society, under these facts, defendants may not insulate their actions under the cloak of the First Amendment."

Moreover, the court noted, such journalistic behavior would be considered unethical under the SPJ code.

Even if the facts in those cases were not precisely as the plaintiffs had described them, they help show that some mainstream journalism has changed in an ethics sense—recall, for example, the special protection the SPJ code of ethics gives children and their privacy—and that this change has led to skeptical courts and lessened legal protection in some cases. In a 2007 decision, too, reflecting the concerns in the *Blagojevich* decision described in Chapter 1, the court bemoaned the difference in current newsgathering policies and ordered that jurors' names be kept secret despite media arguments that courtrooms were necessarily open to the public.[95] Media lawyers had relied upon several older cases, especially one from 1990 in which courts had given media access to such information. But the federal trial court judge explained that times were different now, pointing to a 2006 trial in which he alleged that media had actively pursued jurors and comparing that with more respectful media from the 1990s:

> The events in that [2006] case illustrate that the news media can, and unhesitatingly will, investigate jurors' lives without necessarily ever speaking to the juror. The media may examine all aspects of a juror's background and could, in theory, even wait outside a juror's home to take photographs or request interviews. Today, even a photograph or video of a juror declining an interview or evading a reporter is newsworthy. This is so despite the fact that some might fail to see how it advances the public's understanding of how well our courts do the government's business. The [1990 court] likely envisioned a more-or-less polite request from the media seeking comment, followed by a similarly polite media retreat in the face of a flat "no." It is unlikely that this would be the court's vision now.

That criticism is in line with what many Americans have complained of: to quote columnist Kathleen Parker in 2012, "an increasingly tabloid press."[96] As early as 1997, mainstream journalists who had gathered at Stanford University agreed that they were headed toward such a future and suggested that, even back then, a fair amount of journalism was broken.[97] "Traditional news values are under major assault," the president of CNN had warned at the conference, because, among other things, "[t]abloid shows are providing profit." Others spoke critically of the press's tendency "to flock to stories of lurid sex, celebrity, and crime," and, implicitly, its move away from traditional ethics standards, despite the negative effects on the public perception of journalism.

Recall that in 2013, the Pew Research Center's Project for Excellence in Journalism confirmed the current reality of that negative view. It pointed out

in its annual report that cutbacks in journalism staff, reporting that emphasized sports, weather, and traffic over hard news, a shift toward "talk" coverage instead of more expensive packaged stories, and other economic shifts
in mainstream media had "add[ed] up to a news industry that is more undermanned and unprepared to uncover stories, dig deep into emerging ones or to
question information put into its hands [a]nd . . . that the public is taking
notice" and abandoning news outlets when they feel news is not being covered
in a satisfactory way.[98]

The Pew report also warned that the future did not look much brighter,
given both mainstream media trends and viewer trends in opposition to
that media.

The Future for Mainstream Media

In summer 2013, after a woman's car plunged off the Chesapeake Bay Bridge
in Maryland, the *Washington Post* posted a very short, basic story on the
Internet headlined "Car Plunges from Chesapeake Bay Bridge, Woman
Lives."[99] For those who have driven the bridge, one that is so unnerving for
some that professional drivers stand ready to get behind the wheel for them,
the story was of great interest and of at least some importance: How could
someone survive after a plunge in a car from those heights? How could this
happen on a bridge many drive across each weekend to get to Maryland and
Delaware beaches? Why did so many believe that such an accident would be
impossible? How could the bridge be made safer?

But the story on the *Post*'s website was a mere five short paragraphs, sported
an archived photo of the bridge, and offered no great detail, other than that
"[t]he crash involved a tractor trailer and two cars." Immediately, commenters
began offering theories on how the accident had happened, how the woman
had survived—and why the *Post* had failed to put together a satisfyingly informative story. Eventually, they began to complain that they had paid for their
online coverage and yet no reporter, some sixteen hours after the crash in their
estimation, had bothered to drive the sixty minutes to the scene to do any real
reporting or to interview the survivor. One commenter theorized that the
reason was that the *Washington Post* was going "broke."[100] The *Post* did, in
time, publish longer stories that included more information but, until it did,
the dissatisfaction among its readers was palpable.

That one small vignette both confirms the Pew report on public dissatisfaction with mainstream journalism and suggests that readers who must pay for their online news have higher expectations for the journalists they support, with little patience for those who do not come through.

Shortly thereafter, the newspaper announced that it had been purchased by Amazon's Jeffrey Bezos, a man with no experience in journalism but plenty in the use of digital business models to disrupt traditional markets. He promised a "golden era" at the *Post* but suggested too that news editors must figure out a way to make news profitable again. In an article about Bezos, a *Post* reporter admitted that the newspaper was "beset by Web-based competition that [had] weakened its advertising base and steadily sapped its print readership."[101] Bezos himself appeared skeptical about pouring money into the *Post*'s investigative journalism unit—the group that broke the Watergate scandal—when, he said, others can summarize and report the same information without paying a fee. He called that journalism model "deeply flawed."

A 2013 report by the Tow Center for Digital Journalism at Columbia University, in line with that opinion and other polls, also suggested that a recovery trend for journalism was not on the horizon. It predicted that "journalism in this country will get worse before it gets better, and, in some places (principally midsize and small cities with no daily paper) it will get markedly worse."[102] Public trust in newspapers has certainly fallen: from 51 percent of the public responding in the 1990s that they had "a great deal of confidence" to 37 percent in 2000 to 30 percent in 2006 to 23 percent in 2013.[103]

With economic pressures on news outlets mounting, and growing competition for internet page views and public attention from unconventional rivals and self-styled "citizen journalists" unconstrained by institutional ethics codes, it will be difficult to reverse the fall in public confidence. Indeed, coming innovations in journalism meant to cut costs and generate new sources of revenue seem calculated to compound the problem.

Some well-respected publications, as in the CNN example featuring *Anchorman 2*, have moved into what is known as "sponsored content," a way advertisers can deliver messages to readers through trusted journalists and their publications. Pew explained one publication's sponsored content this way: "In early March [2013], *Fortune* took [a new] step, launching a program for advertisers called Fortune TOC—Trusted Original Content—in which *Fortune* writers, for a fee, create original *Fortune*-branded editorial content for marketers to distribute exclusively on their own platforms."[104] The *New York Times* suggested that such innovations—what it called "advertising wearing the uniform of journalism"—may well be journalism's latest new peril.[105] It offered an example from *Forbes:*

> *Forbes*'s BrandVoice allows advertisers to produce editorial products that reflect their best efforts to engage audiences. The content is clearly labeled advertising, but has the familiar headline, art and text configuration of an editorial work.
>
> As a result, things can get pretty complicated pretty quickly. In addition to staff posts, the site has a roster of 1,200 contributors—consultants, academics, journalists and others—who are compensated according to the audience they attract. And then there are the posts from the marketers, with a current roster of 15 active brands.

The story suggested that Buzzfeed, the *Atlantic,* the *New Yorker,* and even the *New York Times* itself had started to use such journalism-like advertising. "If you are on Buzzfeed," the article explained, "World of Warcraft might have a sponsored post on, say, 10 reasons your virtual friends are better than your real ones." The literal costs are high for such artificial news stories: an advertiser pays $100,000 for four or five posts that are put together by writers at Buzzfeed.[106] "It . . . could kill journalism if publishers aren't careful," one internet expert warned.[107]

Stories that appear as "recommended" for a reader are also connected at times with advertising. The "From Around the Web" stories on mainstream news websites like the *Washington Post,* the *Washington Post* itself reported, are sometimes a form of "an advertising product." Some of the "stories" are created by companies motivated simply to sell something.[108]

Meantime, *New York* magazine reported that Northwestern University's Medill School of Journalism had had a hand in developing a computer program "that writes basic news articles like sports-game summaries and [companies'] earning reports" apparently without the need for a living journalist's touch.[109] The magazine likened the computer program to a robot-journalist and also noted that the developers had at least thirty clients ready to use it.

And there are reports that mainstream news websites are increasingly relying on computer algorithms instead of a human editor's news judgment to "determine the best placements of text, photos, and video for maximum exposure" and maximum profits.[110] In multiple newsrooms too, reporters receive a list of most-clicked stories at least once per day as subtle guidance from editors both that clicks are important and about how they might increase readership through their reporting.

All these technological "advances," as media law scholar Lili Levi notes, put tremendous pressure on journalism's traditional goals including accuracy, accountability, and completeness. She suggests that such changes will lead to still greater legal backlash against the press, in courtrooms, in Congress, and constitutionally by hampering any attempted revival of the Free Press Clause.[111]

But if market pressures and technological developments are encouraging even mainstream news outlets to push the boundaries of news, the threats posed by quasi-journalists are even greater.

At times, in fact, it all makes a gallery of mug shots appear decidedly benign. And courts have already struck back hard.

5

The Rise, and Lows, of Quasi-Journalism

If developments in mainstream media have the potential to push the protective First Amendment bubble even closer to the breaking point, then emerging practices of quasi-journalism seem determined to break it. In some ways, they already have.

Quasi-journalism is a term meant to describe those publishers that publish truthful information outside the context of traditional mainstream journalism; a simple word like "publisher" often serves as a synonym but would be too broad to use routinely here. Traditionally, journalism's qualities are said to be "impact, immediacy, proximity, prominence, novelty, conflict, and emotion."[1] Some experts add "mystery, drama, adventure, celebration, [and] self-improvement."[2] As noted previously, in making news decisions, traditional journalists also exercise ethics-related judgments beyond those qualities, including the story's "truth, its importance, its public value or utility,"[3] and its potential harm. If it is true that the "mystique of the editorial process" is based upon "intuitive judgment and competitive strategy,"[4] then many with the intuition today make competitive judgments far different from those made in the mainstream press.

Though there is no perfect way to draw the line, many quasi-journalists do not seem to follow an established mainstream ethics code—recall, for example, that Gawker's founder boasted proudly that his website publishes truthful information that mainstream publications' ethics standards would not allow—and some of these publishers would not consider themselves journalists at all, even though they publish what many readers consider truth.[5] Here, a tabloid like the *National Enquirer* is a form of quasi-journalism because of its highly sensational stories that at times push the envelope of propriety and truth, even though its reporters work under some editorial control and ethics principles. Websites such as Gawker, blogs that operate more as free-form thoughts or diaries, or those that even more clearly lack an ethics foundation, and many reality television programs also fall into this category. Those sorts of publications contrast with New York's daily tabloids, for example, because the latter report traditional news including crime and political news in addition to more sensational articles and seem generally more restricted by some form of ethics. This quasi-journalism category, in contrast, includes publishers that mostly publish outside the traditional mainstream.

In other words, both mainstream and quasi-journalism publish truth-based information but quasi-journalism (1) often excludes what we might consider traditional news including routine politics and crime stories, sometimes in favor of more sensational news items more likely to inflict emotional harm and (2) often seemingly fails to consider traditional journalistic ethics principles when doing so, sometimes proudly and purposefully so.

This chapter collects numerous examples of push-the-envelope quasi-journalism and courts' negative responses. Today, protection springing from First Amendment principles is not as robust as it once was and quasi-journalism is at least partly responsible.

The Dirty and Communications Decency Act Protection

The Dirty is one of those push-the-envelope publications—but its story is one that has implications for all of internet publishing.

The Dirty, or TheDirty.com, is a website with twenty million monthly views, about two-thirds as many as the *New York Times* online. It was created in 2007 by Nik Richie, a man who maintains that anyone can say whatever they would like to say on the Internet. The website's content includes photographs of women sent by readers along with insulting commentary and bits of information about them. In January 2011, for example, those who visited The Dirty saw a photo of a young overweight woman lying on a floor, one chubby arm raised above her head. Her clothing was disheveled and stained. Near her on the floor and on her shirt was what appeared to be vomit. She looked to be staring directly at the camera through swollen eyes, though it was clear that she was likely too dazed to comprehend her circumstances.

Someone, apparently a person who had had some interaction with the young woman the night before, sent the photograph to The Dirty along with this unedited description:

> Here we have a typical case of a girl who cant handle her alcohol. Me and my best girlfriend threw a small party, and someone invited her. She somehow thought I was her best friend, ive never seen this girl before the party in my life! All she did the entire night was talk sh*t about everyone at the party, my best friend (the host!) and how lame it was, and how she could have better spent her night. To EVERYONE we invited, we made it perfectly clear that it was a SMALL party. (we have crazy neighbors) So tell me why she didn't get the message, and thought it be okay to come up in our house and talk sh*t the whole time. After ALL that, she wanted to show us all up, and drink the most. She wanted to prove how cool she was. This bit*ch threw up all over our room, and pissed herself. We had to have three grown men drag her nasty *ss to the bathroom. Then she woke up in the morning and had the nerve to ask for new clothes to wear and to take a shower. ARE YOU KIDDING ME? Nik, put this bit*ch on blast, please. NO ONE INVITE HER TO YOUR PARTY no matter how big or small.[6]

In comments below the post and the photograph, someone identified as "Anonymous" suggested that the young woman pictured was a "whale" and another commenter, "Doosh Bagalow," implied that she was a cow. "Turdferguson" suggested that he or she would have both urinated and defecated on the young woman while she was asleep and "jessierae" helpfully purported to identify her by name. "Britney" posted that she (or he) hoped the young woman would see the post and cry.

Nearly six thousand people viewed the post of the young woman lying in vomit and, in 2014, more than three years after its initial publication, it was still available online in the archives of The Dirty for additional unrestricted views. There are countless other examples on The Dirty of embarrassing photographs of people, many of women dressed provocatively or nearly nude, people on the toilet, or people who simply appear challenged in some way, followed by a blizzard of hateful or degrading comments.

The *Arizona Republic* newspaper reported in 2013 that "Nik Richie and thedirty.com are flourishing in a world where the Internet and social media sites render privacy more and more irrelevant."[7] But, in a legal sense, at least, the *Arizona Republic* was quite wrong. Richie and the posts and photos he describes as a "reality-based blog" from "civilian paparazzi," have inspired the beginnings of a change in a law that had long been sweepingly protective of expression—a change that, if it continues, would make the law far more protective of privacy and could well have a further dampening effect on his "flourishing."

That potential shift, in fact, may be one reason why the "SUBMIT POST!" portion of Richie's website is set up as it is. It asks for "news tips, pictures and videos" followed by smaller print that informs posters that The Dirty has the right to use the information sent to it "in perpetuity, throughout the world, in any and all media now known or hereafter devised, [and] to communicate [the information] to the public." Moreover, the disclaimer reads, the poster who sends the information will be forced to indemnify The Dirty against all resulting claims.

The indemnification line is necessary—though not necessarily protective of The Dirty—because those featured have sued the website and Nik Richie for torts such as invasion of privacy, intentional infliction of emotional distress, and defamation.

Sarah Jones, a former Cincinnati Bengals cheerleader and former teacher, was one such plaintiff. An anonymous poster wrote to The Dirty in 2009 claiming that Jones had "slept with every . . . Bengal Football player." A second post suggested that Jones had sexually transmitted diseases and had had sexual activity at her workplace. Richie replied, "Why are all high school teachers freaks in the sack?"

When Richie published the information he had received about Jones, he knew that websites like his enjoyed a protective immunity against legal claims courtesy of Section 230 of the Communications Decency Act. The law, passed by Congress in 1996, reads: "No provider or user of an interactive computer service shall be treated as a publisher or speaker of any information provided by another content provider."[8] In other words, any website that allowed non-affiliated others to post on it would be protected from liability for those posts, even when they were privacy-invading or defamatory. The idea behind the law was that the web might thrive with "vibrant" expression and "competitive free market" commerce and not be fettered by significant government entanglement.

Moreover, website publishers would be protected even if they seemingly had had a hand in the mischief: "Merely providing third parties with neutral tools to create web content, even if the website knows those parties are using the tools to create illegal content, does not create liability," one court explained, "nor does refraining from removing objectionable content, despite receiving notice."[9] Websites such as The Dirty that existed nearly solely through content contributions from readers believed that they were protected as long as others wrote the originally harmful information, even if they called themselves something provocative like "The Dirty."

It is doubtful that in 1996, members of Congress imagined that websites like The Dirty would come to exist or that those sorts of websites would successfully argue in the nation's courts that Section 230 offered protection from young mostly female constituents' claims of tortious, hurtful language and embarrassing photographs. It is not difficult to imagine that, given the choice today—in a world of revenge porn and other purposefully humiliating websites that operate literally because the federal law exempts them from liability—Congress would not have sided so strongly with the technology that promised unfettered expression.

In 2012, a federal district court did not side strongly with unfettered expression. Sarah Jones, who would find a different sort of trouble later,[10] would bring claims for defamation, privacy, and intentional infliction of emotional distress against The Dirty and Nik Richie, even though others had posted at least a significant part of what she found harmful. Richie responded that Section 230 immunity protected him, but Jones argued that he had actively encouraged the offensive postings that had made The Dirty infamous and that, therefore, the law should not protect him.

The court sided with Jones. "This Court holds," the federal trial court judge hearing a preliminary motion in the case wrote of The Dirty, that "by reason of the very name of the site, the manner in which it is managed, and the personal comments of defendant Richie, the defendants have specifically encouraged development of what is offensive about the content of the site."[11] The court noted that Richie himself had boasted that he called his fans "the Dirty Army" and that he had said that he loved that those fans had a "war mentality"; Section 230 was not meant to cover behavior that encouraged hurtful posts, the court reasoned. A jury would later award Jones $338,000 in damages.[12] In an opinion following that verdict, the trial court reiterated that the CDA did not protect websites like The Dirty as strongly as Nik Richie believed it did: "[T]he weight of authority teaches that such immunity may be lost," the judge wrote, when "a website owner . . . intentionally encourages illegal or actionable third-party posting to which he adds his own comments ratifying or adopting a post."[13]

By that time, a second court had decided as much in another case brought against Richie and The Dirty, this one in a federal trial court in Maryland. The post at issue there was titled "Chris Hare The Baltimore Stalker" and claimed that Hare "stalked girls kids [*sic*]" at schools and suggested that the people of Baltimore needed to be "wary" of such a "loser."[14] Richie had noted after the post: "Wow, he really looks like a stand up guy." Nearly eighty comments from readers followed. One of them revealed Hare's workplace and said he was a "psychopath" who "terrorizes" people. Two additional posts featured Hare, and Richie wrote some additional comments himself.

Hare brought invasion of privacy, intentional infliction of emotional distress, and defamation claims against Richie who, again, argued that he was protected by Section 230 immunity. The Maryland court also rejected the immunity, however, and ordered that the case continue to trial, reminding the defendants that Section 230 "was not meant to create a lawless no-man's-land on the Internet." "Dirty World's involvement," the court wrote, naming Richie's company, "goes beyond mere editorial functions and extends to the creation of its own content—specifically, Mr. Richie's comments at the end of each post." It also suggested that liability might extend, as in the *Jones* case, to those who encourage harmful content by designing a website as a gateway to defamatory material.

Though Richie settled the *Hare* case before it could go to trial,[15] he appealed the one brought by Sarah Jones. The Reporters Committee for Freedom of the Press, a journalism advocacy group, joined in an amicus brief in Richie's case, praising the public interest in the First Amendment's "free flow of information" while seemingly turning a blind eye to content that included a young woman lying in her own vomit. Gawker, CNN, Facebook, Google, Twitter, Amazon, the Magazine Publishers of America, BuzzFeed, and the McClatchey media company also joined in Richie's appeal.[16] In mid-2014, the appeals court sided with Richie, but Jones promised her own appeal to the Supreme Court.

In the meantime, Richie too has attempted to raise the First Amendment as his website's reason for existence; he told the *Arizona Republic* that The Dirty gives "people a voice where they [can] express themselves and have their freedom of speech and talk about their neighbors, celebrities, friends, politics and what not."

But, as should be clear by now, mere invocation of the First Amendment does not provide absolute protection for all speech, even all truthful speech, and indeed the strength of its shield is weakened by envelope pushers like

Richie. No matter the final outcome in the case brought by Jones, increasingly, it seems, courts are siding with an individual's privacy rights over an opposing publisher's free-speech claims—even when existing law puts a clear weight on the side of expression.

The implications of this shift go beyond extreme provocateurs to include mainstream media. As noted in Chapter 4, most newspapers open even particularly provocative news stories to comments, surely knowing that offensive posts will follow—and newspapers and magazines can be liable for defamatory or privacy-invading letters to the editors that they publish in print. If anything, the Internet, through its reach and its endurance, has greater capacity to harm than a one-time letter in the print edition of a local newspaper. That was the conclusion, after all, of the Ohio Supreme Court when it first adopted the false light tort in an attempt to protect its citizens from internet abuses. Even in dicta in *Snyder v. Phelps*, the funeral protest case, the Supreme Court seemingly cautioned that, while public protests using generic political statements may be protected, websites with more precisely aimed harmful information might not be.

If newspapers are not protected from liability for privacy-invading letters to the editor published in print, a court could well wonder why they should be protected from the virtual equivalent, especially when they seem to be profiting economically from additional comment-based clicks and when, as in the case of The Dirty, nasty comments are particularly foreseeable.

This is certainly part of the reason why media defense attorneys have suggested that the two trial court decisions involving The Dirty and Section 230 described here should cause all those who publish websites to "be alarmed."[17]

Other Websites and Changing Law

The Dirty, of course, is not the only website available on the Internet that intentionally or carelessly pushes the envelope of propriety and civility. As judges and others meld mainstream news media and quasi-journalism, these websites help influence a change in law to make it more privacy-protective than expression-protective. The result is that both quasi- and mainstream journalism are left more vulnerable.

The movement away from granting mainstream news organizations access to mug shots, for example, could well be based in part on websites with little journalistic veneer and significant commercial interests that publish them seemingly for profit. In 2013, a website calling itself MugshotsWorld.com, for example, had a searchable database of mug shots from multiple states. When one clicked on any particular mug shot, information about the arrestee appeared, including a home address. A "Remove this mug shot" link was just below each booking photo and a click took the reader to a webpage that promised that for $200 the photograph would be removed from the website and Google within twenty-four hours with a "100% Success Rate."

A similar website, ARR.st, subtitled "Look Who's Booked," offered viewers a game it called "Guess the Charge." (A similar blog of the same name asked readers to both guess the charges and rate the looks of women who had been arrested; in 2014, though dormant, it was still online with the women's mug shots prominently featured.) When a random arrestee's mug shot appeared, the viewer could guess which of four laws the arrestee was said to have broken. The website also allowed readers to comment under each arrestee's mug shot. One vehicular homicide arrest in Louisiana in 2013, for example, led to multiple comments that called the arrestee names and told her to "rot in jail" and "burn in hell."

Similar websites, like The-Place-for-Mugshots.com, offered readers the opportunity to comment and, for $49.99, offered arrestees removal from the website and Google. As one mug shot was presumably removed, more were added: jail bookings with photos, one website promised, were updated every five minutes.

A New York court decided a freedom-of-information case in 2013 brought by one such website, one described by the court as "a commercial website that generates revenue by posting arrest records of inmates, including their names, addresses, dates of birth, and photographs, and then charging a $68 fee to remove this personal information."[18] As might a mainstream news publication seeking information about an arrest, the website had made a public records request of New York City; here, however, the website had asked for all arrestees' mug shots, not just ones of particular news interest. The city refused and the court upheld that refusal: in a decision with ramifications for mainstream news reporters who use mug shots to illustrate news stories, the court decided that the release of mug shots would cause both personal and economic hardship to arrestees and that, therefore, city officials were correct to refuse to release such information.

A similar decision came from a Kentucky court in 2007, when a quasi-journalism group, described by the trial court as one "closely linked to organizations" that publish public information "for use in commercial ventures," asked for all accident reports from multiple Kentucky counties. The appeals court held that "if [the organization] is nothing more than a sham news organization requesting the reports for the purpose of selling the contents," accident reports would not be made available. The trial court, in similarly rejecting the request, had not been that specific regarding the status of the requesting entity.[19]

This much is clear: mainstream media is concerned about these types of cases. In 2011, for example, a federal appeals court agreed with a lower court that a publication known as *Prison Legal News* should not have access to video and autopsy photographs related to a prison murder, images that court called "grotesque and degrading."[20] Echoing the U.S. Supreme Court in *Favish*, the court ruled that family members had a right to privacy from a sensation-seeking culture and that such visuals were properly kept out of the publication's hands, even though the images had been shown in open court. *Prison Legal News*, a publication that strongly promotes inmate rights with a readership of mostly inmates, might be considered a quasi-journalistic publication here, but the ultimate decision in the case had strong implications for all mainstream news media, as shown by amici that included *60 Minutes*, the Associated Press, the American Society of News Editors, and the Society of Professional Journalists. The court ruled against *Prison Legal News* and all amici media organizations, however, and today in that jurisdiction, it appears that family interests in keeping such crime visuals private will trump news organizations' interest in them—presumably even when they might be considered newsworthy.

Meantime, in 2014, a man featured on JustMugshots.com filed a lawsuit, one he said he hoped would become a class action, "to stop [the website] from profiteering from the public humiliation of arrested individuals."[21] In spring 2014, that website remained online and attempted to spin itself as one that merely offered citizens their "right to be informed" about local arrests. (Important here, it also offered news websites free access to what it said was its more than 17 million arrest records, suggesting that it would pay the newspaper ad revenue should the newspaper integrate the information on the news website.) Also in 2014, a Florida court preliminarily refused to dismiss a misappropriation-like case filed by a man whose mug shot was featured on a website that featured an "unpublish" link.[22]

Today, then, quasi-journalistic online publications have not only conceivably lessened Communications Decency Act Section 230 protection, they have made and have acted in ways that threaten to make public documents including mug shots, accident reports, and prosecution records less accessible. As a result, by limiting access, they have limited what might be considered traditionally reportable news.

So too in a number of recent cases involving, in a broad sense, quasi-journalism (or, better put here in some cases, freelance publishers) and the information beyond mug shots that they wished to use. Consider the implications for what would be considered more mainstream journalism in the following examples:

- In a case involving a so-called for-profit documentary film about Elvis Presley, a court found that photographs and video of Elvis were not inherently newsworthy.[23]
- A federal court in Oregon decided in 2011 that a blogger's posts involving a bankruptcy trustee and his handling of a bankruptcy estate's taxes were not of public concern because there was no evidence that the public had paid any attention to the private company's collapse.[24]
- In California, a state appeals court decided that photographs taken of fully clothed little girls in public places and posted on the Internet on a website run by a self-proclaimed pedophile could be the basis for an invasion-of-privacy claim.[25]
- The federal appeals court for Missouri ruled in 2012 that "the public has no legitimate interest in the private sexual activities of [a woman who had been harassed on a revenge-type website and elsewhere] or in the embarrassing facts revealed about her life," after the website had revealed the woman's alleged child sex victimization, an alleged suicide attempt, and "family secrets."[26]
- A trial court in Washington State ruled that a man who had "persistently posted [neighbors'] names and addresses on the internet" could be liable for such privacy-invading behavior despite First Amendment-based amici arguments from various journalism organizations and a tradition that street addresses are public information.[27]
- A California state court upheld a teenager's privacy claims after a website published her name, address, and directions to her home, along with a seminude photograph purportedly of her.[28]
- And a federal trial court in California wrote that the disappearance of an intern who had had an affair with a married member of Congress was

"not necessarily a political or community issue in which public opinion and input is inherent and desirable," after the *National Enquirer* published an article about the affair.[29]

Each of those decisions has the potential to affect mainstream journalism even though they did not involve mainstream journalism directly—and given the discourse on the Internet today, such anti-media decisions are likely to increase.

Shock Internet and Its Implications

When a court in California rejected a relatively mild website's no-one-believes-it defense based upon its tendency to publish items admittedly in bad taste, its writers' tendency to joke, its hyperbolic tone, and its "edgy and provocative style," and, instead, upheld a plaintiff's claims of defamation and emotional distress against the website,[30] the implications for other such websites were significant. Though courts have long protected satire, when publications seem to have gone too far, they can move from a protected sphere into potential liability.

Nonetheless, many websites seem not to have received that message or others like it. Whether based upon presumed Section 230 immunity or simple misunderstanding of privacy and defamation law, many websites have published items in ways that would likely shock even the most absolute of First Amendment advocates.

Hunter Moore, for example, made his internet mark with the website he called Is Anyone Up, described by the *Village Voice* as "a virtual grudge slingshot of a website that gleefully publishes 'revenge porn' photos—cell-phone nudes submitted by scorned exes, embittered friends, malicious hackers, and other ne'er-do-well degenerates—posted alongside each unsuspecting subject's full name, social-media profile, and city of residence."[31] The *Village Voice* subtitled its article about Moore this way: "The hated revenge-porn profiteer says he wants to teach a lesson with his web site. How long before the 26-year-old learns one himself?" Moore told the publication that those victims of Is Anyone Up who threaten a lawsuit simply would cause him to post the threat, drawing additional attention to their plight, and to further belittle those who claim emotional distress. For those pictured nude, he admitted that things could not get much worse, but, he told the reporter, "[L]et's be real for a second: If somebody killed themselves over that? Do you know how much money I'd make? At the end of the day, I do not want anybody to hurt themselves. But if they do? Thank you for the money."

At first, Moore admitted, he had removed offending posts when people complained, but after he learned of Section 230 immunity for websites that publish others' posts, he republished the offending posts and multiple others. The rights to Is Anyone Up were apparently sold to an antibullying group that immediately shut it down but other revenge porn websites, including one known as Is Anybody Down, continued the revenge porn work. One day in 2013, Is Anybody Down featured a named young woman from Missouri along with five highly suggestive fully nude photographs of her; the website's owner boasted to a reporter in 2013 that the website contained at least 700 different nude photos, many of them sent in by others, and that he, as publisher, was simply "out to make a buck."[32] As had Moore, he explained that he could publish such things because he was protected by the Communications Decency Act's Section 230.

There were and are countless additional examples. A website that called itself UGotPosted.com published similar photographs of young women, identified by name and hometown. The website has been taken down but a mirror site exists. Another, Texxan.com, disappeared after women sued the website and its internet hosting service for emotional distress.[33] More general websites, like 4chan's /b/random[34] and other boards, often contain nudes that seem uploaded by someone other than the subject. Many of them are followed by critical comments regarding the women's looks; other comments explicitly suggest rape and murder.[35]

And in 2014, a website calling itself MyEx.com—one that literally urges its readers to "get revenge"—featured what appeared to be hundreds of photographs of nude women and some men by name and town, including one of a woman from Allentown, Pennsylvania, headlined "Cheating Whore Wife."[36] One click led to explicit nude photographs that appeared to be of the same woman; counters suggested that those photographs had been viewed by more than 30,000 people in fewer than twenty-four hours, and more than twenty commenters had posted that same day criticizing or lauding the woman in sexualized language. A separate "Remove My Name" button led to a link to a service calling itself "Reputation Manager," in which it suggested that one's name would be removed after a $400 payment to an address in South Africa.[37] Without such payment, the Frequently Asked Questions webpage suggested that the website owners would take the images down only for copyright-related reasons. Incongruously, the FAQ maintained that the website owners kept no identifying information from those supplying the photographs, but the submission form warned that the website "has a zero-tolerance policy against child pornography" and that such content and its submitter would be reported to the authorities if discovered.

Meantime, the link for those who wish to upload images of "exes" asked for the ex's name, gender, age, country, state, city, Facebook profile, and Twitter account, making the website searchable by name and state. A search in spring 2014 revealed a photograph of a fully clothed teenager identified on the webpage by name and described as a "slut." The girl, the uploader had written in much more foul language, had had sexual intercourse indiscriminately, presumably with strangers. The post was followed by a February 2014 comment from someone who identified herself as the girl's godmother. She demanded that the image be taken down, explaining in strong language that the girl was only 16. In spring 2014 the girl's name, image, and the insulting language describing her remained. The webpage counter suggested that nearly 25,000 people had viewed the information.

"Sites like th[ese] may be the trigger point for more sweeping legislation that comes in and says, 'Yes, we want immunity for site holders—but there is a point at which you cross the line,'" one intellectual property attorney told the *Village Voice*. To answer the question the reporter posed about when Hunter Moore might learn his lesson, then, the story suggested that a change in the highly protective law might help spark his education. (In 2014, it was not the Communications Decency Act, but criminal law that impacted Moore. Federal authorities announced that a grand jury had indicted him for hacking-related charges, identity theft, and conspiracy.[38])

Like Is Anyone Up, the website Juicy Campus, which asked posters to publish the juiciest gossip from campuses across the country and promised anonymity for those who did, has ceased to exist but other websites have attempted to take its place. Just after Juicy Campus' demise, the category "Tulane University" on CampusACB.com, for example, contained a post naming the hottest freshmen on campus. Anonymous comments after the post pointedly criticized or lauded the seventeen-, eighteen-, or nineteen-year-olds' bodies.[39] A separate post named an individual undergraduate student and anonymous comments suggested that she was promiscuous and that she had a certain type of body odor.[40] Like Juicy Campus, CampusACB seems to have disappeared, but CollegeLeak.com is a newer iteration; a post there in 2013 named a male student, and several commenters used a gay slur describing him.[41] And in 2014 Collegiate ACB contained similar posts and comments, also searchable by school.[42]

College Wall of Shame is another more recent example. "Upload your Shame!" the website urged in 2014 and then asked of the uploader on a form that followed, "What happened to this dumbass? Add your caption here."[43] One upload featured a male student with two broken arms, recognizable to anyone who knew him, apparently passed out and seemingly covered in flour. "Breaded and Deaded," the title read. Another photograph was of another sleeping victim of what appeared to be too much alcohol; he wore Disney mouse ears and had been covered with what appeared to be permanent marker so that he looked like Minnie Mouse. His marked-up torso featured a very large drawing of a penis. "Minnie Marker Rape," the title above the photograph read and "I love boys" was the comment below.

Though considerably less offensive, outside of college, People of Walmart has a similar tone. It features embarrassing photographs of people taken at Walmart stores across the country; many of the subjects are wearing clothing too small for their sizable bodies. In 2011, one posted photograph was of a man who apparently had defecated in his pants and another in 2014 featured a woman lowering the elastic on the back of her sweatpants. "Oh, crap!" was the caption on the former; "Down under" was the caption on the latter.[44] And on DirtyPhonebook.com readers are encouraged to post information about people—something the website called "uncensored people reviews"— searchable using their phone numbers. In 2014, a number of phone numbers had been linked to names and Facebook pages, along with what appeared to be defamatory or privacy-invading information regarding their sexual matters and employment issues.[45]

In a somewhat similar vein, a website calling itself The Secret Files was published in 2013 revealing various celebrities' home addresses and social security numbers. Its motto, published as a headline just over a girl with darkened eye sockets holding a dirty finger to her mouth, was "If you believe that God makes miracles, you have to wonder if Satan has a few up his sleeve."[46] And Who's a Rat, allegedly started by a man who suggested that he had been charged after being named by an informant,[47] promised to be the "largest online database of informants and agents," asking viewers to add to its list of names by clicking "new agent" or "new informant" buttons.[48] The database was said to be available only to those who paid for access, though three ever-changing individuals appeared on the homepage by photograph, name, and hometown.

There are more-mainstream examples that also have the potential to inflict individual harm. Fairfax Underground is one; it is a suburban Washington, D.C., website on which people have posted names of teenagers allegedly involved in drunken sex videos, as one example, and the grades of thousands of local high school students, as another.[49] Its owner told the *Washington Post* that anything that was being talked about on the streets of Fairfax would be fair game for discussion online, and he boasted that posts on the website promoted community free speech.[50] "The Internet is about peer-to-peer communication, without an editor's lens or filters," the website's owner told the *Post*. He had apparently found the grades revelation merely "embarrassing" for students, so the school board successfully asked a court to order the grades removed. An attorney for one of the teens implicated noted that the website had effectively thrown kids "under the bus." Subjects of revelation are not just those in high school, however. One day in 2013 Fairfax Underground featured multiple entries, including one suggesting that a local woman was "a snitch," another suggesting that a different woman was a "crackhead," and a third suggesting that a third woman was "a whore." All women were named and all links for further discussion about each were on the main Fairfax Underground page.

And Reddit, a website where thousands of posters around the world discuss matters by topic, made headlines in 2013 when its members attempted to identify the suspects in the Boston Marathon bombings.[51] The smaller Reddit community that took on the challenge called itself "find boston bombers" and preceded to wade through hundreds of photographs taken on the day of the bombing, looking for men wearing backpacks. Posters republished close-up photographs of a recognizable "guy with heavy backpack in green hat and white earbuds" and a recognizable "guy in a dark aqua jacket with an olive green cap," among others. Several of the photographs and the implicating posts remained online for days after the real suspects had been identified. One of the people accused by Reddit posters was a seventeen-year-old boy who said he felt the "worst feeling" possible when he learned he had been the subject of the internet sleuths' accusations.[52] Another Reddit suspect was a college student whose family had reported him missing days before; he was later found dead from a suicide completely unconnected to the bombing.[53] His family, then, had to live through both the agony of his disappearance and the horror that anonymous internet posters believed him to be a murdering terrorist.

In 1964, the U.S. Supreme Court wrote in *New York Times v. Sullivan* that the Constitution's First Amendment freedoms encouraged "uninhibited, robust and wide open" public discussion so that in the end we would understand more about the world and come to know truth. In 1988, the Justices wrote similarly in *Hustler v. Falwell* that both "rhetorical hyperbole" and "imaginative expression" added much to the nation's discourse. Those two cases and others like them laud the vibrancy of a marketplace of ideas where false information is drowned out by truth and where bad ideas are drowned out by good.

Today, however, such sweepingly powerful language, at times specifically crediting media, seems terribly naïve. And, today, because of media's own indiscretions, that language is not as protective as it otherwise could be. Four more detailed examples of the backlash in law against what is here considered quasi-journalism follow: Girls Gone Wild, Borat, James O'Keefe, and reality television.

The Law and Girls Gone Wild

Long before The Dirty and Gawker and websites with a seeming mission to expose, in 1997, there was Girls Gone Wild. The videotape series was "[c]reated by entrepreneur Joe Francis," one court explained, and "feature[d] young, and sometimes underage, women in states of partial or total nudity."[54] Girls Gone Wild's focus was helped along by the women themselves: they "commonly consent[ed] to be photographed and videotaped in various stages of undress," one court explained, "for a nominal gift in the form of costume jewelry, usually consisting of long strands of brightly colored plastic beads and trinkets."[55] Each videotape in the series consisted of carefully edited clips of girls and young women lifting their shirts to expose their breasts, sometimes interspersed with far more graphic clips of girls and women engaged in sexual activity.

The facts as alleged by the plaintiffs in the cases that made their way to court were often heinous. Some claimed that producers had taken advantage of their intoxication[56] or had provided them with drugs and/or liquor,[57] pressuring them to perform while promising that their images would not appear on the Girls Gone Wild series.[58] Most of the girls who brought claims in reported cases against Francis and his production company were underage: seventeen, sixteen, fifteen, fourteen, and even thirteen years old.[59] Some were stopped by a photographer on the street, while others were brought to a party and allegedly plied with alcohol. Some knew that a photographer was present but others insisted they did not or did not fully understand what the photographer was up to.

In other words, the series seemed designed to give courts good reason to extend privacy law to protect these plaintiffs whose mistakes had life-altering privacy implications: these momentary lapses of discretion by apparently trusting underage girls had been immortalized forever as part of a tawdry series of videotapes.

Nonetheless, Francis had the First Amendment and decades of privacy law jurisprudence on his side. First, he argued that he was simply covering a newsworthy part of American culture—the phenomenon of females willing to disrobe for an item of little value—making the same argument as would a journalist who had covered a riot on the streets. "[T]he defendant [Girls Gone Wild] suggests it merely used videotape of the crowd at Mardi Gras," one court wrote, "as part of a true and accurate depiction of a newsworthy event—much as CBS might cover a presidential speech or Fox might cover the Super Bowl."[60]

Moreover, the defendant producers noted, the girls had exposed themselves in public, either at the beach or at parties, and, therefore, privacy law would not apply. One young woman, for example, was on "a public part of the lake, stood on top of a boat and removed her bikini bathing suit top"[61] and another was "at a 'party' on the second floor of a Bourbon Street bar" in New Orleans.[62] Their "flashing," Francis argued, was a newsworthy, public event[63] and he was but the documentarian.

One court sided with Francis in a case involving a seventeen-year-old who had argued that she would not have exposed herself had she known of the cameraman's plan. The court rejected her privacy claim, finding that the Girls Gone Wild series was "an expressive work created solely for entertainment purposes" in which the girl had "voluntarily participated."[64] The judge wrote that the videotape, like any television news story, was a "truthful and accurate description of [the plaintiff] voluntarily exposing her breasts to a camera just as she did on Labor Day Weekend in Panama City Beach, Florida" in a public place "while several pedestrians were in the general vicinity," even though the cameraman was a complete stranger.

That decision stood alone, however. From the first reported case brought against Girls Gone Wild in 2002, in which the court wrote that "[t]he First Amendment provides no right to make an unconsenting individual the poster-person for a commercial product,"[65] to one of the last, decided in 2013, and involving a fourteen-year-old girl, in which the court reasoned that "[t]he men to whom [the plaintiff] exposed her breasts never indicated to [the plaintiff] that they worked for, had any connection with, or had any intention of giving [the plaintiff's] image to" Girls Gone Wild producers,[66] the decisions at least in part favor the plaintiffs' claims, most of which sounded in privacy and intentional infliction of emotional distress.

The remaining courts in reported cases rejected the Girls Gone Wild producers' newsworthiness arguments either implicitly or explicitly. "Since plaintiff is not a public figure," one such court wrote, the producers are "not participating in a public dialogue about the condition of American society in general."[67]

Two courts also rejected the defendants' argument that they were protected because what had happened with the young women had happened in public. One court held that someone at a party attended by others could, in fact, be in private even though the bar in question was on Bourbon Street in New Orleans and even though the establishment was open to the public and strangers were in attendance.[68] Another flatly rejected the idea that taking off one's top in public automatically puts the person in the public eye.[69]

And one federal appeals court worried openly about what might happen to these girls and young women in the age of the Internet where visual depictions of their indiscretion might remain forever. It warned that Girls Gone Wild girls "faced the very real danger of becoming internet sensations" and it pointed to the example of the seventeen-year-old who had failed to convince the judge to rule in her favor. That plaintiff was now "permanently identified in the IMDb database for one of the Girls Gone Wild movies," the court wrote, by name and with the title of "17-year-old public breast-flasher." For that reason, over First Amendment-based objections by Girls Gone Wild producers, the court held that the plaintiffs in the case could remain anonymous throughout the duration of the lawsuit.[70]

The legacy of quasi-journalist Joe Francis and his Girls Gone Wild series, then, can be seen as three-fold. First, people who are at a public gathering may, in fact, be considered in a private space for purposes of invasion of privacy; second, newsworthiness's sweep is more limited and presumably might not include a news item with video of young women who flash for beads in public; and, third, courts can restrict media from learning lawsuit parties' names if there is a danger that privacy will be forever wiped away by internet mentions.

Mainstream news media organizations recognized the implications these cases had for traditional news gathering and reporting and filed First Amendment amici briefs in at least one of the cases.[71] But, not surprisingly, those arguments, too, were drowned out by the privacy claims of girls who had found themselves more exposed than they thought possible.

The Law and *Borat*

Borat is a 2006 Hollywood film starring Sacha Baron Cohen, subtitled "Cultural Learnings of America for Make Benefit Glorious Nation of Kazakhstan." On IMDb, it is described this way: "Kazakh TV talking head Borat is dispatched to the United States to report on the greatest country in the world. With a documentary crew in tow, Borat becomes more interested in locating and marrying [television star] Pamela Anderson." In the real-life making of the film, Sacha Baron Cohen traveled across the United States pretending to be a foreign journalist and interacting with very real people who had no idea that they were being tricked: what they thought was a Kazakhstan-produced documentary would instead appear in theaters across the United States. The film, then, was very real in that real businesspeople, real etiquette experts, and real fraternity brothers were featured in nonscripted ways, but also quite fictionalized in that Borat, the journalist, was a figment of Baron Cohen's imagination, as was the general script.

After its release, multiple people featured in the film sued for privacy-related reasons. Some argued that they had been made to appear silly, others that their antisocial behavior had been revealed. The trouble was that many of them had signed releases that, upon reflection, should have raised red flags: in exchange for up to $350, the participants had agreed to appear in the film described as one "meant to reach a young adult audience by using entertaining content and formats," and those signing the participation contract containing that language had promised not to sue for invasion of privacy or intentional infliction of emotional distress.[72] The releases mostly protected the producers even though the plaintiffs argued that they had been tricked. In one case, for example, the court analyzed the news value of the film as a trump to the plaintiff's privacy claims, finding it to be a newsworthy "ironic commentary of modern American culture, contrasting the backwardness of its protagonist with the social ills [that] afflict supposedly sophisticated society."[73]

But Borat's travels had led him to a Pentecostal church camp meeting, one attended by a deeply religious woman named Ellen Johnson. As a court would later explain, in the film, "Borat . . . seeks redemption at the camp meeting during which he acts as if he is converted by the minister and begins speaking in tongues along with other Pentecostals doing the same."[74] Johnson appears in the film for three seconds. "While Borat appears to be experiencing this religious conversion," the court explained, "several members of the camp meeting, including the plaintiff, are shown in the film raising their arms to praise God for Borat's conversion."

There was no conversion, of course, and, after seeing the film, Johnson felt that she had been made to look as if she did not take her religion seriously. She sued the filmmakers for invasion of privacy and intentional infliction of emotional distress in a federal trial court in Mississippi. They had, she argued, filmed her without her consent, had portrayed her in a way that suggested that she had knowingly mocked her church, had released the film without her signed waiver, had tricked her into believing that the film was a documentary on American religion to be shown in a foreign country, and had not told her that Borat himself was not real. The defendants, in turn, argued that they were protected by the First Amendment.

The court that would hear the case called it "a battle between the defendants' assertion of their free speech rights and the plaintiff's right to privacy."[75] And here, privacy won out.

The decision is remarkable in that the court found two separate privacy-related torts actionable even though case law supported the opposite conclusion. First, the court agreed with the plaintiff that she had a valid false light claim even though the court found that Mississippi had never before explicitly recognized false light as a valid cause of action. The producers had argued that the three seconds of hand-raising had truthfully occurred and that, therefore, there could be no false light claim, but the court ruled that the issue was whether viewers of the movie might believe that Johnson had knowingly mocked her religion. The court reasoned that the film could well be misunderstood: "There are indeed many reasonable Americans," the court wrote, "especially those who are of an older generation, who are not familiar with the type of humor/satire that is depicted in the film *Borat*."

Even more remarkable, however, was the court's decision to allow the plaintiff's privacy-related misappropriation claim to continue as well, even though it was based solely on a three-second image of the plaintiff in an eighty-four minute film. The court reasoned that those three seconds could support misappropriation because the film itself was a commercial enterprise, because producers had not received her explicit permission, and because producers had misled church leaders. Multiple courts had previously decided that a small focus within a considerably larger project would not support such a claim, but, even so, the court's focus was solely on the film's commercial nature.

As for the defendants' First Amendment shield, the court ruled that Supreme Court precedent that protected fictionalized motion pictures did not apply to one involving "an invasion of privacy claim by a private citizen":

> [T]he nature of the film *Borat* is different from a purely fictional work since, although the viewer is aware that the plot itself is fictional and that the characters of Borat and his producer are fictional, the viewer is also aware that the vast majority, if not all, of the other people featured in the movie are nonpublic figures who are not actors and are likely unaware that Borat is not a Kazakhstani reporter filming a documentary for Kazakhstan.

As in the previous examples in this chapter, the actions of the pretend journalist Borat and the court's reaction to his shenanigans, therefore, have implications for mainstream journalists. First, the court recognized the false light privacy tort in the jurisdiction in order to protect citizens from mischief-making media, here a quasi-journalist. Second, misappropriation was extended to include what many would consider incidental use—three seconds within a much longer film—simply because the end product was a commercial one. And finally, and perhaps most importantly, the defendants' calls for First Amendment protection went unheard because the court's very strong focus was not on freedom of expression but on the protection of the plaintiff's privacy interests.

The Law and James O'Keefe

Unlike the fictionalized Borat, James O'Keefe is a real person. Like the Borat character, he considers himself a journalist. So strong is his conviction and so deep is his apparent need for validation, he has ambushed or confronted multiple journalists and journalism professors in an effort to get them to welcome him into their fold. In a video he posted online,[76] he attempts to get by security at various newspaper offices and journalism schools to meet with those who can validate him; one such attempt appears to be shot using a hidden camera. He also unsuccessfully tries to have a phone conversation with a New York University journalism professor, Jay Rosen, who apparently hangs up when he realizes that O'Keefe has called; Rosen has long advocated for rights for citizen journalists even as others voiced concerns that their misunderstanding of law and ethics could have detrimental effects on all media.

O'Keefe is the man who made headlines in 2009 for pretending to be an extravagantly dressed pimp who, with a less-dressed woman pretending to be a prostitute, entered Association of Community Organizations for Reform Now (ACORN) offices to ask for tax advice regarding what they explained would be an underage prostitution ring using noncitizens. The two used a hidden camera and posted video of what appeared to be ACORN workers at different offices offering advice about how to operate such a business. The video voiceovers use a sometimes mocking tone.

The trouble was that at least one of the featured ACORN workers had immediately called the police when the two left his office; he later explained that he had led them on in an effort to gather more information for the authorities. Others videotaped in a similar fashion claimed that O'Keefe had selectively edited the video to make it look as if they had advocated something they had not. Nonetheless, the videotapes received thousands of internet hits and strong mainstream news coverage.

Some months later, O'Keefe and three others would attempt to infiltrate the phone closet in U.S. Senator Mary Landrieu's office in New Orleans. At least two of them were dressed in coveralls and hardhats and convinced office staff at the Hale Boggs Federal Building that they were there to work on the phone system.[77] O'Keefe had entered earlier to record the events on his cell phone.[78] He would later explain that he and his colleagues were "investigating allegations [that] the senator was trying to avoid calls" critical of a health care issue. He would also argue that such investigative work was appropriate because "[i]nvestigative journalists have been using a lot of these tactics for years."[79] Despite his explanations and protestations, O'Keefe would plead guilty to entering federal property under false pretenses; the judge sentenced him to two years of probation and he paid a $1500 fine.[80]

Most of the descriptions of O'Keefe's behavior, if accurate, seem to violate some of mainstream journalism's ethics provisions, at least as they stand in 2014: hidden camera use, pretending to be someone else to gain access to a building or to schedule a personal interview, and a mocking attack-journalism approach. Moreover, many times in videos and otherwise, O'Keefe's goal seems to be to promote a book he authored; he is seen at various points attempting to give a copy to subjects. He also attempts to interview key people about his arrest in New Orleans: "Did you leak my emails to the press?" he asked a former U.S. Attorney in one published videotape. If one of his goals is to promote his book, such a motivation is also in discord with journalistic ethics: even the citizen journalist whom a seemingly oblivious O'Keefe interviews on that same video condemns those journalists who act as publicists. Moreover, ethics provisions would never allow a journalist to cover a story directly involving himself: his ability to be neutral and, therefore, believable and trustworthy would be at issue.

Such ethics lapses and ethics stances by quasi-journalists surely contribute to journalism's falling reputation, but O'Keefe's contribution to its downfall has a legal aspect as well. There has been at least one successful lawsuit springing from O'Keefe's ACORN stings, one brought on privacy grounds. O'Keefe eventually settled the case, paying $100,000 to the ACORN worker who had called police but whose interaction with the fake pimp and prostitute remained on the Internet even so. As the author of an article about O'Keefe in the *Atlantic* opined, despite numerous other journalistically questionable acts, the "egregiously misleading" editorial decision to retain the video on his website was O'Keefe's "most indefensible thing."[81]

Juan Carlos Vera was the ACORN worker who eventually settled his case against O'Keefe. He had based his claim on a California privacy law that forbids the use of hidden recordings; Vera had told the court that the posted hidden camera video had publically humiliated him and had caused him extreme emotional pain and suffering.[82] Attorneys for O'Keefe argued in response that there should be an investigative journalism First Amendment exception to the privacy law, maintaining that O'Keefe had an "affirmative defense based upon his First Amendment rights including freedom of the press."[83] The court was not moved by O'Keefe's constitutional claims, but it did not dispute his bona fides as a journalist. Instead, it found "no compelling reason" to construe the California privacy law in a way that would give journalistic motives a pass, a ruling with far-reaching implications for news-gathering by mainstream journalists.[84] Now, the interpretation of the privacy statute that rejects a journalism exception is part of a published federal trial court's opinion, certain to be used by other plaintiffs even in cases involving mainstream journalism. As the court made clear, its interpretation of the law was "true even in the context of exposé news gathering."

"The First Amendment protects citizen journalists who expose truthful information for the greater public good," an attorney representing one of O'Keefe's associates had argued before the court. "This lawsuit [filed by Vera] is a direct attack on the First Amendment and an attempt to silence a young citizen journalist and discourage future journalistic inquiry that may shed light on the truth."[85] But the court disagreed and its published decision now confirms that the attorney's interpretation of the law is far too generous.

There are other possible legal repercussions from O'Keefe's moves. A 2012 O'Keefe hidden camera report, for example, focused on voter registration laws; at a polling place, an undercover operative had asked for and had received the ballot meant instead for Attorney General Eric Holder because the operative had not been forced to show any identification.[86] Nine months later, in response to a request from mainstream journalism, a federal appeals court in Pennsylvania closed off all voting areas to journalists and quasi-journalists alike, explaining that

> membership in the Fourth Estate has been democratized. Access to blogs, smartphones, and an extensive network of social media sites (not the least of which are Twitter and Facebook) have transformed all of us into potential members of the media. While in almost any other situation this would be a boon to a free and democratic society, in the context of the voting process, the confusion and chaos that would result from a potentially limitless number of reporters in a polling place would work the opposite effect, potentially creating confusion, frustration, and delay. . . . In this situation, anyone could record in the polling place if the First Amendment protected the right of access thereto.[87]

Meantime, in a video posted on his website, O'Keefe seemed both shocked and scornful that one of the journalists he had attempted to confront had told O'Keefe that his best chance for an interview lay elsewhere: with his lawyer. "This journalist is referring us to his attorney," O'Keefe said incredulously. But, clearly, O'Keefe's stealth recording and his editing and publishing of videos like the one involving the ACORN worker is precisely why many fear his brand of quasi-journalism and why even strong journalism advocates refer him to their lawyers.

The Law and Reality Television

It cannot be good for all journalism that, at a time when courts have moved to restrict police records like mug shots and accident reports on privacy grounds, a series titled *Panic 9-1-1* exists. *Panic 9-1-1* is a cable television show described as one that "take[s] 911 calls to a whole new level never seen or heard before on television. Unlike emergency shows of the past, viewers will live inside the calls and experience every harrowing and terrifying moment along with the caller. Every second is real."[88] The premiere episode made clear that "harrowing" and "terrifying" are apt descriptors: viewers listened to a real 911 tape and watched a reenactment as "9-1-1 dispatchers receive[d] a frantic call from a Colorado mother who [had] barricade[d] herself and her teenage son inside an upstairs closet with no lock as an unknown intruder searche[d] for their hiding place." One clip on the program's website is titled, "Don't Let Me Die." Meantime, a website calling itself Amazing 911 Calls boasted that it too had audio of "the most scariest, most intense, amazing 911 calls out there."[89]

Such sensationalized real-life moments of agonizing terror could make even media-sympathetic courts think twice about releasing 911 tapes to media generally, lest the recorded calls end up as voiceover for a television program more about horror than news.

Most lawsuits brought against reality television programs, however, are those based upon newsgathering and the push-the-envelope production behavior at places like hospitals or with police at crime scenes. Contrary to James O'Keefe's interpretation of constitutional law, most courts have found no First Amendment protection for newsgathering itself, despite the newsworthiness of the underlying story. Even in intrusion-into-seclusion tort cases in which courts could easily decide that the offensiveness of any intrusion should be offset by the value of the underlying news story, most courts refuse to allow newsworthiness to enter the intrusion determination at all.

Most of the intrusion decisions, however, stem not from *60 Minutes* or some other well-respected investigative journalism, but from reality television programming and some from what might be said to be O'Keefe-like behavior.

A California appeals court in 2002, for example, reiterated what the *Shulman* court had held four years before:

> [N]o constitutional precedent or principle of which we are aware gives a reporter general license to intrude in an objectively offensive manner into private places, conversations or matters merely because the reporter thinks he or she may thereby find something that will warrant publication or broadcast.[90]

In that case, the plaintiffs had alleged that reporters had disguised themselves as hospital workers in order to get video for the reality television program *Trauma: Life in the ER*, and had featured within the program itself a man who had ingested a drug known as Blue Nitro. Despite the fact that the court recognized the newsworthiness of the dangers of so-called "rave" drugs, it allowed the lawsuit to continue over the producers' First Amendment arguments.

Even though these programs have had a negative effect on mainstream journalism, they often do not seem to follow the same mainstream ethics restrictions. In a lawsuit brought against the reality television program *Inside American Jail*, for example, the complaint noted that the show's producers had donated money to the sheriff's reelection campaign, suggesting that because the sheriff had agreed to the filming, the producers would therefore help with his reelection.[91] In contrast, mainstream news reporters are strongly encouraged to be apolitical or to keep their political allegiances quiet lest their reporting be perceived as biased and subjective. Many mainstream journalists do not campaign for any candidate and some refuse to vote in primary elections in which they would be forced to reveal their political party. Indeed, reporters have been fired for covering political rallies while wearing political paraphernalia[92] or for revealing their political beliefs in some other fashion.[93]

Even so, when a California court holds that newsgathering itself has no constitutional protection, as did the California court in the Blue Nitro reality television case, the holding applies to all journalism. And when a federal appeals court in California decides that the identity of a police informant is not newsworthy in a case springing from a reality television program's alleged failure to digitize the man's face, the holding can be applied more generally; the court had noted that others' faces had been digitized and reasoned that, therefore, there was little news value in the person's precise identity.[94]

Troubling, too, are those times in which a reality television program aligns itself with mainstream news reporting in an effort to piggyback on mainstream journalism's stronger reputation. In a case from Tennessee heard in federal court in 2011, for example, the plaintiff complained that a reality television program titled *The Squad: Prison Police* had placed her in a false light and had defamed her by suggesting that she had carried drugs into prison while visiting her inmate husband.[95] The court described the program's use of hidden video as it followed the plaintiff, with the voiceover provided by a government agent assigned to the case. "I think we got her . . . inmates have found a weakness in our security," the agent said as the woman's driver's license picture was shown in mug shot-like fashion, "we're expecting this lady today." When there was little physical interaction between the couple at first, the official suggested that "it [the drug exchange] don't look like it's been done yet, so now it's just a waiting game." Later, after the couple kisses, he predicted that time for the "nitty gritty" had begun: "[H]old on now," he noted after the kiss, "she's going to the bathroom [and] [t]ypically these woman hide stuff up in their vaginal cavity and then go to the restroom to take it out." When the woman left the bathroom quickly, he suggested that such a move implicated her further: "She didn't have time to pee. She went in and came right back out." After more kissing, the agent seemed certain that "some [expletive] just happened [and] I think we got 'em." At various points, as the video focused in on the woman and her behavior, the producers used ominous sounds and background music to enhance the crime-fighting theme.

As might be expected given her false light and defamation claims, nothing was found on the woman (despite, as the program explained, a "strip search of the suspect") or on her husband (despite, as the program noted, a twenty-four-hour "dry cell" hold in which he had no access to running water or a traditional toilet). Even so, the agent warned at the end, "We might not get you today, maybe next week, next month, next year, but eventually we're going to catch up with you, and we're gonna get you."

The woman argued that the program had suggested that she had and would smuggle drugs into prison. The court agreed that her case was a valid one and, in doing so, rejected the main defenses put forth by the producers. First, they had argued that a notice at the beginning of the program suggesting that all were innocent until proved guilty and that the ultimate "false alarm" conclusion of the narrative at the program's end negated the overall effect of the videotape and voiceover. The court skeptically rejected that argument, pointing to the heavy focus on the plaintiff and the suggestion at the end that officials had not caught anyone yet, but would. The court also rejected the defense argument that the voiceover comments were merely opinions, noting that even opinions are not necessarily protected when they implicate someone in wrongdoing.

But what the court called the most "important" defense argument was the producers' claim that the program—a reality television show—was merely doing real-time news reporting, as would a television news station during a breaking news event. In effect, the defense seems to have argued, the viewer was carried along by the narrative as the criminal investigation moved forward, just as a television station presumably would cover a bank robbery or some other crime as it happened. But the court rejected this defense as well. It recognized that the program had been taped well in advance and had then been edited down into the thirty-minute program that the viewers saw, with producers having full control over the end product. As a "canned" program, then, the court found that it was very different from typical coverage of a breaking news event in which journalists are given little control over how a suspect might ultimately be portrayed.

That decision, though clearly finding a distinction between mainstream news reporting and this type of reality television, still has the potential to affect future journalism cases in which the editing and narrative of a news story implicates a suspect until the end.

The problem with reality television—one in which its methods have a lasting legal impact on journalism generally—is likely to continue. Today's courts seem quite averse not only to some of its newsgathering techniques but also to its formats and its impact on American values. "In popular culture," one Rhode Island court wrote in 2011, "we see reality television constantly lowering the bar of civility and common courtesy."[96] A court in New York suggested that the genre "offers opportunities for embarrassing and insulting participants and the more outlandish the conduct, the higher the ratings," lamenting that "[t]here does not seem to be a bottom to the viewing public's appetite for this brand of entertainment."[97] A federal court in Indiana— hearing a case involving college students who had lured a fellow student to a fake Facebook page and then had recorded and posted on YouTube the point at which the fellow student learned that the Facebook girl did not exist— linked the students' video prank to reality television. It quoted a psychology article that had characterized such shows as like "'freeway car accident[s] or train wreck[s]' that 'seem to exploit and reward outrageous behavior' and allow viewers to 'take delight in the problems and misfortunes of others.'"[98] "Indeed," the judge in that case wrote, "the very objectionable or offensive nature of the show's subject matter can make it a hit." A federal judge in Kansas joined in the criticism, writing that "the reality TV business . . . (whether the shows involve bachelorettes, stranded survivors on faraway islands, or hunting game in the wild) . . . is inconsistent with the notion of always telling the truth."[99]

That is the real problem with much of quasi-journalism: it cannot be trusted as much as mainstream journalism should be trusted. And yet the negative opinions in its cases can be read to affect even strongly ethical media.

Meantime, a casting call went out for what producers promised would be an "upcoming premium reality television series." It described the planned program in this way:

> The upcoming series will be based loosely on the theme of blackmail and deceit. The series will primarily focus on the entrapment of rich and affluential married men. Chosen actresses will be provided a team of analysts which will generate dossier's on these men in order to aide in each mans entrapment by our actresses. There will also be an added sense of competition between the actresses of different cities revolving around a $500,000 cash prize and vacation to a location of the winners choosing for one week. . . . The overall goal of the actress towards her target should be to entrap the target so much that the target becomes so entangled in the deceit that they lavish the actress with gifts, trips, etc. obsessing with the actress to the point where they are infatuated.
>
> Then comes the blackmail portion[:] the men are given the suggestion of making a substantial donation to a charity or the information being turned over for public viewing.
>
> During the course of the entrapment the gentleman's face will be blurred however if he chooses to donate time or funding to charity his face will not be revealed. If the entrap chooses to refrain from the donation his face will be revealed.[100]

If that "premium reality television series" is not an O'Keefe undercover experiment—or even if it is—the courts are likely to hear more about it and, afterward, be forced to make decisions that will have the potential to harm all reporting.

Quasi-Journalism and Journalism: The Difference between "Reality" and News

The struggle to decide which publications should be considered "true" journalism—how we delineate between mainstream journalism and quasi-journalism or less traditionally journalistic publications—is more than an academic exercise. As discussed in greater detail in Chapter 8, currently, journalists are protected in important ways that quasi-journalists or simple internet publishers are not. State laws shielding them from forced court testimony, for example, recognize that journalists bring something special to society and that journalism's role should be protected so that the public can be informed both about government from press releases and about government wrongs from inside sources who would not come forward but for a shield of protection.

But there is another reason why the distinction is an important one: decisions made by mainstream journalists based on ethics considerations help protect the people who are the focus of news coverage. Ethics considerations will stop many journalists from reporting private embarrassing things about others, even when the revelation would have significant news value. Rightly or wrongly, reporters in Idaho, for example, were said to have known about Senator Larry Craig's alleged dalliances for "decades,"[101] but no one reported on these alleged affairs likely because they felt they needed additional on-the-record sources. There are multiple other examples at all levels of government and otherwise. One cannot imagine many push-the-envelope gossip websites maintaining such standards. In fact, one blogger had outed Craig well in advance of mainstream media outlets, but, apparently lacking additional sources, mainstream media did not re-report the story.[102]

Consider too the ethics of Gawker's campaign in 2013 to raise enough money to buy a videotape that Gawker believed showed the mayor of Toronto, Canada, smoking crack. "We are Raising $200,000 to Buy and Publish the Rob Ford Crack Tape," a Gawker headline at the time read,[103] and the story promised that for a $1000 donation the donor would be invited for dinner with the Gawker staff. While the fundraising effort was successful, a few days later, Gawker reported that the tape was "gone" and, therefore, no longer for sale from the source who had demanded the money.[104] Traditional journalism ethics provisions suggest that exchanging money for information is wrong and would certainly not embrace crowdsourcing such funds.

But aside from such ethics protections, there is also the recognition in law that only newsworthy stories that invade privacy are protected while crass and morbidly sensational stories that invade privacy are not. A word like "newsworthy" necessitates that someone decide what is news and what isn't. The best one to make that call is a practicing journalist who has had experience weighing the private interests in privacy against the public interest in the information, lest the four-million viewers of the Hulk Hogan video be the ones to determine newsworthiness and the future legality of prying into our most intimate private lives.

Recall that the Restatement suggests that news is determined by looking at what is published by news organizations. If we allow all truth publishers, including MyEx.com and Girls Gone Wild, to make newsworthiness determinations, then someone with a laptop but no journalistic training could well decide that private medical information or private family information or private sexual information about anyone is newsworthy. The Hulk Hogan videotape? Absolutely newsworthy in a world where Gawker gets to decide what has news value and what does not.

Consider too those girls outed in the Girls Gone Wild videotape series, or those whose images have been posted on revenge porn websites, or those private persons humiliated because hidden camera video of a private discussion was posted on YouTube. Traditional methods of defining newsworthiness—those that focus on a journalist's discretion—would allow those people to bring privacy claims. If news is defined more broadly, in a way that accepts all publishers as capable of determining news value, then privacy as a legal claim and legal deterrent will all but disappear. If we extend journalism to cover anyone who publishes anything online, then newsworthiness necessarily includes the crass, morbidly sensational "stories" about everyday people that are published on websites like The Dirty and Gawker, but also on websites like College Wall of Shame and 4chan. Moreover, when courts extend the definition of journalist to include everyone—or the definition of news to include everything—the First Amendment is strained. After all, if everyone is a journalist, then the foundational reasons for a reporter's shield law disappear and no one is protected; government officials with insiders' knowledge of real wrongs will fear revealing important information to journalists.

The difficulty in delineation is a key reason why Congress has yet to pass a federal shield law; Congress is worried about potentially protecting those who publish without hesitation, reflection, or a sense of ethics. "There are some major carve-outs in the [reporter's shield] legislation," the *New York Times* reported in 2013 in an article that predicted that Congress was close to enacting such a law, including "limitations on what constitutes an act of journalism, most of which seem aimed at next-generation news organizations that sometimes simply post classified material, rather than report more in-depth articles based on that information."[105]

Toward a Narrower Definition of "Journalist"

Further proof of the need to define journalist and journalism comes from courtrooms. Not surprisingly, judges similarly seem to be inclined toward a narrower definition.

A court in a 2013 case from Texas defined journalist narrowly. There, a labor union for service employees had published website posts as a part of a "Justice for Janitors" campaign and the union argued that such publications made it a member of the news media. It was an important issue because Texas gives electronic or print media special jurisdictional considerations, a distinction based upon the Constitution's press freedoms. The court, forced to define journalism, decided that such posts did not qualify. "A 'journalist,'" the court wrote, quoting Texas law, "is defined as 'a person who for a substantial portion of the person's livelihood or for substantial financial gain, writes news or information that is disseminated by a news medium."[106] It also suggested that other factors would contribute to such a determination: the author's journalistic background, how established in journalism the reporter was, the character of the posts at issue, the editorial process involved including decisions based on the newsworthiness of stories, and the size and nature of the readership. Given the Texas law and those considerations, the court found that the union should not receive the special jurisdictional considerations that a traditional journalist would.

A New Jersey state court facing the definition issue that same year defined journalist more broadly and decided that a blogger who wrote for a website called The County Watchers would be protected under the state's shield law, preventing her from having to testify regarding her journalistic research in a criminal case. The court found that the blogger's posts on something the community called "Generatorgate," her exposé on "Musicfest," and her stories on pension padding and theft of county property, among others, would be considered "news" under the statute. Moreover, the court decided, the blogger's purpose was to disseminate news to the community as opposed to publishing information for a limited audience. Given those considerations, the shield law—one written to protect "a person engaged on, engaged in, connected with, or employed by news media for the purpose of gathering . . . editing or disseminating news for the general public"—protected the blogger. In delineating between journalist and quasi-journalist, however, the court suggested that the definition for the former would not always be inclusive; it reiterated an earlier warning that "new media should not be confused with news media." It also suggested that the legislature might further define the term within the shield law if it found it necessary given the "changing times."[107]

The trend seems to be going the Texas way—toward a narrower definition for journalist—even in cases far closer than that of a service union. Charles Tobin, a chair of the American Bar Association Forum on Communications Law and a media defense attorney, called the trend "disturbing" and worried that courts' or legislators' willingness to define who counts as a journalist would inevitably leave some legitimate truth-seekers outside the scope of protection.[108] These "recent decisions," Tobin wrote, "teach[] us that the First Amendment shield is perhaps less resilient for some classes of journalists than for others."

There are additional reported cases that support Tobin's assessment. In 2012, a federal trial court rejected media protection for a company website that had published a press release, finding that the defendant website owners were "private parties with their own websites" and not news media even though the press release had been picked up by 130 media outlets; the court specifically wrote that it was worried that finding otherwise would "abolish any distinction between private parties and members of the media," a distinction that was important in Florida pre-suit notice law.[109] A federal trial court in Maine made a similar determination that same year, finding that a website that advocated against a gubernatorial candidate was not entitled to a press exemption for election disclosure requirements; the website creator's First Amendment arguments failed because the court found the website much more like a negative campaign advertisement than a periodical publication.[110]

And, in a particularly close case, a website known as Media Takeout, one calling itself "the most visited urban website in the world,"[111] was unable to use a newsworthiness defense because the court, in effect, found its story not journalistic enough: incorrect, too short, and not sufficiently linked with a celebrity. The website had published a piece in which the plaintiff was identified incorrectly as celebrity Kimora Lee Simmons' sister.[112] The woman featured in the story, who was not related to Simmons at all, sued on privacy-related grounds, arguing that the website had used her identity to make money. Media Takeout argued in response that the story itself was not published for commercial reasons because "a news article reporting on a celebrity . . . involves 'a matter of public interest' and thus fits comfortably within the 'newsworthiness' exception."

The court, however, rejected the website's attempt to categorize itself as a journalistic enterprise. "At the outset," it wrote, "Media Takeout's contention that its article 'reported on a celebrity' is greatly exaggerated," finding that the fifty-word article only included photographs of the plaintiff, a quick mention of her desire to get into modeling, and no mention of the celebrity at all other than the misinformation that the two were sisters. The court allowed the plaintiff's invasion-of-privacy lawsuit to continue to trial, finding that the falsity within the article could make it not newsworthy and, therefore, unprotected.

In other words, there is often a need to distinguish between those who are mainstream journalists and those who are not in a legal sense. Courts, therefore, are defining "journalist" and "newsworthiness" out of necessity. As suggested in greater depth in Chapter 8, narrow definitions, ones that exclude some quasi-journalistic publishers and some quasi-journalistic publications, may harm some truthful expression. But narrow descriptions that limit those who can claim journalistic privilege and that reject claims that any publisher can publish anything it wants, can lead to a freer flow of important information and help protect the privacy of many.

6

The New Old Legal Call for Privacy

A California woman who had been diagnosed with bipolar disorder occasionally missed work in 2008 due to her condition. No one in her real estate office workplace other than her boss knew of the diagnosis until he allegedly shared the information with coworkers. After that, one of them asked the woman if she would "go postal" someday. Upset that her boss had apparently violated her trust, the woman sued for invasion of privacy.[1]

This employment privacy case, noted briefly in Chapter 3, had absolutely nothing at all to do with media, and yet, ultimately, a California appeals court seized it as an opportunity to criticize news and other publications and to expand the scope of privacy protection in an effort to combat media invasions. Put another way, privacy was strengthened and media was censured all because a real estate office supervisor had allegedly revealed that an employee had been diagnosed with mental illness.

First, the court quoted Samuel Warren and Louis Brandeis who in 1890 had written in "The Right to Privacy" that idle gossip within newspapers was a threat to domesticity. "Evidently not much has changed in more than a century," the court quipped. Second, it rejected a definition for publication of private facts in which liability attached only when the private information was revealed in writing. "[N]o one has come up with a good reason for restricting liability to written disclosures," the court held, calling such a rule "outmoded" and reasoning that spoken disclosures could be just as harmful. Third, it revealed the media-centric reason it felt privacy violations must include the spoken word:

While this restriction [limiting the publication tort to the written word] may have made sense in the 1890s—when no one dreamed of talk radio or confessional television—it certainly makes no sense now. Private facts can be just as widely disclosed—if not more so—through oral media as through written ones. To allow a plaintiff redress for one kind of disclosure but not the other, when both can be equally damaging to privacy is a rule better suited to an era when the town crier was the principal purveyor of news.

In other words, despite the court's cheeky suggestion that things had not changed much in 120 years, things had changed and, in the court's opinion, for the worse: broadcast media, specifically talk radio, confessional television, and today's news deliverers, had made it necessary to expand privacy law in ways Warren and Brandeis likely would have embraced had they known what journalism and quasi-journalism would come to.

In an age of such push-the-envelope media, invasive technology, and personal revelation both online and otherwise, it is not surprising that courts, lawmakers, and scholars have called for greater privacy protections. Those judges and others driving changes in legal policy may not necessarily see themselves personally at risk from reality television, push-the-envelope quasi-journalism, or paparazzi, but they cannot avoid airport body scanners, computer tracking cookies, traffic cameras, and other ubiquitous intrusions. These can lead many to value privacy and the protection of persons from related emotional harm more, even as they come to value media less.

This chapter explores today's shift toward privacy in the courts, legislatures, and elsewhere. It begins by recognizing privacy values and the sometimes conflict between privacy and the dissemination of information. It then uses language and ideas from "The Right to Privacy" to show that the older, media-critical law review article parallels what many of today's judges, lawmakers, and others have argued is necessary in light of today's strong privacy interests, new technologies, and a sense that media has lost its way.

Privacy and Privacy in Conflict

It is important initially to recognize and appreciate historical, personal, and societal interests in privacy.

In 1811, more than two centuries ago—and nearly eighty years before Warren and Brandeis argued that the right to privacy was a necessary addition to the law—a court in Louisiana decided that it would in fact be "tortious" should a person publish another's private letter, especially a letter "written in mystery and confidence."[2] The court quoted Roman philosopher Cicero and used the word privacy explicitly in its rhetoric: "'How many serious things proper to be communicated in the privacy of one's correspondence are unfit for the public eye[?]'" and later suggested, again by word, that family "privacy" would be at stake should a letter be published revealing family secrets.

That language from the early 1800s, written well in advance of "The Right to Privacy," makes sense given the nation's history; one judge recently suggested, in fact, that "it was a yearning for privacy that caused [many] early immigrants" to come to the United States in the first place.[3]

In other words, the Boston lawyers who defended privacy in 1890 were hardly the first. From Cicero, who connected privacy with the foundational functioning of society, to the mandated arrest in England in the 1300s of eavesdroppers and peeping toms, to the 1811 Louisiana court that punished a newspaper publisher for revealing information in an open-hearted letter, to Warren and Brandeis's time, privacy has been protected, oftentimes revered, sometimes literally over journalists' calls for press freedom.

The reason is fundamental. As Justice Sonia Sotomayor suggested in the introduction to her autobiography, psychologists have found that conceptions of privacy may differ from person to person, but, for all, are built upon respect for oneself and are necessary to psychological and sociological function.[4] Threats to privacy, it has been argued in a legal sense, "threaten our very integrity as persons."[5] Privacy law scholar Julie Cohen links those privacy interests to an informed, reflective citizenship:

> Privacy is shorthand for breathing room to engage in the processes of boundary management that enable and constitute self-development. . . . In a world characterized by pervasive social shaping of subjectivity, privacy fosters (partial) self-determination. It enables individuals both to maintain relational ties and to develop critical perspectives on the world around them.[6]

Law around the world reflects those types of interests, and privacy, in some places, is literally considered a human right. Article 12 of the United Nations Declaration of Human Rights, for example, reads:

> No one shall be subjected to arbitrary interference with his privacy, family, home or correspondence, nor to attacks upon his honour and reputation. Everyone has the right to the protection of the law against such interference or attacks.

But privacy values, as strong as they may be in both an individual and a collective sense, are often necessarily in conflict with other important values that similarly benefit individuals and society: the right of access, the right to learn, the right to know, and the right of freedom of the press. That counterweight is recognized even in Article 12 itself: if no one should be subjected to an arbitrary privacy interference, some interferences must indeed be reasonable.

The struggle for courts that hear cases arising from claims of media intrusion and media revelation, then, is how to draw the proper line, how to strike an appropriate balance between respect for individual privacy and the importance of news coverage of important and everyday happenings.

For some courts today, it seems not too hard a struggle. In an age in which some suggest that the United States is the "wild west of privacy,"[7] their decisions are decidedly in line with two privacy-worried authors who wrote at the turn of the twentieth century.

Privacy Interests in 1890 and Now

In their important article, "The Right to Privacy," Warren and Brandeis had six main points: strong criticism of media, worries about technology, self-interest in defining privacy broadly, confidence in their ability to determine when individuals' privacy interests would trump news value, privacy's importance even for public officials and public figures, and privacy's importance in society generally.

What follows is language from "The Right to Privacy" and case examples that show how some of today's judges echo Warren and Brandeis's concerns and, at times, align current law quite precisely with 1890 ideals.

1. Skepticism bordering on anger at an out-of-control media. *"The press is overstepping in every direction the obvious bounds of propriety and of decency. Gossip is no longer the resource of the idle and of the vicious, but has become a trade, which is pursued with industry as well as effrontery. To satisfy a prurient taste the details of sexual relations are spread broadcast in the columns of the daily papers. To occupy the indolent, column upon column is filled with idle gossip, which can only be procured by intrusion upon the domestic circle."*

An example of the overstepping of bounds of propriety that so worried Warren and Brandeis in 1890 would today be Gawker's publication of a surreptitiously recorded sex tape. Overstepping of bounds would also be inherent in a majority of cases discussed in the preceding chapters, some of which state quite clearly, as did Warren and Brandeis, that media has gone too far.

The implications of courts' wariness and distrust of media are many; they are especially relevant for journalists who cover the courts and journalists who rely on open access to report fully on judicial and governmental matters. If courts do not trust the media to do the right thing with privacy-sensitive information, they can many times simply restrict access to it. That is this section's focus. Compare today's close-to-the-vest attitude among some courts with that of the Wyoming Supreme Court in 1983: it ordered certain police records released to media under the state's freedom-of-information law, recognizing media's failings but trusting media anyway. "The press may be arrogant, tyrannical, abusive and sensationalist," the court wrote, "[b]ut . . . the decision of what, when, and how to publish is for editors not judges or—we might add—the keepers of public records."[8]

Today, some judges more confidently keep certain information out of media and public hands, worried what might become of it. There is an on-point example of this from a 2013 decision of Massachusetts' highest court.[9] The underlying case involved child sexual abuse of a horrific nature; the child victim was two and, among other injuries, she had suffered burns to her genital area, presumably from a curling iron.

After the criminal trial and the accused's conviction, a documentary filmmaker requested both the written transcript and the audio from the trial. He explained that he wished to explore in a documentary the defendant's "continued assertion of innocence in light of the evidence presented at trial." His plan, presumably, was to use certain voices from courtroom testimony—voices described as containing "inflections, nuances, and pauses"—within the film as part of its audio track.

The Massachusetts justices uniformly rejected his plan. It was true, they noted, that public access to judicial records was necessarily broad to allow citizens to keep watch on government. Here, however, the balance between the documentarian's interest in courtroom sounds and the risk of the victims' emotional distress should those sounds be released strongly favored the latter. The child's family, the court wrote, would have their "peace of mind" disrupted if they learned that their actual voices would be heard on the documentary, even if they ultimately chose not to watch it. Such disruption and such emotional distress trumped whatever First Amendment rights would have otherwise given the journalist access. The transcript of the trial would have to do.

For a documentary filmmaker, one who relies on audio and video, a transcript is far less valuable than actual audio from the courtroom; audio would make the trial seem more real to the viewer. Even though producers could well have used courtroom audio in a way that had respected the victims and their privacy, the court decided not to take the risk.

That same respect for individual privacy and concern about media overstepping the bounds of decency also prevented reporters from receiving certain documents in a Washington State bankruptcy case. The papers would have revealed the debtor's "personal financial information, the location of his residence, and the names of third parties who ha[d] assisted him financially"[10] and, therefore, the court reasoned, would have given media a loophole to exploit the downtrodden: "While the press has a right to report on public activities such as a trial," the court wrote, quoting a Missouri court that very clearly distrusted journalists, "'it has less of a right to exploit bankruptcy procedures as a means of delving into the private financial affairs of third parties.'" The Washington court held that a transcript of relevant testimony would have to do, but then suggested that a well-placed (and seemingly judicially-inspired) protective order might well close that to media too.

In the 2000s, then, strains of Warren and Brandeis's much-earlier rhetoric against the press echoed in court opinions that described news publications as "tabloid journalism [with a] celebrity obsession"[11] and "sensationalistic [and] profits-driven" where "'newsworthiness' is not necessarily synonymous with 'of public concern.'"[12] In 2012, the Vermont Supreme Court worried specifically about idle gossip: that the unwary who had embarrassing information on their computers—information that someone needed "medication for a disease," that "someone's child [was] being counseled . . . for a serious problem," that someone was conducting "steamy email correspondence with an old high school boyfriend," or that someone was "looking at dirty pictures"—would be outed by media within days if such information were released at trial.[13] Such a projection, very much in line with worries in "The Right to Privacy," completely discounts modern ethics provisions that would counsel journalists not to report any such tidbits, especially those involving a private person.

Those sentiments from judges, however, parallel the findings in a 2013 poll by the *National Journal* in which nearly 70 percent of respondents answered that they trust the media not very much or not at all to responsibly use information media gathers about them.[14] It is little wonder that media law scholar Clay Calvert advised in 2010 that news media today "must pick, choose and, most importantly, explain their battles wisely when they seek access to [] content" lest courts respond by denying access completely.[15]

Consider Newtown, Connecticut, site of the Sandy Hook Elementary School shooting that left twenty children dead. The Connecticut legislature overwhelmingly passed a law that would keep certain photographs and documents from the resulting police investigation sealed. The legislators, apparently additionally interested in more generalized ways to keep information from media, also created a task force to "consider and make recommendations regarding the balance between a victim's privacy under the Freedom of Information Act and the public's right to know."[16] In early 2014, that task force recommended that all crime scene information in Connecticut, including 911 tapes and photographs, be restricted from public access unless the requestor proved that no privacy invasion would occur.[17]

Such legal outcomes and such legislation seem bound to continue at a steady pace, especially if certain predictions hold true. Recall the suggestion that those who teach constitutional law in the United States currently "tend to view the media as the 'good guys'" but that the British tabloid journalism phone hacking case "changes everyone's view of who the good guys are."[18] Law professors in the United States, the prediction goes, will now reconsider their generally pro-media First Amendment teaching.

If that happens, the next generation of lawyers and judges could well be even more pro-privacy and even less inclined to protect the press and access to information.

2. Worries about the privacy implications of current technology. *"Recent inventions and business methods call attention to the next step which must be taken for the protection of the person, and for securing to the individual what Judge Cooley calls the right 'to be let alone.' Instantaneous photographs and newspaper enterprise have invaded the sacred precincts of private and domestic life; and numerous mechanical devices threaten to make good the prediction that 'what is whispered in the closet shall be proclaimed from the house-tops.'"*

If a traveler aboard a plane opened a *SkyMall* catalog in summer 2013, the traveler would have seen at least six potentially privacy-invading items available for purchase. One was a video-and-audio pen described as "the easiest, stealthiest way to capture true events." It was "sound and voice activated," the catalog promised, and an inset photograph showed a man and a woman whispering to each other, apparently unaware that something that looked like a regular writing pen was watching and listening.

Another surveillance option was a camcorder called "the world's smallest," one that, because it was the size of a pack of gum, could "record video without ever being detected." The description suggested that buyers might "[s]lip one . . . onto a shelf or conceal one behind a picture and see what [they] couldn't see before." A third product was touted as an "affordable way to monitor driving activity using GPS technology," and promised that the buyer would know the routes, speed, direction, time, and duration of stops of those vehicles he tracked.

Each product cost less than $200. Each was sold in a routine way, alongside slippers and reading lights, as if everyone flying would have reason to own a video pen or gum-sized recorder or tracking device.

Meantime, at the dawn of 2014, *Wired* magazine predicted that "wearable tech" such as Google Glass, glasses that have the power to take photographs and video of everything the wearer sees with a subtle swipe of the temple, would soon "be as big as the smartphone."[19] As Slate warned in late 2012, we all must "Prepare for the New Cameras-Everywhere World."[20]

Warren and Brandeis—who worried about the privacy implications of suddenly portable cameras—would be horrified.

"When the First Amendment became part of the Constitution more than two hundred years ago," a federal judge in Pennsylvania wrote in 1996 in language that now seems almost quaint in light of today's technology, "its drafters could not have imagined . . . the sophisticated tools available to T.V. journalists [such as] cameras with powerful zoom lenses, video camcorders that simultaneously record pictures and sound, directional microphones with the capacity to pick up sound sixty yards away, and miniature cameras and recording devices easily hidden in a pocket or behind a tie."[21] The court in that case granted the healthcare executive plaintiffs a preliminary injunction that kept tabloid television reporters away despite the producers' argument that the executives' high salaries and way of life was newsworthy. The judge ordered the program to stop "engaging in conduct . . . which invade[d] the privacy" of the executives and their families.

Today, that technology—and much more—is in many hands. The 2012 Slate article that warned of cameras everywhere explicitly linked the technology explosion to an ethically conflicted and broadly defined media and suggested that "[n]ew technology means we'll only see more images like the *New York Post* subway-death photo," the one that featured the man clinging to the side of the tracks seconds before dying. The author worried about "big brother"—in government surveillance cameras and drones—but also "little brother"—the everyday people with cell phone cameras or wearing Google Glass who could well post whatever they see to the Internet to share with the world.

As for big brother, the *Washington Post* has noted, some technology in which government would be interested is relatively inexpensive, making it possible for government entities to spy in ways that would have seemed highly futuristic just ten years before. Cameras that read license plates, for example, are "cheap [and] powerful," the *Post* explained and suggested that the technology was in use by many police departments not only for parking ticket scofflaws but also in criminal investigations: such cameras take images that end up in databases stamped with date, time, and location, so that police can later return to the scene of the crime digitally and pinpoint those people who may have been present using license plate numbers.[22] A later article revealed that the government planned to begin a three-year test of blimp-like "military-grade tracking technology [aerostat aircraft] floating above suburban Baltimore" in late 2014 with the ability to monitor trains, boats, and cars—and detect cruise missiles or enemy aircraft. The same article suggested that, while high-altitude surveillance capable of spotting people was available, the government had promised that it would not be present on the aerostats during the test period.[23]

There are significant privacy implications in those sorts of cameras and that sort of surveillance, of course, especially relevant as courts move toward accepting the argument that one should be able to maintain some level of privacy while in public. Even eye-level cameras that record cars speeding or driving through red lights have been banned on privacy grounds by at least one court, and similar claims are pending in others.[24] The Ohio Supreme Court refused to intervene when a judge literally ordered that similar cameras be taken down.[25]

Regarding little brother's potential for privacy invasions, and recalling the technology for sale in the *SkyMall* catalog, smaller private cameras, such as those within cell phones, have led to new restrictions in locker rooms, gyms, corporate boardrooms, and, of course, courtrooms. "I think we're seeing an overreaction," one technology expert told the *San Francisco Chronicle* rather myopically. "People generally know what is right and what is wrong."[26] But a reported increase in "upskirting," the act of surreptitiously taking photographs of women's underwear or more using a small camera or cell phone quickly placed under a woman's skirt,[27] conflicts with that assessment. And the technology website CNET.org reported in 2011 that "half of all Americans [are] prepared to use their smartphones to shoot videos of people in embarrassing, compromising, or just plain weird situations."[28] It called such people members of the "Cell Phone Video Spy Club."

Other technology-related privacy concerns involve cell phones more generally. The New Jersey Supreme Court found a constitutional privacy right in the devices because they "trace our daily movements and disclose not only where individuals are located at a point in time but also which shops, doctors, religious services, and political events they go to, and with whom they choose to associate."[29] By the time the court decided that case, one could easily track another by cell phone, in real time through GPS and historically: some phones retained every location its user had visited and stored the data on the phone itself, making it easily available to others.[30] Those interested in such historical information included the Michigan State Police who, at times, used a mobile forensics device during traffic stops that easily bypassed passwords and in less than two minutes could extract all cell phone material from motorists who had agreed themselves or by warrant to a cell phone search.[31]

Based upon that example and others, a huge privacy concern today arises from the power of the Internet and how we use it. Not only can internet searches on a cell phone or otherwise reveal much about us, through the Internet, we can both uncover and reveal much about others in an instant. Consider as one memorable example the Duke University student who in 2010 created a mock presentation that critiqued the sexual prowess of several athletes on campus. She had sent it to only three friends as an inside joke, but within days, her mock presentation, in all its graphic glory, had made its way to email inboxes and multiple gossip websites across the nation much to her distress and the distress of those she had critiqued.[32] Similarly, in 2013, an otherwise unknown public relations executive tweeted in advance of a plane flight to South Africa a racially insensitive message to her fewer than 500 followers. Within hours, she had become so internationally infamous through social media that, as she stepped into the airport lobby in South Africa, citizen paparazzi were there to capture her picture. Her original message, sent just hours before, became known as "the tweet heard round the world."[33]

Courts that recognize the danger of that sort of nearly instant worldwide revelation have ruled, for example, that a deposition be kept secreted, worried that the defendant might otherwise publish it easily to all. "It is," the court reasoned, "impossible to control the editing of such material by others once it has been posted."[34] Sounding very much like a proponent for the right to be forgotten, another court was concerned about the longevity of similarly posted information, suggesting that computers had "long memories" and that retention of such information could lead to significant embarrassment in future years.[35] When a different court rejected a county's internet-based "Wall of Shame" that included those arrested for impaired driving offenses, it too pointed to what it called the Internet's "endless implications": "The Internet has no sunset," it wrote, "and postings on it will last and be available until some person purges the Web site, perhaps in decades to come."[36] Even though the information was of public record, the court held that the county could not reveal the identities of those arrested in such a fashion, lest "search engines, credit agencies, landlords and potential employers" have access to it "for a lifetime, regardless of the underlying outcome of the case."

Those technology-based privacy worries have led to changes in the law, such as the push-back against mug shot releases and the acceptance of the false light tort in jurisdictions that had previously rejected it, but they have also led to the solidifying of older pro-plaintiff doctrines that protect against harmful disclosures.

In a 2013 case from Iowa,[37] for example, the defendants had argued that the court reject the libel-per-se legal doctrine as outdated; libel per se automatically awards damages in defamation cases when the information wrongly published is particularly heinous and very obviously reputation-harming. The defendant author in the Iowa case had argued that libel per se was no longer needed because the Internet allowed anyone to publish anything in response to defamatory information, thereby readily and easily counteracting defamation's sting. The Iowa Supreme Court, however, embraced the doctrine for the very reason that the defendant had argued it was no longer necessary. The justices wrote that they did not believe that "the internet's ability to restore reputations matche[d] its ability to destroy them" and quoted with approval the New Jersey Supreme Court that had similarly re-embraced the legal principle:

In today's world, one's good name can too easily be harmed through publication of false and defaming statements on the Internet. . . . [P]rivate persons face the real risk of harm through the modern ease of defamatory publications now possible through use of the Internet. Presumed damages vindicate the peace-of-mind interest in one's reputation that may be impaired through the misuse of the Internet.[38]

The Iowa court also worried about those internet posters who, because they are able to remain anonymous or lack the backing of a news organization, have no incentive to self-police or to pause to consider the truth of their posts; these are among the persons considered quasi-journalists in this book. "[C]ompared to a generation ago," the court wrote, "nonmedia defendants may have a greater capacity for harm without corresponding reasons to be accurate in what they are saying." "[L]ibel per se," the court wrote in language that echoed what Warren and Brandeis had written years earlier regarding privacy in a technologically advancing society, "plays a useful role in helping to keep our social interactions from becoming ever more coarse and personally destructive."

Additional technology-related, privacy-based legal efforts to keep coarse and personally destructive information off the Internet include legislation and lawsuits that target so-called revenge porn, photographs of a naked person uploaded to the Internet by a former lover. As discussed more fully in Chapter 7, California made it illegal to an extent in 2013,[39] as did New Jersey.[40] Other states promise similar action. Meantime, a number of women have filed lawsuits against revenge porn websites and the internet service providers that host such websites.[41] And, in response to the revelation that the National Security Administration had been snooping into phone calls and other data, a number of groups, already anxious about the expansion of government surveillance after the terrorist attacks on September 11, 2001, filed claims against the NSA on privacy grounds.[42]

Additional lawsuits are sure to follow as courts and lawmakers struggle with consumer issues such as internet tracking and the technology that enables it. A writer for CNN, in an article headlined "The Internet is a surveillance state," listed Google and Facebook among those entities that track users' online habits. "One reporter," the article suggested, "used a tool called Collusion to track who was tracking him; 105 companies tracked his internet use during one 36-hour period."[43]

One of the more troubling tracking methods is known as "scraping," a method in which companies hire so-called "scrapers" to search the Internet for a poster's real name and contact information. Such identifiers are of great value: anonymous posters who reveal online that they have a particular disease or condition can be identified and information about relevant prescription drugs or treatment methods can be advertised to them in a highly targeted fashion.[44] An article on scraping published in the *Wall Street Journal* featured a man whose identity had been scraped after he had posted on a patient-supportive website that he suffered from depression. The *Journal* also reported that the support website itself had sold anonymous information about him to drug companies. Attorneys have suggested that such a practice has significant legal implications, especially privacy-based ones.[45] In 2013, privacy experts suggested that names of rape victims and AIDS patients were also being sold by data brokers.[46]

While there have been some attempts at data-mining legislation generally, including the Federal Agency Data Mining Security Act,[47] many legislators who rely on campaign contributions likely have mixed feelings regarding such practices. The Associated Press reported during the presidential election of 2012 that the Mitt Romney camp had used "a secretive data-mining project . . . to trove through Americans' personal information—including their purchasing history and church attendance—to identify new and likely wealthy donors."[48] Multiple companies exist from which entities such as political parties, charities, and universities can buy similar information, including a company's projections about a subject's personal wealth.

When California's Supreme Court ruled that retailers could not request zip codes from shoppers because of privacy worries,[49] the new restriction seemed but a drop removed, not from a bucket, but from an overwhelming sea of information that is available today through technological advances.

We are far from the world that document leaker Edward Snowden warned of in 2013, one he suggested would feature a system of worldwide mass surveillance, watching everything we do, with children who will "never know what it means to have a private moment to themselves—an unrecorded, unanalyzed thought," but it is clear why many received the message with little humor.[50]

Meantime, on the journalism side, the Nieman Journalism Lab asked various experts to predict important new issues that would confront journalists in 2014. Showing a myopathy similar to that of the technology-confident expert referenced earlier, a journalism professor predicted both that 2014 would bring the "Drone Age of Journalism" and that a paparazzo's drone, a small pilotless aircraft operated from the ground, would soon crash into a celebrity.

This accident, he warned, would lead to "terrible, reactive, and free-press-hostile laws." Nonetheless, he ended his piece with the, for him, hopeful prediction that responsible journalists would "lead the way on the integration of drones into [Americans'] lives" and the suggestion that he was "optimistic for the widespread use of drones in society."[51]

Just a few months later, the FAA banned drones at the University of Missouri after a journalism class there started using the low-flying aircraft to gather news.[52]

At about the same time, *Popular Mechanics* magazine featured on its cover the word privacy in large but eroding block letters. It noted that privacy was disappearing in American society, but suggested that new computer-based technology could help those interested in protecting themselves.[53]

"Privacy," the very first sentence in the *Popular Mechanics* article predicted as if in response to the looming Drone Age of Journalism, "is about to come roaring back."

3. Recognition that those defining privacy in a legal sense could well be victims of privacy invasions themselves. *"For years there has been a feeling that the law must afford some remedy for the unauthorized circulation of portraits of private persons; and the evil of invasion of privacy by the newspapers, long keenly felt has but been recently discussed . . ."*

It was likely Samuel Warren who was the driving force behind "The Right to Privacy." The Boston lawyer had married into a politically powerful family, one that regularly made headlines. Mrs. Warren's father, a former U.S. senator from Delaware and secretary of state under President Grover Cleveland, was a figure of both political and societal interest and his daughter's wedding to Warren had received significant coverage in both the *New York Times* and the *Washington Post*. Many believe that press coverage of Warren's family is what sparked Warren's call for privacy; if so, the "feeling" of "the evil invasion of privacy" by newspapers that the authors described could well have been the feeling Warren sensed from family members and well-connected friends.

Today, it is clear that some judges, like Warren presumably, are conscious that the words they write and the decisions they make regarding privacy could well affect their own lives. This is reflected in the *Blagojevich* decision from Illinois regarding juror privacy in Chapter 1.

It was in Illinois, too, that a parking ticket complaint gave a federal appeals court a self-interested privacy-based opening: the court interpreted a federal law in a way that could well prevent the release of some public officials' personal information. The case arose under the Driver's Privacy Protection Act,[54] a federal law that makes illegal a state's disclosure of certain information contained in driving records and gives those whose information was wrongly revealed a private right of action against the revealing entity.

The facts were as mundane as the legal response was surprising. In 2010, a man parked his car overnight in Palatine, Illinois, apparently in violation of a parking restriction. When he returned to the vehicle five hours later, he found a parking ticket on his windshield. The ticket contained his name and address, his driver's license number, his date of birth, his gender, and his height and weight, all information from his state driver's license; it also included information regarding his vehicle. The man, irritated that the information had been "made public" on a ticket placed under his wiper blade, sued Palatine for invasion of privacy; he based his claim on the federal Driver's Privacy Protection Act.

It would have been easy for the federal appeals court to dispense with the claim rather quickly. The judges could have ruled in a short opinion that the city may have revealed private information in violation of the Act, thereby sending the case back for trial. Or the court could have dismissed the claim as one that the law did not contemplate. As the dissent in the case noted, Congress passed the driver's privacy law in response to the murder of an actress after the California Department of Motor Vehicles had given the actress's stalker her home address. "Only with difficulty," the dissenting judge wrote in the Illinois case, "can one imagine a stalker who, noticing a woman he'd like to stalk get into her car and drive off, follows her and when she parks lurks behind her car in the hope [that] it will be ticketed and that if that happens [that] he'll be able without being observed to peek at the ticket and discover the owner's name and address." When the case was heard at the appellate level originally, the court had accepted that interpretation of the law and had ruled that it did not apply to parking tickets left on windshields by police.

After a full court hearing before an en banc panel, however, the federal judges decided that the privacy law did, in fact, cover tickets left on windshields. The judges' focus was on the possibility of a stalker: "an individual seeking to stalk or rape can go down a street where overnight parking is banned and collect the home address and personal information of women whose vehicles have been tagged," the judges wrote, worried that the stalker would then be able to ascertain "sex, age, height, and weight pertinent to his nefarious intent."

But their concern was also based on what potential impact such information-rich parking tickets could have on those who, like the judges themselves, serve the public but desire privacy. "[A] public official," the judges wrote, "having gone to great lengths to protect himself and his family from the threat of violence that unfortunately every public official faces, bears the risk that an expired parking meter violation might provide an opportunity for an individual intent on causing the official or his family bodily harm or death." Several years before, a federal judge's husband and mother had been murdered in Chicago by what was believed to be a disgruntled litigant, and even though the judges did not mention the crime in their opinion, it reads as though it was at the forefront of their minds.

The police officer who filled out the parking ticket that evening in Palatine likely did not contemplate that federal judges would one day decide that his actions had the potential to place them and others like them in great danger. After all, he too would be a public servant likely desiring of his privacy. The case, however, shows well how privacy worries of judges can play a significant role in privacy-related decisions and lead to greater privacy-based restrictions on behavior.

There are even more precise, albeit unusual and individualistic, examples. Judges have figured as direct litigants in some recent privacy lawsuits and the opinions are often favorable to them. Tennessee, for example, recognized a false light claim in a case in which a judge sued a television station that had used his quick on-camera dismissal of a reporter to suggest that the judge was "uncooperative or evasive" more generally;[55] the same state first recognized the false light tort in 2001 in a case in which a television station had reported that a probation services employee had a "cozy" relationship with a judge.[56]

Relatedly, in 2011, the Supreme Court of Washington decided that media should not be allowed to attend the in-court deposition of a key witness in a case involving a judge who had been accused of soliciting a prostitute. The dissent had argued that justice needed to be administered openly and that the in-court testimony was key because many believed that the witness would later not show up for trial.[57] And an Illinois appeals court found potential privacy-based intrusion and false light claims after an investigative news reporter followed judges home and then suggested that one judge was not in his office when he should have been.[58] "Judges work in their private chambers as well as their courtrooms, and many judges serve on committees in their official capacities or are otherwise involved in the legal community," the judges wrote in somewhat defensive language intended to teach media and others about their work habits. "A judge's official duties do not require a constant presence in the courtroom itself at all times, or even in the courthouse."

The same sensibility and sensitivity about judicial privacy can be seen at the U.S. Supreme Court, a court famous for its close attention to privacy and the secrecy of its own internal works process—and the court that one day will make the ultimate decision on where to draw the line between protected privacy and newsworthy information. At the nation's highest court, distrust of media unites with worries about technological innovations and concerns for the Justices' own privacy, leading Justices to refuse to allow cameras in the most important courtroom in the United States. This anti-media, pro-privacy feeling was surely bolstered in 2014 when an activist group released secretly recorded video of its leader interrupting the Justices during oral argument.[59] One writer on a politics-oriented website later suggested that evolving technology could well make such intrusions ubiquitous: "Just imagine what can be done now with Google Glass," she wrote.[60]

In 2013, Justice Sotomayor, a once camera-supportive Justice, told an audience of writers in New York that she had both changed her understanding of freedom of expression and, echoing the introduction to her autobiography, that she had become less free since joining the Court. She suggested that she had started "voluntarily and scrupulously censoring" herself after she joined the bench and, in large part, she blamed the press. She criticized members of the media for the "sport" and "facile drama" inherent in their Court-related predictions regarding the outcome of cases and their misplaced attempts to read "newsworthy drama into every oral argument." She explained that such media missteps had led her to question her once pro-camera stance: such media behavior, she told the audience, "leads even those of us who value transparency over tradition to think carefully about welcoming cameras into the courtroom."

Justice Sotomayor specifically mentioned the Justices' need for privacy a number of times during her New York speech, once in conjunction with concerns about technological innovations, reminding the audience of her opinion in *United States v. Jones,* a GPS tracking case, in which she worried about the effects government surveillance would have on First Amendment freedoms.

She had learned the hard way, she suggested, that media would take one sound bite, isolate it, and play it repeatedly, so that it would never and could never fade away.

The Justice also distinguished between privacy and secrecy and used as an example an "intimate" conversation she had had with an actress in front of eight hundred people. "The press," she explained, "was not invited" so that the two women could "establish certain parameters of tone and context" there. She had been especially concerned about the "televised press," she explained, criticizing broadcast media especially as changing the "dynamic" of an event. In using this example as one that highlighted the difference between privacy and secrecy, she seemed to suggest that the event itself may not have been secret but that, given her parameters and the apparent lack of media, had been or should have been a private one. It is very likely, of course, that many of the eight hundred gathered for the occasion held smart phones that could record at a moment's notice and upload in an instant.

Even though Justice Sotomayor had professed support for cameras at the Supreme Court in 2009, as had Justice Elena Kagan in earlier years, by 2013, both had apparently changed their minds.[61] And the tone of Justice Sotomayor's speech suggested that she had real concerns about news media outside the courtroom as well.

Ironically, Justice Sotomayor had given her talk as part of a writers' group's "Freedom to Write" lecture series, one advertised as devoted to freedom of expression and First Amendment rights to "protect those who risk their lives . . . to defend free speech."[62]

4. Elites know better than the masses what is appropriate news and what is best for society. *"Each crop of unseemly gossip, thus harvested, becomes the seed of more, and, in direct proportion to its circulation, results in the lowering of social standards and of morality. . . . It belittles by inverting the relative importance of things, thus dwarfing the thoughts and aspirations of a people. When personal gossip attains the dignity of print, and crowds the space available for matters of real interest to the community, what wonder that the ignorant and thoughtless mistake its relative importance. Easy of comprehension, appealing to that weak side of human nature which is never wholly cast down by the misfortunes and frailties of our neighbors, no one can be surprised that it usurps the place of interest in brains capable of other things. Triviality destroys at once robustness of thought and delicacy of feeling. No enthusiasm can flourish, no generous impulse can survive under its blighting influence."*

When Warren and Brandeis, two Boston attorneys who had met at Harvard Law School, wrote about social standards and how the nation's weaker, less smart, and confused population had been misled by newspapers into believing that gossipy and sensational news was important, the implication was that the masses needed to be led to more appropriate reading by elites who knew better. The masses, it seemed to Warren and Brandeis, had no idea what was good for them, and the law could make the nation better by limiting what the many, because of their ignorance and thoughtlessness, felt was appropriate news. Put another way, the elite valued privacy more than gossipy sensationalism and without intervention by the elite, the masses would be led astray to society's overall downfall.

The most profound examples of a similar sensibility today come in cases involving crime or crime-related matters, of particular relevance here because crime has had at least some news value in the United States since at least the early 1800s, sparked in part by one early newspaper's overwhelming success with a column that focused solely on crime.[63] Despite great public interest in crime stories that continues through today, however, some judges, as seen in the *To Catch a Predator* case, have moved to protect the privacy of the accused or the convicted, deciding that those interests trump readers' interest in their misdeeds.

It is remarkable, for example, that a federal appeals court in 2013 sealed from public view certain criminal sentencing documents in a business fraud case—and used as precedent a decision handed down in 1893, just three years after Warren and Brandeis wrote "The Right to Privacy."[64] The contemporary appeals court suggested that the trial court could editorially use redaction to separate information it found "necessary" to public understanding of the sentencing decision and suggested that its own superior privacy sensibilities had led it to trump what it presumed would be media's nefarious intentions: "Courts have long declined to allow public access simply to cater to a morbid craving for that which is sensational and impure," it wrote, quoting the 120-year-old case as if it perfectly described journalism and the reading masses in the United States today.

The same sensibility, in which judges strongly support personal privacy over news value, can be seen in other crime-related cases, including one in which the federal appellate court for Florida decided that a reporter could not have the mug shot of a man who had pleaded guilty to securities fraud.[65] The court reasoned that such a photograph could be withheld even if the person were in prison serving time for the crime, because "it captures a moment that is not normally exposed to the public eye." Moreover, the court referenced the earlier Louisiana mug shot case and wrote with an editor's confidence that there was very little in a mug shot in which the public should be interested. The only value on the other side, the court reasoned, was "perhaps the negligible value of satisfying voyeuristic curiosities."

Even when media is not directly involved, the privacy-inspired rectitude and superior news sense of today's courts is clear, both in cases where the public would likely agree and in cases where it likely would not.

As a 2012 example of the former, a federal appeals court in California decided that the mother of a two-year-old child who had been murdered more than twenty years before had "a common law right to non-interference with [her] remembrance of a decedent."[66] The case had become newsworthy again because her ex-boyfriend's conviction had been overturned and the former prosecutor had sent the boy's autopsy photos to the press. The appellate court, quite obviously horrified for the mother, looked especially to the *Favish* case in deciding that family members had a privacy right in autopsy photos of their deceased relatives. First, the court reasoned, publication of death images affect survivors' privacy in that they often show how much the decedent suffered in his final minutes. There are "few things . . . more personal," the court wrote. Second, in perhaps a bit more of a reach, it pointed to the constitutional notion of family integrity and the interests parents have in caring for their children, including whether to have an autopsy upon that child's death.

Key here, the mother had testified that when she learned that autopsy photos had been sent to the press, she was horrified and worried that she would see the images published on the Internet. Such "intrusion into the grief of a mother over her dead son," the court wrote, "shocks the conscience." Such strong privacy language, paralleling that in *Favish*, could well have a significant effect on publication of crime-related death images in the future.

As an example of the latter, a case in which the public would likely want access to information that the court had nonetheless suppressed in the name of privacy, consider a decision from an Idaho state appeals court. The judges there decided that a man who wished to seal his criminal case file from public view had enough of a claim that his argument deserved a hearing.[67] Twenty years before, the man had pleaded guilty to battery with intent to commit rape but argued that his criminal file should now be sealed to prevent his economic harm. Some of his employer's clients, he explained, had refused to welcome him into their fold when background checks revealed the felony. The appellate court, sounding very much like one that could uphold a right to be forgotten in future years, reasoned that a lower court might well seal the man's criminal record and keep it from public view. It suggested that the would-be employee's interests in privacy could potentially trump the public interest in disclosure of his rape-related conviction.

In contrast with those types of cases, compare decisions from the more pro-media 1980s. An Ohio appellate court in 1980, for example, decided that a newspaper would not be liable for publishing how a seventeen-year-old girl had died in a presumed suicide. After the newspaper reported somewhat gruesome facts involving the girl's hanging death, her parents sued for invasion of privacy. The court, however, flatly rejected the parents' claim, finding that "the event was newsworthy and of possible public interest."[68] Unlike the court in the 2012 case involving a child's autopsy, it did no agonized weighing of competing family privacy values whatsoever. In a similar vein, as noted briefly earlier, a 1983 Louisiana Supreme Court case brushed off privacy claims by former criminals who had turned their lives around; it did not dwell on their privacy interests. The men had sued a newspaper that had published an old story of their arrests for burglary within its "Page From Our Past" series. The reporters may have been insensitive or careless, the court held, but there could be no liability based on privacy because the information was truthful, accurate, and nonmalicious.[69]

Today's sense that the judicial elite better understand news value and should act as a protector of the nation's privacy interests and its media consumption is perhaps best revealed collectively in a 2007 survey of the members of the Connecticut judiciary.[70] In response to the question whether there were instances in which news media should exercise discretion even when they had a legal right to publish, nearly every judge responded that, yes, the media should use restraint. The comments showed some exasperation with media's choices:

- "It is probably useless to suggest that the media exercise any restraint or good taste."
- "Of course—but that's not the mindset of the media."
- "Sure, but they won't if it's a hot topic since they fear their competitors might scoop them."
- "Yes—just because you can—doesn't mean you should."

- "Of course. Sir Edmund Hillary may have climbed Mt. Everest 'because it was there' but journalists don't have to print the latest gossip for the same reason, even if it is heard more than once. A measure of discretion would be welcome in this no-holds-barred age."

Some of the judges gave specific instances where they believed that media outlets had overstepped bounds: stories that involved juror identification, victim identity, child identity, sordid sex cases, personal safety, and "information that would affect the fairness of [a] trial."

One judge wrote simply that media missteps "[w]hen [the story] serves no public interest," quite nicely implying a superior judicial notion of that phrase just as had Warren and Brandeis.

5. All persons, even public officials and public figures, must be protected in some way. *"The design of the law must be to protect those persons with whose affairs the community has no legitimate concern, from being dragged into an undesirable and undesired publicity and to protect all persons, whatsoever their position or station, from having matters which they may properly prefer to keep private, made public against their will. . . . Some things all men alike are entitled to keep from popular curiosity, whether in public life or not . . ."*

Warren and Brandeis urged that even public officials (politicians and others who serve the public) and public figures (usually celebrities and others in the public eye) had the right to keep some things private, a notion perhaps rooted partly in their revulsion to the scandal-mongering surrounding President Cleveland's relationship with the much younger Mrs. Cleveland, his once-charge. Today, it is likely that we would regard such a relationship by a sitting president to be securely a legitimate matter of public interest, but there are cases suggesting a stiffening resolve to draw a line on reporting on public officials, as with the judges mentioned previously in this chapter and the Texas prosecutor caught up in a child-sex sting, and public figures, as with at least one court deciding the case involving Hulk Hogan and his unwitting sex tape.

Traditionally, public figures and public officials, described more officially as those who "voluntarily place[] themselves in the public eye by engaging in public activities or by assuming a prominent role in institutions,"[71] have had less privacy protection in the law. News media could more deeply intrude into their private affairs because, often, their private matters are of public interest. "Revelations that may properly be made concerning a murderer or the President of the United States would not be privileged if they were to be made concerning one who is merely injured in an automobile accident," the Restatement reads, delineating between those who are voluntarily in the public eye, especially those who serve the public, and those who are not. To show the breadth of such appropriate revelations, Dean Prosser wrote in his 1960 law review article "Privacy" that there would be "very little in the way of information about the President of the United States that is not a matter of legitimate public concern."[72]

Compare, however, a 2013 case from the federal trial court for the District of Columbia, in which the judge wrote that should President Obama be found to have been born outside the country—a suspicion among some partisans that seems to refuse to die despite the publication of his birth certificate—the background check records showing as much would be protected from public disclosure for the president's personal privacy reasons.[73]

Compare, too, another 2013 case from New York in which a federal trial court refused to allow access to records of research requests made on behalf of George W. Bush and Dick Cheney at the National Archives.[74] The requestor had asked for information regarding those times in which Bush and Cheney designees had accessed records that, under the Presidential Records Act, were not yet available to the public, arguing that information regarding the presidential requests would help show what each regarded as key points in the Bush administration and how they wished to shape public perception of their time in office.

The court, however, flatly refused to release the records, deciding that such revelations would "constitute a clearly unwarranted invasion of personal privacy." It held that the former president and vice president had "obvious" and "great" privacy interests in their research designees and in their areas of research interest, presumably for memoirs and other written works. On the public interest side, the court wrote that the balance clearly favored the former leaders because "[t]he American public stands to gain little from knowing what the former officials are researching." It is true that the person seeking access to the material worked for Gawker (he called himself a political reporter) and it is possible that the court's worries about the website's ethics played a role in the decision. If so, the decision may reflect another instance of quasi-journalism undermining what could well be legitimate access by recklessly pushing boundaries elsewhere. But it may be simply that the court's sensitivity to the legitimate privacy interests of a former president and vice president would have led it to reject the same request from the *New York Times*.

There is proof of that increased sensitivity in other cases involving politicians. A state court in New York, for example, protected records of an ethics board investigation involving a former mayor of White Plains even though the requestor was mainstream media.[75] The court held back sworn interviews with the mayor and also documents that included financial records, canceled checks, and bills, finding that the public interest in the documents did not outweigh the mayor's privacy interests in them. It protected the mayor's sworn statements under a different privilege.

In Texas too, in a case involving a conversation between a Houston city official and a police sergeant that took place in an open courtyard within earshot and the secret recording equipment of a reporter, the court found that the city officials had a valid privacy claim.[76] The reporter had been assigned to investigate the city official's work habits and had argued that the men had no privacy in their conversation because they were in a public courtyard where others could hear their conversation. The court, however, sided with the city officials, looking to their intention not to be overheard and to their body language to find that the conversation could well be considered a private one even though it was seemingly in public:

> Viewed in the appropriate light, a factfinder could reasonably infer . . . that [the city officials] were speaking in a tone that could objectively be considered private, that they did not intend to be audible, and that might not actually have been fully audible, given (1) their location in the courtyard, (2) the manner in which they were standing there, (3) [that fact that one of them] look[ed] around periodically, (4) the din around them, and (5) the conversation's alleged, possible [private] content.

In upholding the officials' privacy claim against the news station, the court explained that it refused to find that conversations in public are necessarily not private.

Meanwhile, in a case against New York police officers brought by the mother of a murder victim who claimed that police had mishandled the investigation, a federal trial court judge protected the officers' privacy by deciding that an internal investigation into the murder and the police response could be kept from media.[77] In doing so, the court "sought to protect the named police officers' privacy more than ... the disciplinary process within the department," the plaintiff-mother had argued. The court, however, responded that public interest in an investigation does not mean that the press will have a right of access to everything within the trial.

And in Montana, the Supreme Court blocked newspaper access to an investigation into misuse of state-issued computers by public employees—including some said to hold high-level positions—who had accessed pornographic websites on their computers during working hours. The majority suggested that public disclosure was "clearly" not in the public interest but noted critically and somewhat incongruously that the revelation would make "interesting or sensational news copy." The dissenting justices argued that protection from embarrassment was insufficient grounds to protect those high-level employees whose salaries were paid by taxpayers, noting that the workers had been warned that their computer usage would be monitored.[78]

Perhaps today's most surprising example of legal protection for those in the public eye, however, involves Hollywood celebrities, those who make their living based in large part on public interest in their activities. In 2013, the California legislature added a criminal law that protected children from harassment based upon the work that their parents do, a law meant specifically to protect children of celebrities. The amendment included greater penalties and gave parents the right to sue for "actual damages, disgorgement of compensation, punitive damages, reasonable attorney's fees, and costs" presumably from invading paparazzi.[79] It also broadened the definition of "harassment" to include "conduct in the course of actual or attempted recording of children's images and/or voices ... by following their activities or lying in wait." The bill had been backed by high-profile actors, including Halle Berry, Sandra Bullock, and Jennifer Garner, whose children are often featured in celebrity magazines,[80] mostly innocuously (though a January 2014 tabloid featured five children of celebrities on the cover and used the word "crazy" to describe what it reported to be their extravagant lifestyles).[81] A reporter who covers celebrity issues expressed confusion over what would now be permissible under the law and concern that such surprisingly strong legal restrictions would soon spread to other states. Perhaps in response to the new law and the lobbying that led to it, some celebrity publications announced in 2014 that they would no longer publish photographs of celebrity children.[82]

Children and their celebrity parents were already protected in California by an earlier statute enacted in 1998 that makes certain paparazzi-like behavior unlawful when the celebrity is with family or doing something private:

> A person is liable for constructive invasion of privacy when the defendant attempts to capture, in a manner that is offensive to a reasonable person, any type of visual image, sound recording, or other physical impression of the plaintiff engaging in a personal or familial activity under circumstances in which the plaintiff had a reasonable expectation of privacy, through the use of a visual or auditory enhancing device, regardless of whether there is a physical trespass, if this image, sound recording, or other physical impression could not have been achieved without a trespass unless the visual or auditory enhancing device was used.[83]

The statute also enjoins the publication of any such photograph if the publisher knows that the photograph was taken in violation of the law.

More than hardened paparazzi are affected by such laws. A 2007 *New York Times* article noted that celebrity chasers now included anyone with a cell phone and suggested that the new amateur paparazzi had "intensified [the] already aggressive atmosphere" around celebrities.[84] A college student mentioned in the story had earned $780 for thirteen street photographs of actor Dustin Hoffman.

In Hawaii, a similar measure to protect celebrities stalled in the legislature in 2013. The bill was known as the "Steven Tyler Act," named after the Aerosmith band member who had purchased a home on Maui and who was said to have been photographed drumming on the beach in a revealing bathing suit.[85] If eventually passed, the law would impose liability against anyone who "captures or intends to capture, in a manner that is offensive to a reasonable person, through any means a visual image, sound recording, or other physical impression of another person while that person is engaging in a personal or familial activity with a reasonable expectation of privacy."

Meanwhile, as noted in Chapter 3, some courts hearing cases involving celebrities or would-be celebrities have erred on the side of privacy in its conflict with public interest. A California court initially ruled in 2013, for example, that an actress could bring a claim against the Internet Movie Database for posting her real age online; the actress had maintained that she was representing "[a]nyone who values their privacy" by bringing the lawsuit.[86] In a misappropriation action brought by former professional wrestler and former Minnesota governor Jesse Ventura, a court ruled that an approximately page-long passage within a Navy SEAL's autobiographical book that mentioned Ventura could well be the misappropriation of Ventura's name for its value.[87] Linda Tripp, a woman made famous through tangential involvement in the Bill Clinton-Monica Lewinsky scandal, convinced a federal trial court that she had a viable privacy-based claim when federal officials disclosed information from her government security clearance to reporters, including her answer to a question regarding previous arrests. She had answered no to that question, while the journalists alleged that she had been arrested for grand larceny many years before.[88]

And courts in First Amendment cases have upheld contracts signed by those employees or relatives who promise celebrities that they will not share private information with media.[89] A former employee with Harpo, Oprah Winfrey's company, had signed such a contract and later argued that the First Amendment made the contract void because the agreement was to last for the employee's lifetime and throughout the world.[90] The court disagreed:

> [W]e find unpersuasive plaintiff's argument that the confidentiality agreement is too broad because it remains effective for all time and with no geographical boundaries. Whether for better or for worse, interest in a celebrity figure and his or her attendant business and personal ventures somehow seems to continue endlessly, even long after death, and often, as in the present case, extends over an international domain.

Because the contract was one that the plaintiff had initially agreed to, the outcome itself had less serious First Amendment implications, but the court's sensibility regarding celebrity privacy protections was clear.

Compare those cases and that pro-celebrity legislation with a 1980 case that flatly rejected a privacy-related claim brought by actress Ann-Margret against *High Society* magazine, a publication that features nude photographs of women. Ann-Margret had appeared partially nude in a film and the magazine had published a still image taken from one of the reels. The court was far from star-struck: "[T]he fact that the plaintiff, a woman who has occupied the fantasies of many moviegoers over the years, chose to perform unclad in one of her films is a matter of great interest to many," the court held, explaining that it was "not for the courts to decide what matters are of interest to the general public."[91]

Today, in contrast, a book published by a well-respected university press suggests that Hollywood celebrities are due even greater privacy rights than they already have in the United States. "The natural impulse of today's celebrities to garner recognition for their hard work and contributions," Robin Barnes wrote in *Outrageous Invasions: Celebrities' Private Lives, Media, and the Law*, "is severely frustrated when the rewards of Hollywood appear commensurate with their level of willingness to reveal salacious tidbits about their private lives in television and magazine interviews." Barnes suggests that European law "get[s] it right" when it protects "human dignity, liberty of conscience, free expression, respect for private life, and personal data" over press rights and freedoms. The European law, one that naturally has no First Amendment concerns, is much more protective of celebrities. Barnes described the law this way:

> Constitutional recognition [in Europe] of privacy, autonomy, and freedom of choice in intimate associations protects the individual from unreasonable intrusion in secluded space, misappropriation of an individual's name or likeness, extensive publicity of elements of a person's private life, and publicity presenting the subject in a false light. . . . Legally mandated zones of privacy include boundaries for the safety of persons, their property, and their personal and family dignity . . .

"European courts," she further notes, "have taken judicial notice . . . that these guarantees may be even more essential for [public] figures of contemporary society."

Courts in the United States have not openly embraced such European laws because of freedom-of-the-press concerns; as will be explored in greater detail in Chapter 8, the zones of privacy suggested seem far too sweeping to be constitutional, given the way the First Amendment is interpreted today. Even so, a number of legal commenters have joined Barnes in suggesting that a move toward the European model would strengthen privacy for everyone,[92] despite in turn weakening First Amendment freedom of the press.

6. Modernity makes privacy even more essential. *"The intensity and complexity of life, attendant upon advancing civilization, have rendered necessary some retreat from the world, and man, under the refining influence of culture, has become more sensitive to publicity, so that solitude and privacy have become more essential to the individual. . . ."*

Warren and Brandeis argued that the circumstances of modern society were increasing the value of solitude and privacy, both for the individual and society.

They worried that the frenetic pace and growing connectedness of 1890's post-industrialized, urbanized society had made it increasingly essential to cordon off some realm where individuals could step away from the scrutiny of their neighbors and be let alone. The greater vulnerability to public exposure in modern society, then, made privacy all the more precious, requiring a call for new and clearer measures to draw the boundaries of public decorum.

However strongly Warren and Brandeis's alarm resonated when they wrote what they wrote at the dawn of the twentieth century, it had lost its sway for most of the century that followed, especially as the call concerned media. Even with the unrelenting pace of social and technological change that followed from the jazz age to the space age, most courts, especially later courts, seemed inclined to steer clear of policing the decorum of the press. The tone was set in rulings such as the Supreme Court's 1948 *Headquarters Detective* decision in which it spurned legal controls over a tawdry pulp magazine that it freely acknowledged seemed to revel without any redeeming social value in showcasing the tragic suffering of crime victims.

To courts of the Prosser era that followed—guided by the Berkeley law dean's pro-press sensibilities in the Restatement of Torts and in his scholarly writing—it seemed all the better to suffer the occasional excesses of bad media actors than to risk public controls that might temper a generally responsible press from zealously doing its job.

More recently, however, there seems to be a modern-age shift back toward 1890s sensibilities; courts are signaling a new sensitivity to threats to privacy posed by evolving social and cultural conditions. And, not unlike Warren and Brandeis, they are showing a willingness to expand privacy protection from its traditional confines of the home and other quintessentially private places into streets, cyberspace, and other spaces of public life.

In 2012, the U.S. Supreme Court, for example, decided a criminal case that in a way recognizes privacy in a public space. Justice Scalia, writing a plurality opinion in *United States v. Jones*,[93] the GPS case noted earlier, described the underlying issue this way: "We decide whether the attachment of a [GPS] tracking device to an individual's vehicle, and subsequent use of that device to monitor the vehicle's movements on public streets, constitutes a search or seizure within the meaning of the Fourth Amendment." The Justices ultimately concluded that, yes, it does constitute a search and seizure. Therefore, even if the plurality opinion did not address privacy directly, the reasoning behind it seems to suggest that there can be privacy in public.

In the case, police had installed the tracking device on a vehicle and had monitored the vehicle as it moved openly in full view of anyone around it. In finding that there was a Fourth Amendment violation, some Justices characterized the issue as one of trespass regarding the placement of the GPS device and brushed aside the argument that, because things happened in the open, the defendant had no reasonable expectation of privacy in his movements.

Justice Sotomayor, writing in concurrence, noted even more strongly that "GPS monitoring generates a precise, comprehensive record of a person's public movements that reflects a wealth of detail about her familial, political, professional, religious, and sexual associations." These and other considerations, the Justice argued, should be remembered when courts consider the expectation of privacy in an individual's movements in public:

> Awareness that the Government may be watching chills associational and expressive freedoms. And the Government's unrestrained power to assemble data that reveal private aspects of identity is susceptible to abuse. The net result is that GPS monitoring—by making available at a relatively low cost such a substantial quantum of intimate information about any person whom the Government, in its unfettered discretion, chooses to track—may "alter the relationship between citizen and government in a way that is inimical to democratic society."

A 2013 decision by the Court seems at least partially in line with that conclusion; the Justices held that drug-sniffing dogs could not be used outside a house without a warrant because of keen privacy interests that extended beyond the front door and onto the property itself.[94] There, too, Justice Sotomayor joined a concurring opinion written by Justice Kagan that suggested that the use of dogs would be similar to a person peering with binoculars, "learn[ing] details of your life you disclose to no one." Such behavior, the concurrence maintained, was a privacy invasion because the one peering had "nos[ed] into intimacies [the victim] sensibly thought protected from disclosure."

And also in 2013, outside the criminal realm, the Court decided a Freedom of Information Act case that makes FOIA requests more difficult, restricting access by media and others and protecting at least in part the privacy of those individuals mentioned in state documents.[95] The Virginia legislation, which allows public records access only to Virginia citizens, "provides a service that is related to state citizenship," the Court reasoned in upholding the law. Fifty-four media organizations had filed an amicus brief in the case that had argued that without full access "coverage of important national stories could be sty-mied by virtue of a discriminatory citizenship requirement in a state's public records law" and had offered multiple examples of stories that would have been affected had the law been in place at the time. The Justices, however, did not mention press access in their opinion at all, signaling that perhaps they found the argument of little importance and of little concern.

There are examples from lower courts as well of individual privacy deci-sions that seem an effort to better society by bolstering individualistic retreat-from-the-world privacy in, at times, surprising ways. In Nevada, a federal trial court suggested that the plaintiff who alleged that the defendant had stopped and stared menacingly at him while he was at home and at work several times a day over some months had a valid privacy claim.[96] A reasonable jury could find that the defendant had intentionally and offensively intruded into the plaintiff's seclusion, the court ruled, even though the facts suggest that the defendant was doing so from a public area without the use of special devices.

A federal appeals court sitting in Illinois ruled that medical records of women who had obtained abortions should not be accessible to the govern-ment even though the records had been redacted. "Even if there were no pos-sibility that a patient's identity might be learned from a redacted medical record," the court wrote, "there would be an invasion of privacy." The court likened the release of such records to that of nude photos taken of a woman's body and published on the Internet by an ex-boyfriend to be downloaded by those in another country to be viewed by those who did not know her. "She would still feel that her privacy had been invaded," the court explained, and "[t]he revelation of the intimate details contained in the record of a late-term abortion may inflict a similar wound."[97]

A Kansas state appellate court dealing with precisely that case—one involving nude photos—found just such an invasion through its own expan-sion of privacy.[98] In the case, a woman had brought a publication-of-private-facts claim against her ex-boyfriend who had allegedly left at a tavern a sex video featuring her and had also allegedly scattered her nude photos around her new boyfriend's car. The tavern owner was the only person to see the tape and the new boyfriend was the only one to see the scattered photographs and, traditionally, that sort of "publication" would fail to satisfy the tort's publicity requirement. But the Kansas court reinterpreted the state's privacy law to expand protection, reasoning that, had the tavern owner and the boyfriend not done the right thing by securing the images, publicity as it has been traditionally defined (to publish to approximately ten or more people) would have occurred. The tort's publicity element therefore was satisfied and the plaintiff had a valid claim even though only one person had seen the video and only one person had seen the photographs.

There are multiple examples of courts' attempts to protect privacy on the "public" Internet too, at times expanding the scope of privacy protection in a similar fashion and reaching out to protect paternalistically those who, seemingly, had not embraced privacy themselves. A federal trial court in New Jersey, for example, ruled that a Facebook post could well be private in a case in which the defendant faced liability for intrusion into seclusion for reading the post.[99] The plaintiff had argued that the comment posted to her Facebook wall had been made accessible only to those she had invited to be her Facebook friends. The defendant argued in response that the comment could not be private if it had already been shared with possibly hundreds of people. The court sided with the plaintiff: "Plaintiff may have had a reasonable expectation that her Facebook posting would remain private," the court wrote, "considering that she actively took steps to protect her Facebook page from public viewing."

A federal trial court in California was similarly protective and expanded the boundaries of privacy when it upheld a misappropriation-like action brought by everyday people who had been featured in Facebook's so-called "Sponsored Stories" advertisements; when Facebook users "liked" certain products or services online, their endorsements would appear on their friends' Facebook pages.[100] Likewise, a federal trial court in Pennsylvania found a valid misappropriation claim in a defendant's alleged use of its former employee's LinkedIn account.[101] Someone searching on the Internet for the plaintiff, the court reasoned, would instead find information about the defendants because the defendants had allegedly configured the LinkedIn page that way. And there was a similar outcome in a case brought by a former Air Force Academy cadet who argued that the use of his name and the story of his trouble at school was misappropriation; the defendant company had used a blurb about him as one of several "renowned cases" it had been assigned.[102]

Most of these cases help show courts' seeming recognition that privacy must be configured in new ways to better protect individuals, their right to be let alone, and their security in society. By recognizing privacy interests in the comings and goings of individuals on the public streets and in the musings they cast out into the porous world of Facebook and other social media, courts are embracing a new and more extensive conception of legal privacy rights. Just as Warren and Brandeis suggested, courts have found that today's complexity of life and the dangers of greater publicity have made solitude and privacy all the more essential, and they have expanded privacy accordingly.

Lasting Influence of "The Right to Privacy," Plus More

Today, in multiple ways, parts of Warren and Brandeis's vision for American society seem to be coming true. Concerns about technology and what an ethics-complacent media might do with it mixed with a general sense that individual privacy is being rendered both more vulnerable and more precious by the interaction-intensive conditions of modern society have led today's courts to echo implicitly or explicitly the reasoning and sensibilities of "The Right to Privacy." This is significant as it relates to media, of course, because more than 120 years have passed since the two authors published their law review article and because the U.S. Supreme Court in the intervening years embraced robust First Amendment protections even over gut-wrenching intrusions on the privacy of rape victims and others. Today, courts seem to be moving instead toward protecting not only those victims, but their families, and, at times, even their attackers—a decided shift toward a "Right to Privacy"-like privacy.

But it is also significant because it seems that not even Warren and Brandeis would have gone as far as some of today's courts. What is often overlooked about their article is its conclusion, in which the authors suggest that there would be and should be key limitations on the right to privacy as they imagined it, limitations that have special relevance to media:

- "The right to privacy does not prohibit any publication of matter which is of public or general interest," they wrote. It is important that the authors' focus was on public *interest* rather than public *need* because the public, as noted earlier, may be interested in a celebrity wedding, but it does not need to know about it. The 2014 SPJ code of ethics, in contrast, high-mindedly advises that only an overwhelming public *need* is reason to invade another's privacy. Warren and Brandeis's focus on public interest as the appropriate test for news value, therefore, appears broader than the SPJ privacy provision and some courts' recent focus on what the public needs to know.

- "The design of the law must be to protect those persons with whose affairs the community has no legitimate concern, from being dragged into an undesirable and undesired publicity and to the protect all persons whatsoever," they wrote, but then they qualified that rule by noting that only when those persons had "properly" preferred to keep the information private would the law find liability against someone who had revealed it. Here, too, they recognized that some news could be reported by media even though those at its focus would prefer that it not be.
- The authors differentiated between those people who had "renounced the right to live their lives screened from public observation" and those persons out of the public eye, suggesting, somewhat incongruously given their earlier sensibilities to protect public officials, that such persons could indeed be "the subject of legitimate interest to their fellow citizens" and that any notion of the "private life" of such public men should be defined in "its most limited sense."
- Warren and Brandeis also maintained that news coverage of a person's speech impediment or spelling problem would be perfectly appropriate regarding a "would-be congressman," warning that "no fixed formula can be used to prohibit obnoxious publications" and that any rule needed "an elasticity which [would] take account of the varying circumstances of each case."

Finally, the two authors suggested that "only the more flagrant breaches of decency and propriety" would be reached by their proposed privacy law and warned that it would not be desirable "to repress everything which the nicest taste and keenest sense of the respect due to private life would condemn."

Today, then, in an age in which courts have denounced stories of more generalized public interest, in which they have suggested that it might be proper to have one's public felony criminal record sealed because of employment difficulties stemming from its availability, in which legislatures have deemed "private" celebrities' actions that take place in public, and in which courts have raced to protect politicians, including those public officials accused of crimes, we could well be moving toward a time in which privacy is protected even more stridently than a significantly strident Samuel Warren, fed up with coverage of family and other matters, would have protected it.

In 2012, a Florida court paraphrased and credited "The Right to Privacy" when it wrote that "[t]he right to privacy is, essentially, 'the right to be let alone, the right to live in a community without being held up to public gaze if you don't want to be held up to public gaze.'"[103] Today, that language seems to describe the utopian privacy-protected society in which some judges and others seem to wish to move: one in which an individual can decide for himself or herself how much information is appropriately revealed by media. It does not recognize, however, the significant qualifications placed upon the right to be let alone proposed by the very men many consider to be the fathers of the right to privacy.

7

The First Amendment Bubble, Absolutism, and Hazardous Growth

At a time when a perfect storm seems to be brewing against journalism—including disruption of its business model by technological change and shifting market tastes, intensifying competition from a diverse range of digital rivals, and rising concerns in courtrooms and otherwise about threats to privacy—many in media appear not to fully comprehend the welling danger, trusting in the First Amendment to fend off the new demands for public accountability.

This self-confidence is based in part upon the broad terms of the First Amendment and the bulwark of protective constitutional doctrine built up by the U.S. Supreme Court during the twentieth century. In fact, the vaunted place of press freedoms in the American tradition predates the Constitution, as reflected in the celebrated trial of publisher John Peter Zenger in New York in 1735. Zenger's jury acquittal on seditious libel (he had repeatedly ridiculed New York's colonial governor in the *New York Weekly Journal*) is said to have helped establish truth as a defense to libel in the United States and, thus, the right of journalists to pursue the truth without fear of reprisal. Fifty years later, that notion informed the adoption of the First Amendment, which guaranteed press freedom in broad and unqualified terms: "Congress shall make no law respecting an establishment of religion, or prohibiting the free exercise thereof; or abridging the freedom of speech, or of the press."

The majestic sweep of First Amendment freedoms of speech and press has been rationalized by a multitude of sometimes overlapping theories—as enabling the realization of individual dignity through unimpeded self-expression, or of truth through the contest of ideas in an uninhibited "marketplace," or as empowering the people to rein in abuses of power through a free flow of information about the conduct of public life. By every account, however, both deontological and consequentialist, the scope of First Amendment freedoms was necessarily broad and fundamental to the constitutional design. Freedom of speech and the press, wrote "Cato," whose essays on political theory were widely published in pre-revolutionary America, "is the great Bulwark of Liberty; they prosper and die together."[1]

Though fundamental, press freedoms were never absolute, however. Even Cato's essay articulating the freedom to pursue and publish the truth—published by Zenger and often said to have laid "the intellectual foundation for Zenger's acquittal"—acknowledged that "[t]here are some truths not fit to be told" and that press freedoms would extend to revelations of wrongdoing in the public realm, but not to "private and personal Failings":

> A libel is not the less a libel for being true. This may seem a contradiction; but it is neither one in law, or in common sense: There are some truths not fit to be told; where, for example, the discovery of a small fault may do great mischief; or where the discovery of a great fault can do no good, there ought to be no discovery at all: And to make faults where there are none, is still worse.
>
> But this doctrine only holds true as to private and personal failings; and it is quite otherwise when the crimes of men come to affect the publick. Nothing ought to be so dear to us as our country, and nothing ought to come in competition with its interests. Every crime against the publick is a great crime, though there be some greater than others. Ignorance and folly may be pleaded in alleviation of private offences; but when they come to be publick offences, they lose all benefit of such a plea: We are then no longer to consider only to what causes they are owing, but what evils they may produce; and here we shall readily find, that folly has overturned states, and private ignorance been the parent of publick confusion.
>
> The exposing therefore of publick wickedness, as it is a duty which every man owes to truth and his country, can never be a libel in the nature of things . . .[2]

Moreover, First Amendment theorist Frederick Schauer has argued, the precise takeaway of the Zenger Trial was not that the press was unaccountable in its pursuit of the truth, but rather that it was accountable to the public acting through a jury, rather than to the government acting through a judge.[3]

Yet, in time, constitutional doctrine added by the courts has embellished and strengthened press freedoms significantly to ensure its ability to perform its essential democratic functions—safeguarding the press in publishing even certain falsehoods and largely immunizing the press's judgments concerning the "newsworthiness" of reported truthful information from easy second-guessing by juries or government officials.

Given the rising tide of press freedoms through much of American history, journalists today might be forgiven for appearing complacent in the face of mounting calls for public controls on media's freedom to publish truth. They may believe that they know better.

But things are different today: as shown throughout this book, not only is the law shifting to favor privacy, journalism itself is shifting away from it. The industry's pressures are enormous; news is being rocked internally by intense and growing market pressures which question the very viability of its business model. With advertisers and consumers alike finding ready alternatives to traditional print and broadcast media outlets, there is a scramble to transition to digital platforms, slash costs, and find new ways of packaging, delivering, and pricing news content in a world already saturated with information.

At the same time, with leaner operations and resources, media outlets find themselves desperate for revenue and competing fiercely with an explosion of new, unconventional rivals for the attention of consumers who have never had more options. Predictably, even understandably, these pressures have led to a broader commercialization of journalism—to a blending of news and entertainment programming, to a fuller surrender of editorial news judgment to market forces, and to the encroachment of moneymaking ventures into news operations. These efforts to firm up journalism's financial position have also eroded its privileged status as a public-interested profession above the fray of politics and commerce.

Yet, faced with declining public respect and mounting calls for accountability through legislation and lawsuits, many in journalism continue to put undue trust in the First Amendment. When television news reporters were called to task for allegedly asking teens to chew tobacco to generate video for a news story, for example, or for informing children on-camera that their next-door playmates had been slain to capture their reaction, each group argued that, even if the descriptions of their behavior were accurate, the First Amendment put their news judgment that such behavior was necessary beyond reproach. The same sensibility is echoed in Gawker's steadfast claim that First Amendment press freedoms protect its right to publish whatever truth it would like.

The reality, however, is that the Supreme Court has never suggested that the First Amendment erects an absolute barrier to second-guessing the media. Even when it construed speech or press rights broadly in past cases, the Court always allowed that First Amendment rights could be overborne by compelling public needs on exceptional facts. In *Florida Star*, for example, the case in which the Justices decided that it would be unconstitutional to punish a newspaper for reporting the name of a rape victim, the Court took care to insist that its decision went no further than the precise facts and suggested that different facts might well remove the protection of the First Amendment:

> Our holding today is limited. We do not hold that truthful publication is automatically constitutionally protected, or that there is no zone of personal privacy within which the State may protect the individual from intrusion by the press, or even that a State may never punish publication of the name of a victim of a sexual offense. We hold only that where a newspaper publishes truthful information which it has lawfully obtained, punishment may lawfully be imposed, if at all, only when narrowly tailored to a state interest of the highest order, and that no such interest is satisfactorily served by imposing liability under [the Florida statute] to appellant under the facts of this case.[4]

Today, the Constitution's protection for the disclosure of truthful information, therefore, is not absolute and categorical, but ultimately must be determined case by case according to the particular facts and the balance of public and private interests. Nonetheless, some members of the media hold fast to a more simplified takeaway from cases like *Florida Star* and *Cox Broadcasting* and *Bartnicki*—that the First Amendment protects reporters who report truthful information—and do not bother with the significant qualification repeatedly noted by the Court.

Journalists might be forgiven for glossing over the qualifying language and reading the holdings broadly because, until recently, the results of many decisions of the past half-century have tended to expand the scope of protection under the First Amendment, and sometimes in surprisingly generous ways. At the Supreme Court and otherwise, whether in the context of construing speech to include nude dancing, or in broadly construing the rights of the press to publish private information, decisions have tended to broaden protection for First Amendment expression.

Emboldened by this record, then, or at least seemingly confident regarding their important place in a democratic society, media defendants are pushing First Amendment claims into new territory—the posting of celebrity sex tapes, for example, or the treatment of a helpless accident victim within the confines of a medical helicopter.

In doing so, they have sometimes succeeded in extending boundaries. On one front, some have successfully pressed for an essentially boundless conception of "newsworthiness," insisting, like Gawker, upon a constitutional entitlement to publicize virtually any information that might be of passing interest to the consuming public, no matter how salacious. On another, some have insisted successfully on a nearly boundless conception of the "press," sweeping traditional news outlets together with bloggers, self-styled "citizen journalists" of every stripe, and most other publishers.

Consider, for example, the parallel reasoning of the federal district court and the state appeals court in the case involving Gawker's internet posting of the surreptitious sex tape. In refusing to block the tape, the two courts readily accepted both that Gawker was acting in a journalistic capacity (in pursuit of its "news reporting function") and that its privilege to publish newsworthy matter encompassed what the federal trial court suggested was "'all matters of the kind customarily regarded as 'news' and all matters giving information to the public for purposes of education, amusement or enlightenment, where the public may reasonably be expected to have a legitimate interest in what is published.'"[5] Those are extremely broad definitions for both journalist and for news.

In some ways, this dynamic again suggests a First Amendment bubble, not unlike those seen in other contexts, such as housing, the tech industry, and financial markets, where heedless expansion ultimately proved unsustainable. The scope of reporting and claims for constitutional protection both are continually expanded—encompassing a broader range of push-the-envelope publishers and reckless disclosures—until First Amendment freedoms so far exceed their original foundation that they are at risk of a calamitous collapse, jeopardizing all future protection.

"First Amendment rights of the press," the Rhode Island Supreme Court warned in 1996, "are as much endangered by its zealots as by its critics."[6] That is the gamble of a First Amendment-righteous media that continues to push at the boundaries of an ever-expanding First Amendment at a time when courts seem especially concerned about privacy protections. When the "press" is construed to include every person or entity with access to a web portal, and when "newsworthiness" is taken to encompass any nugget of informational or amusement value published to a rapacious worldwide readership, the rights of the press are effectively all-consuming, squeezing out any room to recognize legitimate interests in privacy. Such a state of law will prove unsustainable given the mounting concerns about the invasive harms caused by an increasingly diffuse and adventurous media.

This chapter looks critically at zealous calls for First Amendment protection. It considers first the expansion of First Amendment rights through a capacious conception of "newsworthy" information, to shield everything from the publication of a videotape of an alleged rape to a newspaper's sale of novelty items bearing a photograph of an accident victim. It next considers the expansion of constitutional press rights to shield not only traditional journalists but also a limitless range of unconventional upstarts, from citizen-journalist bloggers to operators of websites that trade in revenge porn and the abusive mockery of ordinary people surreptitiously caught on video. And it considers these developments against the backdrop of First Amendment jurisprudence that has already pushed the protection of speech rights to controversial and perhaps unsustainable lengths.

Here, at least some level of court intervention seems to have been appropriate because the privacy interests are markedly strong. These examples and their outcomes could well capture the overzealousness of which the Rhode Island justices warned.

The First Amendment and the Rape Tape

The story of the rape tape helps illustrate why the Rhode Island Supreme Court may be right that the First Amendment is as endangered by its zealots as by its detractors.

The story begins in Oklahoma City, a municipality incorporated in 1890, the year "The Right to Privacy" was written. There, in 2003, an accused rapist left behind proof of his alleged crime: a videotape of him allegedly sexually assaulting his estranged wife. The woman, who was incapacitated and unconscious during the alleged attack, found the tape several weeks later and turned it over to police. She recognized the investigative value in the recording, not only for her own case, but also in two more rapes currently under investigation. Police apparently assured her that the videotape would remain private aside from police and courtroom use, and she agreed to press charges.

But police did not keep that promise. Instead, they showed the videotape to a camera crew from a local television station and, with what a court suggested was "a wink and a nod," allowed the reporter and her photographer to copy it for their own use later at the television station. The officer did so, the court would later explain, because he wanted to appear on television; the television news reporter's goal, in turn, was to receive a copy of the videotape, perhaps in a bid for ratings attention. That night, the reporter included various segments of the videotape throughout her television news story about the alleged rapes.[7]

The reporter did not reveal the woman's name or any other identifying information, but the victim argued that the reporter did not need to because the woman's privacy had been shredded just as effectively. The video segments that the reporter chose to include in her story were "shots of [the alleged victim's] feet and calves" and images that "depicted [the alleged rapist] moving above and around [the alleged victim's] obscured body." They also included portions of the videotape showing the alleged attacker's face. Anyone who knew her husband and knew about the criminal charge, the alleged victim argued, would have known that it was her body allegedly being raped onscreen.

The woman brought two main privacy claims against the television station: intrusion into seclusion and publication of private facts. She faced unreceptive judges, however, and a television station that eventually hired perhaps the nation's best First Amendment law firm. Despite shocking facts involving an alleged victim who, it seemed, had been re-victimized, and despite her status as a seemingly highly sympathetic plaintiff who had been wronged in a profound way—recall that a federal appeals court held that even redacted impersonal medical records would be a privacy invasion and that the Supreme Court suggested that publication of a victim's identity could well be the basis for a successful privacy lawsuit at some point—the courts that heard her case found that she had no valid privacy claim whatsoever against the television station.

First, the court rejected her intrusion claim in an early motion to dismiss: the fact that the tape's release by police may have been improper "does not make it improper for the media defendants to seek or acquire the information from police," the court wrote. The opinion discounted the strong argument that she was, in fact, secluded in her home when the alleged rape occurred and that the media had intruded into that seclusion by sharing the alleged sexual attack with viewers of the nightly news. The appellate court would later uphold that decision with a similar matter-of-fact analysis.

But her seemingly stronger publication-of-private-facts claim ultimately fared no better. The trial court had initially allowed the claim to continue, but called it a close question because of strong First Amendment protection for media. "A video depiction of a violent, sexual act, committed in a non-public setting," the court reasoned in surprisingly vivid yet stubborn language, "might *conceivably* constitute [the] extreme case" in which the victim's privacy would trump First Amendment protection, but certainly not necessarily.[8]

After hearing the television station's motion for summary judgment at a later date, the court decided that the airing of a tape of an alleged rape did not constitute the extreme case after all and ruled that the news value in the videotape trumped any concerns for the plaintiff-victim's privacy.[9] The court wrote that it recognized that the videotape was "intensely private and personal" but it also found it to be decidedly newsworthy. "Part of the story's newsworthiness," the court reasoned, "involved the fact that the alleged rapist had videotaped the incident." By showing the videotape during the course of the television news program, the court reasoned, the journalists had proved its existence to viewers. By showing the alleged attack and the alleged attacker, the court held, the journalists had "strengthened the impact and credibility of the story" and, ultimately, had connected it up with a "matter of legitimate public concern": the alleged rapes of three women.

As for the television station's news judgment in airing such a videotape, the court noted that while it would have made a different call had it been the news editor that evening, it refused to stand in judgment of those who did. In fact, it wrote that it *could not* stand in judgment: "[T]he court . . . may not appropriately engage in after-the-fact judicial 'blue penciling,'" the judge wrote, "which might have a chilling effect on the freedom of the press to determine what is a matter of legitimate public concern." Even though the Supreme Court had suggested in *Florida Star* that that sort of blue penciling could be appropriate when courts found that privacy rights trumped press rights, and even though the Restatement and multiple courts had decided the same in arguably far less invasive cases, the court suggested that its hands were tied, almost as if it were deciding a case involving the revelation of an individual's case of the common cold.

The trial court was not alone in its refusal to recognize the plaintiff's privacy claims, however. The federal appellate court hearing the case on appeal similarly rejected the victim's publication-of-private-facts claim, also crediting the station for proving to viewers that the tape existed.[10] "By airing the videotape," the court wrote, "the media defendants heightened the report's impact and credibility by demonstrating that the allegations rested on a firm evidentiary foundation and that the reporter had access to reliable information." Moreover, just as had the trial court, it found that "[e]ditorial judgment is a matter that courts have generally left to the press."

Had the television news report gone further, the court reasoned, there could have been liability. It suggested, for example, that the plaintiff would have had a viable claim if facts about her were revealed that were "too tangential to the prosecution of the perpetrator" to have been of legitimate public interest. The court did not attempt to delineate between facts that were too tangential and a videotape of an alleged rape that a journalism expert found exploitative and not newsworthy, however. In the end, as had the trial court, the appeals court sided with the television news reporter and the First Amendment.

Such defense arguments and such a pro-media decision, supporting a news judgment that many journalists would likely find in violation of multiple ethics code provisions by further victimizing an alleged victim, involving videotape that was likely a never-before-used element of a television news story on an alleged crime, could well push fed-up courts toward a different outcome in future cases. Indeed, it is difficult to imagine the court in the *To Catch a Predator* case hesitating to rein in misbehaving media after learning of that decision, or the Illinois court deciding not to question the *Chicago Tribune*'s news judgment to include a grieving mother's words in its front-page story.

And it is not difficult to imagine this particular case to be one that Justice White would have described as hitting the true bottom of the slippery slope—and one that could lead similarly inclined judges to force journalists back up the mountain of propriety to "draw the line higher on the hillside," just as Justice White had wished.

Coffee Mugs, Commenters, and Creative Cameras

Perhaps encouraged by favorable decisions like the one from Oklahoma City, mainstream media continues to push for First Amendment protection and for an expanding definition for newsworthiness in ways certain to inflame those already convinced that modern media has lost its ethical compass. Three examples follow: a newspaper's claim that the First Amendment protects its sales of souvenir coffee mugs featuring news photographs; another's argument that the reporter's privilege entitles it to shield the identity of all reader-commenters; and a third, a photographer's stance that the First Amendment entitles him to take and publish photos of unknowing individuals inside their homes at night.

First, the coffee mugs. In 2008, a man in Massachusetts was involved in a serious automobile accident; another driver had crossed the centerline and had struck the man's vehicle head-on. The man was injured, but conscious, and when he realized that his family had arrived at the accident scene, he lifted his hand and waved to signal that he was okay. At that moment, a news photographer took his photograph. The newspaper published the photo the following day along with a news article about the crash. The paper then offered readers the opportunity to purchase the image of the injured victim waving to his family emblazoned on a T-shirt, mouse pad, or coffee mug.

The man, horrified that his image at the accident scene would be for sale to others, sued the newspaper for negligent infliction of emotional distress and invasion of privacy. Even though he recognized the news value in the photograph published in the newspaper itself, he explained, the photographic reproductions on the various products had caused him significant emotional harm.

The newspaper argued in response that the First Amendment gave it the right to sell items featuring such images. "In essence," the court hearing the case wrote, "Defendant [newspaper] alleges that any publication of the accident photograph, even in the context of commercial product sales, is not actionable because it is related to the automobile accident, a matter of legitimate public concern." The court quite aptly called the newspaper's legal response "a blanket defense of newsworthiness."[11]

Sparked by such a blanket defense, the court undertook a standard newsworthiness analysis, weighing the plaintiff's privacy against the news value inherent in the photograph. It did so as if it were balancing the newspaper's right to publish an accident scene photograph in the paper, not an accident scene photograph made available on products for the home. "To be sure," the court wrote, "accidents are traditionally contemplated to be 'news'" but then noted that a commercial enterprise could well be where the law would draw the line.

The court, however, hesitated to draw that line itself. It "t[ook] no position" regarding the news value stemming from the photograph on the coffee mug and other products, but found that reasonable minds could disagree over whether "the sale of an accident photograph unaccompanied by any information regarding the accident, sold exclusively for commercial purposes disconnected to the dissemination of news . . . crosses the line from the mere 'giving of information' to a 'sensational prying into private lives for its own sake.'" It denied the defendant newspaper's First Amendment defense—for the moment, at least—and allowed the plaintiff's case to continue to trial.

A second example of a recent First Amendment boundary push involves the Indiana reporter's shield law, a law enacted by the state legislature to protect journalists who promise confidentiality to news sources who give them secret information.

There is a backstory relevant here. In *Branzburg v. Hayes,*[12] the Supreme Court decided that there was no First Amendment protection for reporters who refused to turn over to the government information that they had uncovered during crime-related newsgathering. The reporters had argued that they could refuse to testify because they were protected by the Constitution's promise of a free press, but the Justices for the most part disagreed. In the end, according to *Branzburg,* the public's right to evidence of crime trumped First Amendment newsgathering freedoms.

But *Branzburg* can be interpreted in different ways. Despite the Court's refusal to give reporters First Amendment protection to protect their sources in the context of a criminal investigation, the majority suggested that newsgathering had some First Amendment protections: "without some protection for seeking out the news," the Justices wrote, "freedom of the press could be eviscerated." That, and Justice Powell's concurrence suggesting that journalists did, in some cases, deserve protection from having to testify, led some courts in some cases to find constitutional shield protection. Meantime, many legislatures responded to *Branzburg* by enacting media-protective shield laws in their states.

But even courts that have accepted a reporter's privilege have limited it when pushed too far. In 2005, Vermont's Supreme Court, for example, rejected its own precedent when it held that a Vermont television station had to turn over to police videotape of a sports celebration-turned-riot in which revelers damaged property. In doing so, it suddenly and explicitly shifted away from Justice Powell's concurrence and moved toward the majority's holding that no reporter's privilege existed in the Constitution. The videotape was evidence of a crime, the court decided, and the station was entitled to "no privilege, qualified or otherwise, to refuse to disclose [such] evidence."[13]

Back in Indiana, "DownWithTheColts," the pseudonym for an everyday reader of the *Indianapolis Star*'s website who apparently had negative feelings for the Indianapolis football team, likely knew nothing of the historic discord regarding the reporter's privilege and, perhaps, knew nothing of the Indiana statute. Yet, following a news story about Junior Achievement, he or she posted that money missing from a local office could be found in the former president's bank account. The former Junior Achievement president, angered at the suggestion that he had taken money from the organization, sued DownWithTheColts for defamation.

In order to figure out who DownWithTheColts was, however, the Junior Achievement president needed cooperation from the *Indianapolis Star*. DownWithTheColts had registered identifying information with the newspaper's website and the website's privacy policy at the time had explained that the newspaper would reveal a poster's identifying information if it felt that it should for legal or business reasons. Nevertheless, the newspaper refused to reveal DownWithTheColt's identity—and it based the reason on constitutional principles. The newspaper argued that the Indiana shield law and the First Amendment from which it sprang protected its relationship with reader-commenter DownWithTheColts just as the law would protect a traditional reporter-source relationship.

It was as if DownWithTheColts was the *Star*'s "Deep Throat." And, just like Woodward and Bernstein in the Watergate investigation, the newspaper fought to protect the identity of its anonymous "source." Trouble was that this particular source, unlike Deep Throat, had not offered important information about government misbehavior and corruption in a secret meeting with reporters but, instead, had posted an anonymous comment on a news website as likely had hundreds of others that day. Trouble was that DownWithTheColts, unlike Deep Throat, had not been promised anonymity but had instead agreed to a privacy policy that explained that his identifying information could be turned over to authorities at the newspaper's discretion. Trouble was that the newspaper, unlike the *Washington Post,* had not used the anonymous comment in any investigative manner at all and likely did not even know of its existence before the Junior Achievement president filed his lawsuit. Trouble was that the commenter's intention, unlike Deep Throat's, was likely not to share important secret insider information with a newspaper reporter who would then act upon it, but to publish to the entire world potentially false information meant to anger, irritate, and embarrass another.

Consider the implications of the *Indianapolis Star*'s First Amendment argument. Under the newspaper's interpretation of reporter's privilege statutes— laws already facing renewed scrutiny in some jurisdictions as noted earlier— each time an anonymous commenter posts a racist or otherwise hateful message or simply a hurtful or off-topic message on a newspaper's website, the First Amendment springs forth to protect that person as if he or she were a white knight courageously revealing a public wrong, instead of, more likely, an internet troll.

The appellate court deciding the case did not focus solely on the First Amendment in the way the defendant newspaper would have liked but, instead, turned to the meaning of the word "source."[14] It defined a source as a person who gives information to a reporter so that the reporter can publish an accurate story. In doing so, it rejected the newspaper's argument that the reporter's privilege protected an anonymous commenter like DownWithTheColts who had posted a potentially random comment in cyberspace. Instead, the court ruled that as long as the plaintiff was able to show that the comment was defamatory, the newspaper would be forced to reveal the commenter's identity.

Aside from that individual result, the *Indianapolis Star*'s argument that the reporter's privilege should be extended to include protection of anonymous newspaper commenters could well have lasting national impact—and not in the way the *Star* would like. Such an argument for the extension of the privilege to protect as sources the hundreds of thousands of online commenters to news websites is especially dangerous at a time when federal lawmakers cannot agree on the parameters of a federal reporter's shield law, worried that it would protect too many in an age when to some the word "journalist" seems incapable of definition.

Meantime, in New York, there was a different sort of identity revelation in a case in which the defendant similarly attempted to push the boundaries of the First Amendment. Like the coffee mug case, it involved images taken and used in an unsettling way.

The photographer, Arne Svenson, shot a series of photographs over the course of some weeks in 2012 he titled "The Neighbors." The photographs, some of which were still available online in 2014,[15] are gauzy, ethereal images of people inside their apartment homes. One photograph, for example, is of a man who stands behind a curtain near a window; though the image is not revealing, he appears not to be wearing pants. Another is of a woman bending over, also in front of a window. Her large bottom, covered in what appears to be a billowing green skirt, is the focal point of the photograph. A third image is of a pregnant woman, her hands clasped behind her back in what appears to be a yoga pose; she, like the others, appears oblivious to the camera's lens.

The court hearing the case explained why the pregnant woman was oblivious: "Defendant did not have permission to photograph [his] 'neighbors.'"[16]

Svenson admitted as much and more when he described his project to a newspaper reporter. "The Neighbors don't know they are being photographed," he explained. "I carefully shoot from the shadows of my [high-rise apartment] home into theirs." His careful shooting required a bird-watching telephoto lens, and, just as photographs of rarely seen birds in their natural habitat are shared in nature magazines, he captured his neighbors' images and put them on display.

Some of the Neighbors sued Svenson under New York's Civil Rights statute, New York's version of a privacy law, arguing that the photographs, some of which contained identifiable images of children, were privacy-invading. They demanded that Svenson stop showing them. Svenson countered with the First Amendment, arguing that he was constitutionally protected from being punished for peering into their apartments with his high-powered lens, taking photographs of what he saw inside, and publishing the results.

The court, obviously taken with the First Amendment argument, found for the photographer. Here, the court decided, the defendant's right to expression trumped the plaintiffs' right to privacy: "While it makes Plaintiffs cringe to think [that] their private lives and images of their small children can find their way into the public forum of an art exhibition, there is no redress," the court wrote. "Simply, an individual's right to privacy . . . yield[s] to an artist's protections under the First Amendment under the circumstances presented here."

But the court ventured into news judgment as well, suggesting that publication of the intimate photographs of everyday people within their homes were similarly protected for their news value. "[P]rivacy rights yield to free speech rights in the context of newsworthy events," the court wrote, and newsworthiness itself is "interpreted broadly and includes reports of political happenings, social trends, and articles of consumer and public interest."

In the end, the value of the photographs—be it artistic or journalistic—trumped the Neighbors' right to privacy.

The legacy of the court's extraordinarily broad language in The Neighbors case could be this: in New York, one may be protected by the First Amendment if one looks into another's window using a powerful lens, takes photographs of the people inside who are oblivious to the camera, and publishes the images. The court seemed to make no real distinction between an official art photographer and a more nefarious one; the holding, it seems, could well protect photographers who capture images of celebrities inside their homes or of visitors in New York City's high rise hotels, even when those individuals consider themselves to be in private spaces inaccessible to the unaided human eye.

And it is precisely that sort of boundary-pushing behavior by photographers that led the California legislature to pass laws regulating news photography and sales of privacy-invading photographs.

Meantime, a photography magazine reporter equated the Svenson photographs with government surveillance photos, suggesting that she found similar images taken by the government to be less intrusive:

> [T]he images begin to make you slightly uncomfortable in the way seeing surreptitiously shot footage and pixelated stills from surveillance cameras wouldn't. How are you supposed to react to stunning surveillance, moments that are stolen and then impressively crafted? Should knowing beauty has dubious origins make it less beautiful? Of course, these are questions Svenson's project doesn't even attempt to answer, but they're there, hovering over the work.[17]

There too is the suggestion that if we welcome such privacy-invading inside images under the First Amendment, it makes it easier to accept seemingly less intrusive surveillance images taken outside by the government. The strength of this First Amendment holding, then, arguably helps weaken the Fourth.

These three cases, in which the defendants raised First Amendment arguments in novel ways, are examples of what the Rhode Island Supreme Court would likely consider constitutional overzealousness. The court warned of such boundary-pushing when it found for the first time that the press could be liable for negligently causing a person to commit suicide. Its language seemed to be a warning to the media litigants in front of it and otherwise—and perhaps the sentence directly preceding the justices' warning of overzealousness is just as important in context:

> We realize . . . that there are those both in and out the press-media field who insist that the First Amendment is an impenetrable shield from both press criticism and civil liability. We also realize that First Amendment rights of the press are as much endangered by its zealots as by its critics.[18]

The Rhode Island Supreme Court sent the case back to the trial court to examine whether the suicide had been caused in part by the television reporter who reported on a newscast live at 6:04 P.M. that she was obviously speaking with "a very troubled man" who was angry at the world and quite possibly on the verge of suicide. The man killed himself at 6:07 P.M., just after the interview ended.

In returning the case for trial, the court rejected the journalist's argument that the First Amendment always protected her and other journalists from claims of negligence. Such a zealous interpretation of press freedoms had apparently pushed the court too far.

Dirty Websites and First Amendment Blindness

An important question is why the media is doing such seemingly overzealous pushing in a way that puts the protective First Amendment bubble at risk. The answer, again, may be something other than an intentionally constitutionally manipulative defense strategy: journalists could well strongly believe that the First Amendment protects them from just about any claim. If reporters are taught in the classroom and the newsroom that the First Amendment protects the press, and they forget about or never learn about its growing nuances, their First Amendment arguments may be seen by those who know better as overzealous foundationless attempts to expand the bubble of protection. Media, however, may be simply unaware that they are pushing or have pushed too far.

This is a sort of First Amendment blindness and it is apparent not only in court but, at times, in news coverage.

"Nik Richie and thedirty.com are flourishing in a world where the Internet and social media sites render privacy more and more irrelevant," the *Arizona Republic* reporter wrote in 2013 in its gushing article headlined "Website The Dirty Flourishing with New Scandals."[19] The newspaper had interviewed Richie both because he had some days before posted new "sexting" messages from Congressman Anthony Weiner and because Richie had started his web-based publication locally.

Recall that in the article Richie described his website as "reality Internet" with a constitutional marketplace-of-ideas dynamism. "I wanted to give people a voice where they could express themselves and have their freedom of speech and talk about the neighbors, celebrities, friends, politics, and whatnot," Richie had told the reporter, describing his contributors as "civilian paparazzi."

The article could well have questioned Richie's First Amendment rhetoric. It could have critiqued his venture and acknowledged the harm its posts had done to some. It could have described the full content of the website and noted that such content had led some courts to limit Communications Decency Act protection. Instead, the article as published online is laudatory, aside from a quick mention of the website's "gossip and racy photos." It reads as if The Dirty's Richie is today's version of the lonely pamphleteer and as if his website is one that could change a nation.

The Dirty could change a nation, of course, but not in a good way.

The article lauding Richie could well be an example of First Amendment blindness: when the First Amendment is raised, some journalists and others assume that it should rightly deflect all inquiry, criticism, and legal claims. Why raise complaints about a particular publication when the broadly protective nature of the First Amendment makes it pointless or when the complaints would reveal you to be an opponent of First Amendment principles? For journalists, most of whom are not lawyers and many of whom were taught media law, if at all, by nonlawyers who are potentially more likely to focus strongly on Supreme Court cases to the exclusion of more recent lower court opinions, to question the power of the First Amendment is an anathema that may also weaken one's professional standing. In the *Arizona Republic* article, Richie spun his website as one offering freedom of speech for average citizens. That, seemingly, was enough to halt criticism and further inquiry.

This First Amendment blindness appears further proved by comments in the article from an ethics expert at the Poynter Institute, the well-respected journalism and journalism ethics think tank. The Poynter expert also apparently lauded The Dirty, calling it today's "fifth estate," "valuable," and a source for traditional fourth estate coverage. Perhaps the ethics expert did, in fact, note the everyday ethics lapses in The Dirty and the way it humiliates its hapless targets, especially women. If so, the reporter chose not to include that part of the interview. Instead, as the article stands online, it appears that one of the nation's leading journalism ethics experts failed to question the ethics of one of the websites that has so great an ethics problem that it could well change the course of media-protective First Amendment law by changing courts' interpretation of the CDA. If it is an accurate assessment of her response, that too is First Amendment blindness: how can journalists convince judges that they can be trusted to do the right thing if not even ethicists appear to question a website like The Dirty?

"Too often," famed journalist and author Anthony Lewis wrote in reviewing a book on free press concerns, "the press cries 'First Amendment' as if it gave an absolute answer—as if freedom of the press trumped all other values."[20] This complete adherence to the First Amendment, then, is the way many journalists see the world, not just the way they respond to a lawsuit. It is also part of the reason the First Amendment bubble is in danger of collapse today.

There are examples of this from the classroom as well. Consider a submission to the 2010 "Best Ideas in the Teaching of Communication Law and Policy Competition" sponsored by the law division of the organization that accredits college journalism and communications programs. The teaching idea, the submitter explained, was to assign the students a project that "tests the limits of free expression, tests others' understanding of the First Amendment and/or measures how well society and/or individuals are able to understand First Amendment situations." It further suggested:

> Possible approaches include, BUT ARE NOT LIMITED TO:
> * conducting a survey of people's attitudes toward free expression/ the First Amendment.
> * creating a forum for public expression.
> * *creating something that pushes the limits of legally and/or morally accepted expression (e.g., film, poster, essay, photo, etc.).*
> * arranging a situation that tests tolerance/limits (e.g., a protest, reading banned books out loud, etc.).[21]

The professor had further explained to his students that "all proposals must be legal under First Amendment case law as well as under any state and local laws." Trouble is, of course, as shown throughout this book, the boundaries of the First Amendment and media law are changing and only, it seems, a First Amendment attorney with a finger on the pulse of all courts can advise whether any project pushing the limits of legally and morally accepted expression falls within federal, state, and local laws. Sometimes that attorney may only know for sure after a trial's outcome is upheld on appeal.

Moreover, if one is told to "push[] the limits of legally and/or morally accepted expression," one is necessarily expanding the bubble of First Amendment protection, and hoping that it does not burst.

It is not just one media law professor who believed that such an assignment was an important part of the media law curriculum. The teaching idea that literally urged that students "test[] the limits of free expression" won first place in the competition that year. It is quite possible, therefore, that media law students across the country have experienced the push-the-limits-of-the-First-Amendment project on their own campuses.

The First Amendment project did not always go smoothly. The professor who won first place would later explain that one First Amendment student project involved "a sale of cookies in vulgar shapes and with vulgar sayings." Coincidentally, the bake sale occurred when a group of children was visiting campus on a field trip. Parents and university administrators were outraged—and the professor expressed frustration that the university's president did not rally around First Amendment principles.[22]

A similar sort of First Amendment blindness outside of the journalism world occurred during the debate over the revenge porn law eventually passed by the California legislature, legislation originally introduced to criminalize those who post nude photographs of ex-loves as revenge. The law as enacted reads:

> Any person who photographs or records by any means the image of the intimate body part or parts of another identifiable person, under circumstances where the parties agree or understand that the image shall remain private, and the person subsequently distributes the image taken, with the intent to cause serious emotional distress, and the depicted person suffers serious emotional distress . . . [is guilty of disorderly conduct, a misdemeanor.][23]

The law is not as strong as it could be, however. In limiting liability to scenarios in which images were taken by another, it seemingly does not encompass a typical revenge porn scenario: a woman who takes nude photographs of
herself and sends them to a boyfriend who, later dumped by the woman, posts
the images that she took herself.

The law was weakened after First Amendment-based arguments came
from groups like the American Civil Liberties Union. In its letter in opposition to the law as it was originally introduced, the ACLU argued that the
First Amendment protected such revenge porn publications, citing as precedent a case involving an offensive blog post, one that had absolutely nothing
to do with revenge porn. Instead of recognizing that the publication of a nude,
intimate photograph could well be considered at the heart of an individual's
constitutional right to privacy and, therefore, should be a publication without
as much, if any, protection, the ACLU wrote that the First Amendment
trumped individual privacy. It used language that interprets free speech very
broadly:

> The posting of otherwise lawful speech or images even if offensive or emo-
> tionally distressing is constitutionally protected. The speech must consti-
> tute a true threat or violate another otherwise lawful criminal law, such as
> [a] stalking or harassment statute, in order to be made illegal. The provi-
> sions of this bill do not meet that standard."[24]

In its own version of First Amendment blindness, then, the ACLU failed
to note the extensive jurisprudence that finds some claims based upon privacy-
invading speech to be viable despite First Amendment protections. In fact,
some key examples of viable claims within the Restatement involve nudity or
partial nudity and most courts have traditionally protected nudity in a privacy
sense. Moreover, in his important concurrence in *Bartnicki* that effectively
created a 5–4 majority for personal privacy above publication rights, recall
that Justice Breyer explained that the Constitution was flexible enough to
restrict some offensive or emotionally distressing speech, including publication of intimacies in the bedroom. Consider again the language he used and
how it suggests that California legislators could do precisely what they had
tried to do:

> [I]n my view, the Constitution permits legislatures to respond flexibly to the
> challenges future technology may pose to the individual's interest in basic

personal privacy. Clandestine and pervasive invasions of privacy, unlike the simple theft of documents from a bedroom, are genuine possibilities as a result of continuously advancing technologies. . . . Eavesdropping on ordinary cellular phone conversations in the street . . . is a very different matter from eavesdropping on encrypted cellular phone conversations or those carried on in the bedroom. Legislatures also may decide to revisit statutes such as those before us, creating better tailored provisions designed to encourage, for example, more effective privacy-protecting technologies.[25]

The ACLU later seemingly recognized its First Amendment mistake and changed its mind about its opposition. Just before the reworked bill passed the legislature, the *Deseret News* contacted the ACLU to inquire further about its stance. An ACLU official explained that the organization did not oppose the bill and "could not offer any explanation for why the initial objection letter was sent, nor what changes in the bill altered [its] viewpoint."[26] It was as if the organization's First Amendment-wrapped initial response had been decidedly knee-jerk. After all, not even strong First Amendment proponent and scholar Eugene Volokh saw constitutional issues with the law, suggesting that it was "a suitably clear and narrow statute banning nonconsensual posting of nude pictures of another, in a context where there's good reason to think that the subject did not consent to publication."[27] Volokh, then, draws a First Amendment line at least at the nonconsensual posting of another's nude photos.

As this book shows, that same sort of line-drawing—a reasoned decision about what types of publications should be legally untenable in spite of the First Amendment's promises—is necessary more generally as well. If media is absolutist in matters regarding newsworthiness and other journalism-related judgments, it will lose its chance to help draw a media-friendly line that divides the appropriate from the inappropriate. And it will, instead, leave the work to skeptical and blue pencil-ready judges.

In some cases, media has already left such line drawing to the courts, leading to decisions it would surely point to as evidence of a collapsing First Amendment bubble if it dared to look.

"We Are All Journalists Now"

A 2013 article in the *Columbia Journalism Review* focused on what it called a counter-media movement in Turkey.[28] The article explained that during the trial of an alleged terrorist, reports regarding the trial kept appearing on Twitter. Courtroom officials including the judge asked that they stop, but the tweets continued. The authorities were confused because they knew that no journalist was in the room. What they did not realize is that it was a non-professional, a twenty-one-year-old student in the courtroom, who was tweeting the details. Because he was young, others, if they recognized that he was tweeting at all, likely thought that he was communicating with a friend. Instead, he was communicating against the judge's wishes with the entire world.

"We are all journalists now," the young man told the *Review*. "What we have is our own devices [and] it actually removes the barriers between the person who sees the news and who creates the news."

The we-are-all-journalists mantra is not limited to Turkey. In 2005, the director of the Nieman Foundation for Journalism at Harvard suggested that it had become fashionable among working journalists to "hail the emergence of citizen journalism,"[29] and, indeed, CNN's use of iReporters, as but one example, elevates anyone with a story to tell to a journalistic status. Joe Francis, creator of the Girls Gone Wild videotape series, argued that his published images of girls lifting their shirts made him a journalist and that his publications should, therefore, be protected as newsworthy. Recall too that James O'Keefe also believes he is a journalist and has repeatedly attempted to confront journalism professionals in an effort to get them to agree. If all are journalists, then Julian Assange and other government secrets-leakers—those who post secret documents with no accompanying analysis or context—have clearly joined the ranks of the profession.

Indeed, the former general counsel for the *New Republic* argued that we are all journalists now in a book of the same title.[30] "The lines distinguishing professional journalists from other people who disseminate information, ideas, and opinions to a wide audience have been blurred, perhaps beyond recognition," its author maintained, adding that "the First Amendment is for all of us."

Eric Deggans of the Poynter Institute too "tend[s] to side with thinkers such as New York University's Jay Rosen and City University of New York's Jeff Jarvis, who note that tools available through smartphones and the Internet allow anyone to become a reporter."[31] And in a disparaging Salon article titled "Meet the 'Journalists Against Journalism' Club,"[32] David Sirota slammed the

Washington Post for making a distinction between regular *Post* journalists and leakers like Edward Snowden. "Such an unprecedented move," Sirota wrote in response to a *Post* editorial that suggested that jail might be appropriate for those who reveal some government secrets, "exposes the intensity of the paper's—and the larger establishment media's—ideological antipathy to journalism."

The we-are-all-journalists mantra, after all, is built upon First Amendment principles and journalists apparently dare not suggest anything that might limit it.

Such a powerfully seductive notion—that we are all journalists—fails to recognize, however, the important contributions that statutes like reporter's shield laws help provide—and how, as Congress recognizes as it continues to debate a federal shield law proposal, such statutes necessarily depend upon a more limited definition for the word "journalist." Those journalists who rely on the shield law usually have access to government or other insiders and the reporters, and ultimately the reading public, rely on the secrecy promise that they can make to their confidential informants. If even a somewhat journalism-hostile Justice White in *Branzburg* recognized that some newsgathering should be protected, then it is important to define who the protected news-gatherers are.

On the other hand, if we are all journalists, then, ultimately, not a one of us is because the law simply will not protect every single person who declines to testify when government attorneys come calling.

Indeed, in 2014, litigants that included a music downloading website and a construction industry research company had at least initially attempted to shield themselves from discovery rules using different iterations of the reporter's shield law.[33] Each time one of these entities, some far from what would be considered traditional journalism, raises the shield, a court must decide if the entity is journalistic.

Yet some in journalism and elsewhere continue to push for inclusivity. Such an openness to all is at least somewhat surprising given the supportive language from the Supreme Court about journalism's role in a democracy, news-worthiness, and the need for robust protection so that citizens may come to find the truth about government and other institutions. Such rhetoric seemingly recognizes that there is something special within journalism and its practices; that specialness is what laws that include shield laws, special rights for media in some freedom-of-information access situations, and special legal protection from intrusion claims spring from. Some procedural laws and notice laws in some states are similarly journalism-specific. These laws, built upon constitutional principles, by their very language require that we decide which ones of us are journalists and inherently reject the notion that everyone is.

But even more importantly, if everyone is a journalist, then privacy as it has come to be known in a legal sense is dead. The reason is this: if everyone is a journalist, their published work is journalism and therefore newsworthy because the current Restatement suggests that journalists themselves define the term. Under the Restatement definition as it currently stands, then, journalism would necessarily include revenge porn, Girls Gone Wild, Nik Richie's and his readers' musings on women's bodies, surreptitiously recorded sex tapes, and anything else posted on the Internet or published elsewhere. In fact, many of these publishers, like Richie and Is Anyone Up's Hunter Moore, could point to millions of readers for their brand of "journalism."

Privacy, then, has been protected in a legal sense through news decisions by mainstream journalists necessarily tempered by ethics considerations. Ethics is stressed within the industry. Many journalists have taken special classes in ethics, in school or elsewhere, in which they agonizingly discuss with others the reasons to publish certain stories or not, and many working journalists operate under the SPJ code or another like it designed for their particular newsroom. A citizen journalist or quasi-journalist, in contrast, may well have no ethics code, may not take ethics seriously, and, as some courts have noted, may have no professional restrictions whatsoever in deciding what might be appropriate to publish. In other words, without some form of legal line-drawing, they answer to no one.

Many would-be journalists, to be sure, are upstanding individuals who simply do not understand the practice of journalism. A highly accomplished academic, for example, once drafted a newspaper editorial with a particularly remarkable story at its start. When questioned, she admitted that she had created the story but argued that such fiction was perfectly appropriate in order to draw the reader in. Another published on the Internet a photograph featuring a man about to jump from a bridge. Mainstream journalists who follow ethics codes would have known better.

As would the *New York Times*. The newspaper, as noted earlier, decided not to publish government information that it had recognized as potentially harmful to U.S.'s relations with other countries. Likewise, CNN editors decided not to publish the full reasons behind a terrorist warning because the government had asked them to keep it secret, presumably for security reasons. That, then, is why the *Washington Post* wrote the editorial that it did, differentiating between its journalists and those who post for reasons including the thrill of celebrity or to humiliate others. Those news outlets recognize the public interest in some information but also that they should use restraint in publishing if harm would come to one or many. Those are the sorts of worries that seemingly do not keep Julian Assange, Hunter Moore, or Nik Richie up at night.

There is, then, a need for line-drawing, as the *Post* indicated, for both "news" and for "journalist." An absolutist definition for either could well expand the First Amendment to its breaking point and could well lead to protection for no one.

The potential for that result can be shown, at least tangentially, by returning to the story of the rebel courtroom tweeter in Turkey. Ultimately, as inspiring as his rallying cry that we are all journalists may be, his story is a reminder of why we all cannot be journalists without harm befalling the profession. Now, the judge who sat in that courtroom that day in a country known for governmental efforts to control news media[34] may work to keep all electronic devices out of his and other courtrooms. Indeed, just a few months later, as elections neared, the government in Turkey banned YouTube; officials suggested that some users had posted top secret security information.[35] This and related media crackdowns there have very likely hurt the young man's career as a citizen journalist and have likely brought mainstream journalists straight down with him.

The Expanding Speech Bubble: Of Corporate Speech and "Crush Videos"

Journalism is not alone in its sometime readiness to expand the boundaries of the First Amendment to the breaking point. The Supreme Court itself has recently taken a similarly expansive approach to defining the scope of "speech" protected by the Amendment in other contexts, with arguably similarly destabilizing consequences for the future of speech rights.

In recent years, the Justices have held that corporations have the First Amendment "free speech" right to donate money to political campaigns;

they have decided that the First Amendment protects those who create so-called "crush videos" in which small animals are crushed to death on film to satisfy the sexual fetishes of viewers; they have ruled that a hateful church could protest military funerals in a way that distressed grieving loved ones; and they have decided that the First Amendment protects the practice of pharmaceutical-related data mining.

It was a documentary titled *Hillary* that sparked the First Amendment right to free speech by corporations. An earlier court opinion had described the film as one "susceptible of no other interpretation than to inform the electorate that Senator Clinton is unfit for office, that the United States would be a dangerous place in a President Hillary Clinton world, and that viewers should vote against her."[36] A group calling itself Citizens United backed the film but feared liability under the legal ban on corporate-funded political expenditures for "electioneering communication."

It need not have worried. The Court, warning of chilled political speech, held that corporations do not lose First Amendment free speech just because they are corporations.[37] "[B]rooding governmental power cannot be reconciled with the confidence and ability in civic discourse that the First Amendment must secure," the Justices wrote. "The government has muffled the voices that best represent the most significant segments of the economy," they added, warning that the government must not "prevent[] [corporate] voices and viewpoints from reaching the public and advising voters which persons or entities are hostile to their interests."

Reaction to the decision came swiftly and strong. Many opposed suggested that free speech had been pushed too far. President Obama, for example, criticized the opinion as one that would allow giant corporations' voices to drown out those of everyday Americans.[38] And *Roll Call*, a Capitol Hill newspaper, similarly worried at the prospect of equating a corporation's voice with that of a single voter: "Corporations aren't people deserving full First Amendment rights," it wrote. "They already have ample opportunities to express themselves in the media and marketplace of ideas" outside of funding political campaigns.[39] Indeed, the backlash to the Court's expansive ruling was so strong that some feared—or actively promoted—a reactive effort to contract First Amendment speech rights.[40]

That same year, the Supreme Court ruled that an animal cruelty statute violated the Constitution because the law suppressed some expression.[41] The statute was one designed to criminalize sickening so-called "crush videos." One crush video was described by the Humane Society this way:

> [A] kitten, secured to the ground, watches and shrieks in pain as a woman thrusts her high-heeled shoe into its body, slams her heel into the kitten's eye socket and mouth loudly fracturing its skull, and stomps repeatedly on the animal's head. The kitten hemorrhages blood, screams blindly in pain, and is ultimately left dead in a moist pile of blood-soaked hair and bone.

The Court's majority decided that a statute prohibiting such behavior was too broad and, therefore, constitutionally invalid under the First Amendment, even though the law offered various exemptions, including those for recordings with educational or journalistic value. Those Justices worried that hunting videos could be circumscribed under the statute, but the dissent disagreed. It wrote that the majority opinion had "the practical effect of legalizing the sale of [crush] videos and [was] thus likely to spur a resumption of their production."

Even before the decision was released, a Humane Society official suggested that he could not imagine a society "that can't balance robust, free expression with a need to criminalize that utterly outrageous conduct that has no socially redeeming value."[42] *Washington Post* columnist Kathleen Parker agreed, writing that "[t]he high court's opinion is surely of a kind that prompted Mr. Bumble in "Oliver Twist" to assert: 'The law is a ass—a idiot.'"[43]

There was a similar response to *Snyder v. Phelps,* the military funeral protest case in which the Court allowed a group to protest carrying signs such as "God Hates Fags" on a funeral procession route. An editorial writer called it one of the court's most controversial decisions in the opinion of the general public.[44] Even though it is understandable on a scholarly level, many hear only that such disgusting protests can proceed and are left wondering why the First Amendment would favor such emotionally harmful speech over grieving family members' rights to bury their loved ones in peace.

There was less of an outcry, perhaps because of fewer news stories, when the Court that same year ruled that Vermont's Prescription Confidentiality Law, one designed to keep pharmaceutical records out of the hands of marketers, violated the First Amendment. "Speech in aid of pharmaceutical marketing," the Court ruled, "is a form of expression protected by the Free Speech

Clause of the First Amendment." It found that a law that prohibited data miners from selling such information to drug companies for marketing purposes was unconstitutional as one that burdened protected expression.[45]

If there is pushback against the First Amendment in the opinion of the American people, it is likely based in part upon decisions like those, ones that seem far removed from traditional individual speech freedoms and ones that in most of the cases seem to favor speech by corporations so strongly that they drown speech and privacy interests of individuals. Until just a few years ago, First Amendment freedom of speech was routinely relied upon by courts to promote democracy and democratic ideals. Today, its embrace of corporate speech interests has aroused concerns that the Constitution is being used to quash individual speech and undermine democracy. "Here, as distorted beyond recognition by the Roberts Court," a reporter for the *Nation* fumed, "the First Amendment becomes not the guardian of democratic discussion but the guarantee of unequal protection for well-born and wealth-backed politicians."[46]

Rebecca Brown, a law professor at the University of Southern California, has warned that adopting an expansive conception of what qualifies as "speech" under the First Amendment comes with consequences for the future strength of speech rights.[47] Surveying the Supreme Court's recent cases, Brown observed that an absolutist insistence that corporate political largess and animal crush videos are constitutional "speech" stretches the concept beyond the comprehension of most citizens and inevitably pressures the Court to water down the strength of constitutional protection afforded speech in order to mitigate the extremism of its doctrine. Pairing a broad and absolutist conception of the scope of protected speech with an unyielding conception of the absolute strength of speech rights would make First Amendment rights so socially costly as to be unsustainable.

The observation offers a lesson for the scope of press rights as well. First, the backdrop of the Court's absolutist approach to speech rights suggests that embracing a similarly sweeping conception of press rights compounds the danger of backlash. Second, the scope of First Amendment rights cannot be expanded without limit. Given the very substantial countervailing interests potentially at stake—freedom from defamation and harassment, and individual privacy, to name some—allowance must be made to balance the social costs, one way or the other. To barrel ahead heedlessly is to risk a sharp correction.

Meantime, in 2014, the Supreme Court decided that limits on political campaign contributions in aggregate restricted the First Amendment free speech rights of individual donors.[48] Coincidentally, the case was the one in which the protestor had disrupted oral argument and was promptly arrested for his speech.

Risking a Calamitous Collapse

A journalism professor once rallied a group of students during a talk on press freedoms by urging them to "Get out there and defame someone!" He may have done so in good humor—or he may have actually meant to suggest that an inspiration to defame would make them bold and better reporters, believing that the First Amendment would protect them from consequence for their boundary-pushing behavior. The students responded with thunderous applause, as if the professor were a charismatic preacher who had told them to go forth and spread the gospel.

Either way, the professor would likely want to know that in the November 2012 edition of the American Bar Association's *Communications Lawyer* magazine, one of the founding partners of one of the best media defense firms in the country wrote that things were not so easy. The article, titled "Selling the First Amendment to a Jury,"[49] opened this way:

QUESTION: How do you sell a First Amendment argument to a jury?
ANSWER: Beats me.

The attorney then advised others representing media to avoid simplistic pro-media arguments that "boil down to '. . . but we're the press. . . .'" And even though he did not write so explicitly, the reasons seemed to be based upon a sense of a public backlash against media and perceived overly expansive First Amendment rights: "You should start from the premise that the jurors really do not care a great deal about the First Amendment rights of the press," he wrote, "and that may be even truer these days than in the past."

The professor's boundary-pushing suggestion is therefore risky at a time when there is pushback against media's excesses and when the public and many courts seem far less receptive to their First Amendment freedoms than ever before. In 2013, the First Amendment Center's finding that one-third of all Americans believed that the First Amendment offered too much freedom, a number that was up 13 percent from 2012, the largest jump in survey history,[50] provides similar evidence of a shaky time for media. Moreover, only 1 percent of those potential jurors said that freedom of the press was the freedom they most enjoyed. Given those numbers, it is no wonder that one study showed that media won only one-quarter of the cases against it that went to trial[51]—and that study was from the mid-1980s, when media generally was perceived as more Woodward and less wicked. The author of the study assumed that this meant that jurors were more hostile to media than were judges.

As this chapter has argued, an overarching reason for both the backlash and the resulting overzealousness by media is the growing First Amendment. When some courts find that free apartment guides found on racks in cities across the United States deserve First Amendment protection so that the "newsworthiness" of their apartment listings could not be questioned[52] or that a businessman's lack-of-a-release misappropriation claim arising from the reality television series *Family Jewels* starring rock musician Gene Simmons failed because of the strong public interest involved in the "unscripted" everyday life of a celebrity,[53] it suggests that the First Amendment bubble is growing perilously large in some courtrooms.

As noted throughout this book, there are signs that a correction is already underway. In recent years, courts have stepped forward to circumscribe the publication of even truthful stories, to protect even public figures from unwanted press intervention in highly newsworthy stories, and have exposed media to new curbs by recognizing a tort remedy for false light, while withdrawing previous safeguards for journalists such as the reporter's privilege. Even in the expansive funeral protest case, the Supreme Court noted that there could well be a different outcome for targeted emotionally harmful speech.

And in some places, the bubble has apparently contracted to at least the time of Warren and Brandeis's "The Right to Privacy." In 2013, a federal trial court in New York quoted a case from 1893, one written well more than a century before, during a time when newspapers lacked significant ethics guidance (and the same case relied upon by a 2013 Massachusetts federal appeals court that had earlier limited access to criminal sentencing documents). The federal trial court complained about media's use of public records for what it considered improper purposes and worried that access to such records would give the media the ability to—quoting the much earlier court—promote public scandal and lead to "sensationalized and potentially out-of-context" reporting.[54] While the New York court limited news access to documents in a criminal case, the much older case had merely suggested that some information regarding a divorce should be private.

Media would do well to head off a calamitous collapse of the First Amendment bubble by yielding some ground in their insistence on press autonomy and developing strong self-restraint, both in their reporting practices and in their claims of constitutional privilege. The following chapter offers more concrete suggestions.

8

Drawing Difficult Lines

In 1956, William Prosser, the scholar whose research shaped the way we define privacy wrongs today, suggested that legal protection against intentional infliction of emotional distress was receiving greater acceptance in the nation's courts as a freestanding tort.

He noted that the law in general often changed in response to social conditions, as it had with the acceptance of the tort of intentional infliction of emotional distress. There, interest in protecting individuals from emotional harm began to trump concern rooted in First Amendment freedom of expression when the challenged actions were horrendous enough. "[A]s in many other hard cases," Prosser wrote, "the enormity of the outrage overthrew the settled rule of law."[1]

We again stand at the beginning of a realignment of First Amendment freedoms sparked by outrage. Indeed, it appears that the realignment is already underway.

Despite early years of deference, some outraged courts have moved away from more absolutist notions of First Amendment protection and have subjected journalists and quasi-journalists to greater scrutiny and legal control. Suddenly, it seems, the sweeping definition for newsworthiness that once gave journalists virtual immunity for disclosing private information has narrowed, putting even well-accepted crime coverage at risk. The once highly protective Communications Decency Act may well no longer immunize all website owners from posts created by others, and celebrities have new legal rights to keep photographers at bay even when they are in a public place.

In each of those examples, the enormity of the outrage overthrew what had been the settled rule of law. And in each of those examples, it happened—at least in part—in the name of privacy.

Yet, some journalists and other First Amendment advocates add to the peril by clinging at times to claims of absolute First Amendment privilege and by seeking to extend the boundaries of press rights to cover an ever-expanding universe of bloggers, activists, web merchants, provocateurs, and other quasi-journalistic publishers. Given that a loss of faith in media's own capacity for self-control seems to be a root cause of the courts' new assertiveness, the belief that media can do as media pleases only confirms that suspicion.

This is, therefore, not a time for First Amendment absolutism. Instead, the path to saving journalism from yet more draconian intervention to come is, as Justice White suggested in his *Florida Star* dissent, to begin the process of drawing lines somewhere above the bottom. Scaling back media's claims of First Amendment immunity, and rebuilding faith in the journalism profession's capacity to rein in its own and, hopefully, others, provides the best hope of avoiding a potentially disastrous collapse of journalism's First Amendment bubble.

To draw those lines, journalists need to begin making hard choices in the way they conduct their business, as well as in the ways that they define themselves and their craft. In this era of media pushback and increased privacy protections, they must tread more carefully in their news choices, and they must also refuse to be led along blindly by unethical publishers who call for continually extending press rights to shield every conceivable disclosure of information, no matter the source and no matter the resulting harm. Quasi-journalism, in a legal sense, has harmed mainstream journalism far more than helped. Rod Smolla, a First Amendment scholar, warned of this in 1998 when he wrote that the growth of tabloids would result in decreased overall First Amendment protections.[2] Because of wrongs on the Internet, that is coming true on a much grander scale—and for journalism to align itself with even more shocking push-the-envelope publishers in the name of freedom of the press or freedom of speech or freedom of expression will serve only to draw the lines more narrowly.

This means that courts will need to make difficult choices as well, drawing lines in a way that recognizes truthful expression's real harms while continuing to offer protection for some truthful, hurtful—but responsible and newsworthy—reporting. Such delineation is the first step toward a fairer and more sustainable constitutional protection, one that will protect journalism but will also help those who feel the Internet's sting.

This final chapter looks at what journalism, quasi-journalistic publishers, and courts must consider as the difficult process of line drawing begins. It emphasizes some ideas collectively, including definitions for terms such as "newsworthiness" and "journalist," and a lessening of Communications Decency Act protection, but it also offers more focused recommendations, including the ways journalism might help teach nonjournalists appropriate publishing and how courts might better consider the impact of their decisions on the media and ultimately the public.

It begins with perhaps this book's most controversial point: that journalism is special, important, and basically good.

Journalism Is Special and Important and Deserving of Protection

Throughout its history, the U.S. Supreme Court has shown that it mostly understands the craft of journalism and its, at times, necessary sting. As early as 1845, the Court noted that candidates for public office put their character at issue and suggested that "publications of truth on [the] subject, with the honest intention of informing the people" were not unlawful since such matters were in the public interest.[3] There were some bumpy periods around the time of "The Right to Privacy," including prohibitions on stories regarding executions[4] and paranoia about the "evil" of moving picture newsreels that were, the wary Justices suggested, "more insidious in corruption" than printed news.[5] But, for the most part, the Court has credited journalism even when it caused some harm. We might regret "miscreant purveyors of [truthful] scandal," the Court wrote in 1931, but to suppress stories of malfeasance was an "even more serious public evil."[6]

By the 1960s, then, when the Court began its string of memorable rhetorical flourishes that credited journalism with the promotion of democracy and other nation-building work, there was a firm foundation for journalism's news choices. In 1964, in *New York Times v. Sullivan*, the Court rationalized protection for some falsehoods that would include even perhaps abusive "vehement, caustic, and sometimes unpleasantly sharp attacks on government and public officials" because First Amendment press freedoms require "breathing space" and that without such protection a "pall of fear and timidity" and press self-censorship would occur.[7] Three years later, the Court recognized that we live in a society in which some will suffer some exposure but noted that the risk of that exposure "is an essential incident of life in a society which places a primary value on freedom of speech and of press."[8] Moreover, it wrote, freedom of the press should be broadly defined because a broad definition "assures the maintenance of our political system and an open society."[9]

The reason the press deserved such freedom, the court reminded in *Sullivan*, is that it is critical to democracy: "[T]he people of this nation have ordained in the light of history, that, in spite of the probability of excesses and abuses, these liberties are, in the long view, essential to enlightened opinion and right conduct on the part of the citizens of a democracy," it wrote. In the 1970s, too, in the Pentagon Papers case, after the Court's short per curium opinion, Justice Black credited journalism with great courage that had helped develop the nation:

> In the First Amendment the Founding Fathers gave the free press the protection it must have to fulfill its essential role in our democracy. . . . The press was protected so that it could bare the secrets of government and inform the people. Only a free and unrestrained press can effectively expose deception in government. And paramount among the responsibilities of a free press is the duty to prevent any part of the government from deceiving the people and sending them off to distant lands to die of foreign fevers and foreign shot and shell. In my view, far from deserving condemnation for their courageous reporting . . . newspapers should be commended for serving the purpose that the Founding Fathers saw so clearly. In revealing the workings of government that led to the Vietnam war, the newspapers nobly did precisely that which the Founders hoped and trusted they would do.[10]

In line with that language, in the 1980s, the Court again reminded that " '[An] untrammeled press [is] a vital source of public information,' and an informed public is the essence of working democracy."[11]

Seemingly smitten with journalism, then, the newsworthiness determinations to which the Justices deferred included not only the names of rape victims, but information from juvenile hearings and the names of juvenile offenders, a class traditionally protected not only in law but also in journalism.[12] By the 1990s, the Washington Supreme Court synthesized the Justices' holdings and found no qualification: "[I]n order to uphold the circulation of ideas," the Washington court wrote, "the editors of a newspaper must be free to exercise editorial control and discretion."[13]

Journalism, then, may be criticized for blindly focusing on its at times laudatory treatment in the Supreme Court, but that is understandable: the Court throughout history has often written that journalism is special. The Justices have deferred to journalism and its news choices not only to further democracy, but also, seemingly, because of the distinctive nature of journalism as a profession. They and other judges that followed knew that journalists brought expertise and discretion to the tasks of newsgathering and news reporting that judges or other members of the public were less likely to share.

Journalism's special status extends in most states and some federal courts to the constitutional and statutory idea of a reporter's privilege. It extends to some freedom-of-information statutory provisions that give the press certain, arguably special acknowledgment because of its work on behalf of the people, and it extends in some states to offer unique procedural rights when the press is named as a defendant.[14] With regard to newsworthiness, too, recall that the Second Restatement of Torts suggests that "publishers and broadcasters have themselves defined the term."[15] News, at least as it currently stands in a legal sense, is what newspeople say it is—so much so that the Restatement authors suggest that First Amendment interests could well make the publication-of-private-facts tort unconstitutional to the extent that it invites judicial second-guessing of reporters' news judgment.

In a 2012 report, Columbia University Journalism School's Tow Center for Digital Journalism focused on journalism's extraordinary work in explaining why it holds such a special status:

> Journalism exposes corruption, draws attention to injustice, holds politicians and businesses accountable for their promises and duties. It informs citizens and consumers, helps organize public opinion, explains complex issues and clarifies essential disagreements. Journalism plays an irreplaceable role in both democratic politics and market economies.

First Amendment scholar and president of Columbia University Lee Bollinger too has written that journalism is "suffused with a strong sense of mission to serve the public interest," "largely able to maintain editorial independence" from commercial interests, and, therefore, is and should be "shielded by a constitutional cocoon of protection from the legal accountability" that other businesses face.[16]

It is that sort of audacious work that has led the powerful in other countries to try to suppress journalism. According to a United Nations report, fewer than 14 percent of people around the world live in a place like the United States where "coverage of political news is robust, the safety of journalists is guaranteed, state intrusion in media affairs is minimal, and the press is not subject to onerous legal or economic pressures." The report suggested that from 2011 to 2012, 127 journalists were killed on the job worldwide, most murdered by those who did not want stories written. It also suggested that resulting press freedoms around the world had suffered significant declines in recent years. "Attacks on journalists are an attack on the freedoms of opinion and expression and the public's right to know," the UN report maintained, and "society suffers."[17]

And no matter how many citizen journalists or quasi-journalists exist in a given town, and no matter how strongly some should be commended for their work on behalf of their readers, most will not have the same access to government insiders, to public officials and public figures, to foreign travel, or the time or money to report more complex and important stories.[18] They may try to pick up the reporting slack as mainstream publications wither, but with a lack of resources and, sometimes, credibility, they will be limited in what they can achieve.

That means that, when mainstream news leaves town, citizens do not know as much as they otherwise would. In 2009, the director of the Pew Research Center's Project for Excellence in Journalism suggested that as newspapers die, more important information is kept and left in darkness. "More of American life now occurs in shadow [a]nd we cannot know what we do not know," Tom Rosenstiel, executive director of the American Press Institute, testified at a congressional hearing about journalism's future.[19] The *Christian Science Monitor* too noted significant repercussions when newspapers left particular towns, finding multiple examples of government and other corruption that took years to uncover once the watchdog newspaper ceased to be.[20] And a study by a Tulane University communications professor found a slackening of ambitious reporting and an increase in "lighter subjects such as sports and entertainment, as opposed to politics, education, courts and other traditional core newspaper beats" in New Orleans after the *Times-Picayune* newspaper slashed its experienced reporting staff and abandoned daily print editions for greater reliance on digital reporting.[21]

Not surprisingly, then, and as suggested both explicitly and implicitly by the Supreme Court in its jurisprudence, when mainstream news media falters, some community citizenship dies. The *Christian Science Monitor* story pointed to two different studies that show that published newspapers are particularly important support for democratic vitality:

> New research suggests that fewer people vote after their communities lose a daily print newspaper. Fewer run for office. Fewer boycott—or buy— something based on what they think of a company's values. Fewer contact public leaders to voice opinions. Fewer pitch in with neighborhood groups. More incumbent politicians get reelected.

In other words, there is a special place for the regular mainstream press in the hearts and minds of the public that apparently cannot otherwise be filled: mainstream journalism teaches more people about government and, apparently, makes them care. It is, as courts note, "the eyes and ears of the public."[22]

Economically healthy newspapers also help protect the constitutional rights of everyone. Media law scholar RonNell Andersen Jones has shown that when news media have taken First Amendment cases to court, often to the highest levels, they have helped to protect First Amendment rights more generally. The death of newspapers in the United States, she has argued, will likely result not only in fewer efforts to demand government accountability and accessibility, but also in weakened rights to expression for all.[23]

And finally, at least for now, some mainstream journalism has the economic strength to back important stories. ProPublica, for example, an independent, nonprofit news organization, recently put at $750,000 the amount it took to uncover and report a story about the dangers of acetaminophen. The story took two years; editors and reporters believed it was worth significant costs because it saved lives.[24] It is difficult to imagine an independent citizen journalist who would be economically capable of doing a similar level of reporting.

"Usually dirty secrets must be 'found out,'" a report on media access by the Federal Communications Commission admitted in 2011, "and the people who are most likely to have the time, independence and skills for the job are full-time professionals: police, prosecutors—and reporters."[25] A former reporter for the *Baltimore Sun* would agree. He testified before Congress and predicted that for the next ten or fifteen years, "[i]t is going to be one of the great times to be a corrupt politician" in the United States.[26] Without mainstream journalists' work, he suggested, corruption in government will grow.

Given the remarkable role a journalist plays in the community—described by one author as "the member of the tribe" who, in part, "is sent to the back of the cave to report what is there" for the good of others[27]—and the apparent link between a robust democracy and mainstream journalism, many fear newspapers' demise for reasons that go far beyond the ability to read a daily morning paper.

Journalism Is Not That Special and Journalists Must Act Accordingly

That said, the U.S. Supreme Court has emphasized that "[t]he First Amendment does not grant the press . . . limitless protection"[28] and noted that it, as a court, has "consistently rejected the proposition that the institutional press has any constitutional privilege beyond that of other speakers."[29] However essential the role of the press may be to a well-functioning democracy, it must be held to respect the rights of others much like any other member of society.

As an example, in 1972, a television news crew in Ohio traveled to a local county fair to do a report on a man who called himself the Human Cannonball. The event was decidedly newsworthy; it is not every day that a man launches himself from a cannon. The nightly newscast featured a fifteen-second video clip of the Human Cannonball—from his launch to his landing. What was news to the journalists, however, was an intellectual property violation to the Human Cannonball. Who would pay to see him launch himself in person if the newscast instead gave viewers a front row seat for free?

The press rights/property rights case made it to the Supreme Court—and the Court, led by Justice White, sided with the Cannonball.[30] "Wherever the line in particular situations is to be drawn between media reports that are protected and those that are not," the opinion read, "we are quite sure that the First . . . Amendment[] do[es] not immunize the media when they broadcast a performer's entire act without his consent." The Court, displaying either ignorance or sarcasm given journalism's ethics rules against buying stories, suggested instead that an interested news station simply pay to report on the Human Cannonball's act.

A few years later, in another Justice White opinion, the Court held that a newspaper that had promised confidentiality to a source and then had later published the source's name could be held liable for breaching its promise.

Any notion that the press might enjoy exemption from any law "which in any fashion or to any degree limits or restricts the press' right to report truthful information" was incorrect, Justice White wrote for the Court.[31] There are other examples.[32]

Despite its special constitutional standing and its important place in a democratic order, then, the press is not completely free in seeking and publishing the truth, even when the truth relates to matters of public interest. This book is full of examples from lower courts, both trial and appellate, that span the country. The 1977 Restatement may suggest that news media themselves get to decide what is newsworthy, and Gawker may with certainty claim as much, but many of today's courts have the temerity to disagree in cases ranging from mug shots to court hearings and from baseball team photos to troubleshooter television news segments.

Moreover, news media today has lost significant ground regarding reasons for deference. Modern trends in journalism, including the blurring of news and entertainment, what some see as the competitive race to the bottom in allowing market demand to dictate news coverage, instantaneous posts without editorial review, and the willingness of traditional news media to welcome bloggers and other untrained citizen journalists and quasi-journalists into their fold, have made the claim to journalism's special expertise more tenuous. That deference is now slipping away in the courts is not only because privacy has become profoundly important but also because journalists are becoming profoundly underprotective of their own distinctive identity and responsibilities as a profession.

Meantime, people today are turning to the mainstream media less than before because they trust it less. In Spring 2013, a Gallup Poll showed that those who professed "a great deal" of confidence in newspapers had slipped to 23 percent, continuing a downward trend from 51 percent in the late 1970s.[33]

Media attorney Bruce Sanford has called that discord a "canyon of disbelief and distrust" between the public (including judges) and media, one he suggests started in the 1980s.[34] "A golden age that for fifty years saw the creation and expansion of a First Amendment right of the public to receive information has concluded," he warned at the turn of the end of the twentieth century, noting that the public's anger and resentment was also being reflected in court decisions.

It does not seem that things will turn around much. A Fall 2013 survey predicted a "perilous future for news" as younger audiences showed little indication that they would change their minds to suddenly acquire a bigger appetite for mainstream journalism.[35] "Younger generations just don't enjoy following news," one of the subheadlines in an article about the survey read.

Today it is possible to watch the shift away from the mainstream in a digitized map measuring consumption of internet media in real time across the United States.[36] *Forbes,* one of the map's sponsors, introduced it by writing, "Oregonians love NPR; Wisconsinites adore the Onion; the Huffington Post is widely read in Appalachia."[37] The article noted that traditional newspapers were finding it difficult to break into the increasingly national market for information despite the ease of internet publishing, and in October 2013 the map revealed as much. The task proved not so difficult for the Onion, however, a mock news site that features headlines like "God Reveals He Occasionally Eats Humans." In October 2013, the Onion was the leading online-only news source in 15 states.

Watching the internet media traffic also shows how diffuse media is today; if a reader or a viewer is dissatisfied, there are many, many other options. On the digitized map, each news outlet is given a different color designation and a new media hit showed up as a different color. The map lit up like a multicolored Christmas tree.

As one of the nation's top First Amendment attorneys explained in his *Communications Lawyer* article about selling the First Amendment to a jury, courts and citizens today do not share the same awe that they once had for the press—and they are less enamored with the First Amendment as well.[38] The press may retain a special status for some legal purposes, but Americans do not necessarily see it that way.

Journalism would be wise, then, to recognize that the Supreme Court has, at times, refused to treat it as special and different from any other speaker. If Judge Mikva is correct, such a superior attitude and its resulting confidence in publishing have led to a pushback from courts and could, perhaps, lead to a greater calamity to come. Journalists would be wise to yield some ground and demonstrably practice self-restraint, as suggested in this chapter and elsewhere, both in their claims of constitutional privilege and in the ways they report stories.

Not Everything Is Newsworthy and
the Law Must Reflect That

At the end of 2012, a CNN news story focused on secrets.[39] The story was headlined, "Shhh . . . Some Secrets You Might Need to Keep." The reporter interviewed a number of experts who told her that everyone has secrets; the experts suggested that the wish to keep some things private was simply a part of the human condition. "Shame, fear of embarrassment or fear of not being accepted often are the motivation behind keeping something secret," the reporter wrote.

And then she—or someone else at CNN—added in italics at the end of the story: "Are you holding on to a secret? Tell us in the comments."

That contextually incongruous demand, that secrets are good but that readers should reveal theirs in the comments, did not go unnoticed: "Kind of counter to the main thesis of the article, isn't it?," one of the first commenters asked.[40]

The information within the story itself about the psychic value of secrecy was newsworthy, though timeless. The concluding encouragement that readers confess their private tales online, perhaps including the intimacies of others, was the sort of provocative baiting that has the potential to push through the protections of the Communications Decency Act.

Moreover, would such comments be news themselves? Would it be newsworthy that an everyday person had a venereal disease or had cheated on a spouse? The Restatement authors would likely say no, that a comment about an everyday person's health affliction or love affair is not newsworthy. The 1977 Second Restatement of Torts may define news broadly to include even things that are "of more or less deplorable popular appeal,"[41] but it draws the line at "morbid and sensational prying for its own sake."[42] The latter seems to cover much that could be reported about the private life of an average citizen.

And yet the answer is not completely clear. In 1977, when the Restatement privacy provisions were written, media could be trusted to be more circumspect. Restatement authors, therefore, focused much more on media freedoms than on an individual's personal right to be let alone; the Restatement does not consider at length the emotional well-being of a story's human subject, other than circumscribing non-newsworthy "offensive" material.

Today, given that focus, Gawker's first response was to raise a First Amendment newsworthiness defense when it published the Hogan sex tape. If a court had asked, Gawker would likely have pointed to its four million views as evidence of the tape's "more or less deplorable popular appeal." Thus, at least in theory, newsworthiness might well be proved by the story's apparent market.

But so too could newsworthiness be proved by the supposed 30,000-in-a-day views of the nude photographs of the Pennsylvania woman on MyEx.com.

To avoid such pitfalls from an overbroad definition for newsworthiness, consider the following language that attempts to draw a different line between newsworthy stories and those that invade privacy excessively. Here, unlike traditional privacy law jurisprudence in the United States,[43] the language alerts the court to the importance of a human dignity consideration. By focusing on dignity in conjunction with news values, it attempts to recognize the very real harm that some publications, even those with large readerships, can cause. But it also attempts to give news media support in close cases through a strong presumption of newsworthiness:

> Because the Supreme Court has warned courts to be "chary of deciding what is and what is not news,"[44] the publication of any truthful information is presumptively newsworthy and of public interest and, therefore, is protected from tort-based and related claims. This presumption of newsworthiness may be overcome only in truly exceptional cases, when the degradation of human dignity caused by the disclosure clearly outweighs the public's interest in the disclosure.

Publications that degrade human dignity could thereafter be described to include those that involve depictions of sex, nudity, deeply private or deeply embarrassing medical conditions, private expressions of grief, and other similar parts of humanness generally not exposed to others. They could include aspects of what most would consider private life not revealed in public by the plaintiff and that private information that is generally protected by tradition in the United States. To paraphrase one federal appeals court, a successful privacy-related action here, therefore, would include those intimate details, the revelation of which is not merely embarrassing but deeply shocking.[45]

Moreover, newsworthiness here would be a question of law and, therefore, one for the court. The burden of proof regarding the degradation of human dignity, the lack of public interest in the matter, and the exceptional nature of the case at bar would be the plaintiff's.

Here, concern for human dignity plays an important role, but so does the value of truth, for some the most important of values.[46] Therefore, dignity interests trump a truthful news item only when those dignity interests clearly outweigh public interest in the material—an exceptional case. Such a presumption would help alleviate concerns like those expressed by privacy law scholar Neil Richards and others about inconsistent results that result from too-subjective privacy standards.[47] To that end too, the decision would be one of law and would be made by a judge who best understands the strength of a presumption.

If such or similar language were accepted by courts, stories like the Hulk Hogan sex tape would, in fact, be presumptively newsworthy, but concerns for his dignity in an area traditionally shrouded in privacy in the United States would trump public interest in the material. (Indeed, even as the Hogan case continued, a very certain New York court wrote in an unrelated case that "posting an explicit sex tape cannot be . . . newsworthy . . ."[48]) A court deciding a publication-of-private-facts case under the definition here would not weigh the "popular appeal" of such a publication against its "morbid and sensational prying," in contrast with current law, but, instead, would be forced to consider the importance of the human dignity involved.

In the *Conradt* case example, in contrast, because the arrest of a prosecutor on child sex solicitation charges would be presumptively newsworthy, a court would be forced to consider quite carefully not only human dignity but the implications of a decision against media, implications that would evade the country's important and longstanding tradition of crime coverage, especially as regarding public officials. The prosecutor's dignity would weigh in the balance, but would not clearly outweigh the news value in the arrest of a prominent law enforcement official for a sex crime against children. In other words, *Conradt* would not be the exceptional case in which dignity-related notions of privacy outweigh news value.

Considerations of human dignity are, admittedly, a part of certain European privacy laws.[49] In Germany, for example, the law reads that "[h]uman dignity shall be in violable" and dignity is prioritized above other fundamental rights.[50] The European Convention on Human Rights offers protection for "private and family life"; Article 8 maintains that "everyone has the right to respect for his private and family life, his home and his correspondence."[51]

Such broad privacy protections, however, despite some additional First Amendment-like language regarding free expression, led a European court to decide that famous model Naomi Campbell had a valid claim against a newspaper for publishing photographs of her leaving a drug treatment center.[52] Princess Caroline of Monaco, too, successfully sued for photographs taken of her in public, shopping and vacationing with her family.[53] Pressures favoring dignity more than press freedoms in Europe make photographs of the German Chancellor's family life unusual and their publication scandalous for media,[54] and they create liability known as "parasitism" for the publication of photographs taken at a public fashion show.[55] They similarly emboldened France's president to threaten to sue on invasion-of-privacy grounds when a magazine published a photograph of him outdoors paying a social call on an actress who was not his long-time girlfriend considered the First Lady of France;[56] the actress herself later successfully sued for invasion of privacy based upon the publication of similar outdoor photographs and won the equivalent of $20,000 in damages.[57] And in 2014, in a right to be forgotten-like ruling, a European court held that Google could be forced to remove links regarding a man's past that caused him embarrassment; the links had led to information regarding financial difficulties from approximately fifteen years before.[58]

So strong is the sense that protection against media is needed, legal scholar Gavin Phillipson has explained, some scholars in Britain now question whether truth should remain a viable defense to libel claims,[59] an exception that has existed there for centuries. "EU nations," one media attorney put succinctly, "have been willing to give their citizens a right to control information about themselves."[60]

Those examples from Europe reveal the dangers of an excessive focus on dignity to the seeming exclusion of information of public interest. Under the language helping to guide newsworthiness determinations put forth earlier here, in contrast, the presumption would favor newsworthiness and it is likely that not one of them would be the basis for a successful privacy-based claim in the United States.

Meantime, news media would also necessarily need to embrace considerations of dignity to avoid liability and a further loss of their First Amendment freedoms. Such attention would not be completely foreign; it would merely sharpen the focus on dignity as a limit on disclosure. Presently, the Society of Professional Journalist's code contains a number of directives related to the dignity of news subjects, but it does not expressly recognize dignity as a counterweight to news value. Recall that the current code directs broadly that journalists "minimize harm" in their reporting and states that "[e]thical journalists treat sources, subjects and colleagues as human beings deserving of respect." It also urges journalists to "[s]how compassion for those who may be affected adversely by news coverage," to "show good taste" and "[a]void pandering to lurid curiosity," and to "recognize that gathering and reporting information may cause harm or discomfort." The code thus recognizes the potential human costs of newsgathering and reporting and suggests strongly that journalists minimize those costs in pursuit of news.

As regarding those provisions, however, reporters could currently rationalize their obligations as requiring only that they impose no gratuitous harm in reporting a newsworthy story. The code does not clearly acknowledge that dignity-related costs might properly suggest that a story of public interest not be reported at all.

An important media ethics textbook for college students, *Media Ethics*, suggests that journalism's dignity consideration be defined this way: "Dignity [is] leaving the subject of a story with as much self-respect as possible."[61] That is far too broad and too subjective to be definitional in a legal sense; indeed, as suggested here, the law should not protect dignity at all costs but should instead focus on what has traditionally been sheltered or protected for dignity-related reasons. Such mention by name nonetheless helps provide evidence of journalism's strong ethical interests in the preservation of human dignity.

The news media tasked with weighing the costs of their disclosures to human dignity would necessarily include producers of reality programs that currently push the envelope of propriety and, arguably, law. Television shows that use gut-wrenchingly invasive 9-1-1 calls, for example, without explicit permission from those featured, would potentially be liable, as would true-crime programs that feature wailing family members who have just learned that a loved one was murdered or those showcasing the agony of mentally ill hoarders who, at times, seem to have little or no capacity to waive their privacy rights. Legally, under the definition here, those publications would be presumed newsworthy, but plaintiffs could well convince a court that harm to their individual dignity had clearly exceeded the public value of such disclosure.

In an ethics sense, such a focus on human dignity could well lead news publishers to follow the lead of some others in mainstream media to put an end to some reader comments,[62] especially those after news stories that will obviously invite defamatory or privacy-invading posts, even though the law as it currently stands would likely not require it.

Such line drawing to determine newsworthiness is difficult, to be sure. Those inclined toward more absolutist conceptions of the First Amendment may protest that a balancing test of any sort inevitably opens the door to an endless whittling away of protected rights. That objection, however, presumes that an absolutist conception of press rights remains a viable alternative. In reality, the social, technological, and market forces that have combined to expand enormously the scope of claimed First Amendment rights have made an absolutist conception increasingly untenable. Striking the balance between the societal values in truthful information and individual privacy rights is unavoidable. Making that balance point more transparent and more properly focused on human dignity, with a heavy presumption on the side of disclosure, could help channel editorial judgment constructively and, by providing a remedy for the worst breaches, relieve pressure from the increasingly fragile bubble of First Amendment protection.

Finally, it seems important here to address what some might consider a profound irony: that a distrust of jury review of news judgments seems to coexist with an expansive definition for news based in part upon information that is of interest to the public. Deciding what news is fit to print, however, is not only a matter of confirming a public appetite for it (web sites like BestGore.com, for example, a website that promises readers "[i]ncredibly [g]raphic [v]ideo" and "[i]mage and [m]ovie [g]alleries of [b]lood," confirm that there is a public appetite for almost anything), it requires an examination of countervailing values. Newsworthiness as it stands today is a delicate balance between press freedoms and privacy considerations that can be difficult for jurors, especially in a case involving a highly sympathetic plaintiff with a claim against a giant media corporation. The nature of the legal process, therefore, leaves significant risks that the very small sample of the public composing a jury may be readily swayed against the press when the privacy costs of a newsworthy story are instantiated in an individual.

Even Difficult Stories Are Newsworthy, However

"News is something someone somewhere doesn't want printed," a British newspaper pioneer once wrote.[63]

In the case of U.S. privacy law, of course, the someones who would not want things published include government officials, those convicted or accused of crimes, those involved in accidents, those running for office, celebrities, and many more. The items that they would rather keep private include incidents of crime and mishaps, politicians' gaffes, and celebrity gossip that may not interest all but would surely interest some. Nonetheless, news outlets have traditionally reported such information without legal trouble. These stories may be difficult or distasteful for some, but, by tradition and otherwise, they add to our understanding of culture and community.

A description of news in the context of U.S. privacy law, therefore, cannot be limited to disclosures that are *costless* to human dignity because that would suppress the publication of anything that would anger or embarrass or upset another. If news reporters were bound to consider only the feelings of news subjects, for example, stories such as those concerning Elliot Spitzer, the New York Attorney General who dallied with prostitutes, or Congressman Anthony Weiner, the prolific "sexter," would remain unknown even though both were public officials. To many, those stories are not simple sensationalism meant to drive up newspaper sales or website clicks, they are revelations that provide invaluable insights into the true character of politicians. In Weiner's case, this would include his wildly reckless indiscretions, and, in Spitzer's case, his calculated lawbreaking.

Recognizing that a definition for news and newsworthiness must be broad enough to cover those times in which someone is harmed by the publication of information, consider the following language meant to supplement the provision that would presume newsworthiness. These additions address some specific concerns noted throughout this book and are meant to guide especially those judges who might be inclined to more strongly focus on human dignity and privacy interests:

- For an item to be newsworthy, it need not be something that the public needs to know, but merely information in which some members of the public are interested. News, in keeping with its traditional definition, includes "crimes, arrests, police raids, suicides, marriages and divorces, accidents, fires, catastrophes of nature" and their victims, "a death from the use of narcotics, a rare disease, the birth of a child to a twelve-year-old girl, the reappearance of one supposed to have been murdered years ago, [and] a report to the police concerning the escape of a wild animal."[64] This is not an exhaustive list but it recognizes that even early courts saw value in community knowledge of crime and other information of public *interest* not necessarily of public *need*. Judges must resist the temptation to determine news value based upon on their own sensibilities and the news they might consume themselves, and remember the Supreme Court's admonition that judges often have a different sense of newsworthiness than does the public.[65]

- Information from public records, from public sources, and as regarding public officials is of public interest and, barring the exceptional case, not private. An example of newsworthy public information is an arrest with supporting material that includes a mug shot, which, traditionally in U.S. law, is both of public interest and of public record. Crime coverage warns others but also makes them aware of important overarching issues that affect community, including racial profiling and drug-related violence. The Supreme Court has noted that even tawdry crime coverage deserves protection, writing that though some community members may see "nothing of any possible value to society" in such coverage, it is still "entitled to the protection of free speech as the best of literature."[66]

- Matters that are of public interest will sometimes necessarily invade certain aspects of personal privacy, even when the person who is the focus of a news story is an otherwise private figure and even when the information does not come from a public record. In these cases, if the information is true, newsworthiness is presumed and, except in the extraordinary case in which the plaintiff is able to overcome that presumption, the news value in the story protects the publisher from liability. One example of this is an accident that is of public interest despite a family's tragedy and turmoil. While the publication of certain dignity-protective information regarding such an accident will potentially cause some additional emotional distress, such knowledge makes individuals within the community safer and could well inspire others to act to make it so collectively.

- Political scandal of all types, too, is generally of public interest and newsworthy as it directly or at times indirectly involves those elected by or under consideration for election by the people. This would include scandals such as criminal behavior by public officials, but also dignity-protective, non-invasive coverage of personal scandal as well, such as a politician's love affair, especially but not exclusively when the politician's behavior is hypocritical in some way.

- If dignity-protective, information regarding Hollywood and other celebrities is also newsworthy. Such stories amuse and entertain, but they also expose the culture of Hollywood and of celebrity and give the community fuller information about lifestyles of those who have chosen careers dependent upon community attention.
- Information once made public retains its news value in future years, lest members of the community, including community publications, be forced into silence, ordered in effect to forget or erase from their minds truthful information of public interest published in the past.
- Examples such as these and others help promote truth, an important legal and societal interest. This is why a truthful story is necessarily presumptively newsworthy.

Such language is also meant to help those publishers who may similarly be inclined to focus on human dignity to the exclusion of public interest. Those publishers will recognize that they can indeed cause some level of emotional harm through their necessary reporting and that the law as described will not hold them liable.

Here, the definition for newsworthiness is broad, but in *Snyder v. Phelps*, the funeral protest case, the Supreme Court in 2011 seemed to suggest in dicta that it would continue to define news broadly today. The Justices there focused on public *interest* rather than on a public *need* to know, admittedly with some qualifying language: "a subject of legitimate news interest," the court wrote in the case that had very little to do with news coverage, is one "of general interest and of value and concern to the public" and, they added, even the "inappropriate or controversial character" of such a publication is "irrelevant to the question whether it deals with a matter of public concern."[67] The language can certainly be read to be limited only to news stories of "value" and "concern," but its focus on public interest over public need—and its inclusion of inappropriate or controversial material within the definition—suggests that the Court may well continue its more expansive definition for news when it one day decides where to draw the line between newsworthiness and privacy interests.

All of this is also why any court's use of journalism's aspirational ethics codes against journalism is wrong both in a constitutional sense and in a practical sense. Not only does the Court's broad definition for news seemingly include even stories that the public does not "need" to know (interestingly, that language had been stricken from a draft version of the revised SPJ code that was circulating in mid-2014), it would also include stories that seemingly lack compassion, stories that seem insensitive, stories not in good taste, and stories that seemed sparked by nothing more than lurid curiosity. Moreover, recall that the Court in 1989 explicitly refused to use any ethics code standard as sole proof against journalists in a defamation action, leading lower courts to call it settled law that expert testimony on journalism ethics standards was an inappropriate inquiry—even in cases in which the information that was published was false.[68]

Defining news in a broader sense—in a way that a journalist steeped in the traditional, ethics-abiding mainstream journalism world might well define it—would lead to news that is richer, more important, and, for some, more interesting. News would necessarily include stories that would do some emotional harm, as it has historically, both legally and journalistically. But, in conflict with some judges' suggestions that accidents are not newsworthy,[69] and despite some judges' handwringing concerns about coverage of waterskiing squirrels, such a definition would be broad enough to include those types of stories too: stories simply of public interest, including dangers within the community and including the sort of frivolous coverage that is of at least passing interest to some and may well give them reason to reach out to others to marvel at the silliness in the world. Journalists and quasi-journalists would not be chilled, other than when necessarily considering the human dignity at stake.

In his important book on media theory, *Understanding Media,* Marshall McLuhan recognized those benefits of news, credited journalism, and chided those who refuse to see news broadly. "Those who deplore the frivolity of the press and its natural form of group exposure and communal cleansing," he wrote with some humor, "simply ignore the medium and demand that it be a book, as it tends to be in Europe."[70]

United States courts may wish to keep that in mind when deciding a case involving newsworthiness, recognizing its reference to core First Amendment values and the promising end result. They may also wish to be reminded of it when others suggest that the United States look more strongly to Europe for help in determining what news stories in the States should be legally newsworthy.

McLuhan's musings can also help guide on another important front, one that echoes the quote that started this section: "Real news is bad news," he wrote, "bad news *about* somebody or bad news *for* somebody."[71]

Journalism Must Embrace Privacy

In *The Elements of Journalism,* a book subtitled "What Newspeople Should Know and the Public Should Expect,"[72] a "right to privacy" is mentioned in substance only once, in the context of a television station's "Bill of Rights" for viewers.[73] This placement reveals how privacy considerations naturally come second to news considerations within the minds of many journalists: "The list," the authors wrote of the station's Bill of Rights, "included a right to privacy with the explanation that 'our journalistic duty and the public's right to know often require us to place people and organizations in the news who don't wish to be there. We will never do so in a cavalier or insensitive fashion and will always consider privacy concerns as we weigh the importance of a story.'"

That mention in the textbook comes just after a section titled "Journalists have final say over news." Meantime, "public interest" receives seventeen mentions, most of which are of substance.

Consider too that the television station viewers' "Bill of Rights" noted in the book seems to give the journalist more rights to publish than it gives the subject of the news story his or her privacy. The privacy "right" at issue, after all, is the reporter's "duty" to report news that news subjects do not want them to report, appended with the secondary promise that reporters who work for the station will at least consider privacy concerns as they go.

In line with those examples, in *News Reporting and Writing,*[74] a different book used in journalism classes, privacy is covered as a potential tort claim against media, but consider the matter-of-factness within this paragraph:

Privacy Guideline[:] Here is a useful guide from a federal appeals court ruling:

A reporter or publication that gives publicity to the private life of a person is not subject to liability for unreasonable invasion of privacy if the material (1) is about a newsworthy person—who need not be an elected official or a celebrity—and (2) is not highly offensive to a reasonable person, one of ordinary sensibilities[,] and is of legitimate public concern.

It is of note that here too that the focus is on what the reporter may publish as opposed to what the reporter may not. The brief notation, moreover, would seem to favor the NBC journalists who had covered the story of the prosecutor who eventually killed himself, even though that case ended badly for the network.

It is true, of course, that these books on reporting are not the sole sources of journalism education and that they are often supplemented in even basic reporting classes with others that focus much more purposefully on privacy-centric matters. Moreover, in many journalism programs, ethics is taught as a freestanding course, so these texts would deliberately not cover such issues in depth. Nonetheless, they offer an important window into the way reporting is learned in the United States: with a decided focus on the news story itself rather than on the privacy and dignity interests of the news story's human subject.

Meantime, in contrast, and as noted earlier in Chapter 6, privacy is burgeoning in the outside world and in law. Though admittedly an imperfect measure, a Lexis database search of reported cases shows the word privacy mentioned in nearly 150,000 federal and state court decisions, with a decided uptick at about the year 2000.[75] First Amendment scholar Robert O'Neil, noting the same trend, has written that it was at the turn of the century that two things occurred: journalists found that they could no longer rely on the strong shield of the First Amendment and that "[t]he quest for protection of privacy reached unprecedented levels."[76]

Privacy in a legal sense has become of such great concern that even constitutional law scholar Erwin Chemerinsky has called on courts "to rediscover Warren and Brandeis's right to privacy."[77] He wrote in 2007 that the publication-of-private-facts tort was especially in need of growth, given the increased ability of others "to learn the most intimate and personal things about individuals." Sixteen years before, he had been much more focused on press rights, suggesting that courts would chill journalism if they attempted to decide news values themselves.[78] And a decade ago, even before revenge porn websites had made significant headlines, privacy law scholar Lior Jacob Strahilevitz suggested that courts develop "a more rigorous . . . notion of privacy for the purposes of the privacy torts," lest public revelation cause "catastrophic" damage to people who wished to keep information secret.[79]

Meantime, many law schools have added privacy-related courses to their curricula where, previously, the topic would have been covered at the end of a first-year torts course only if the professor had time or special interest. In 2005, privacy scholar Daniel Solove explained the reasons he supported the curricular change on a website for law professors:

The field is growing . . . big time. There are many new jobs in privacy law—
jobs at privacy advocacy organizations, most major companies, financial
institutions . . . health institutions . . . and the government. . . . Many new
laws are being passed regarding privacy, and cases involving these issues are
multiplying.[80]

He also explained there that the course could well be taught with a special
focus on "media and entertainment issues."

Many attorneys, therefore, are leaving law school today with a solid understanding of privacy law and media law shaped in large part by those outside
the journalism field. Those attorneys will likely feel at least somewhat confident in bringing privacy-based lawsuits against media in the future.

And, of course, privacy is a concern of the American people, those who
perhaps will one day find themselves the subjects of news coverage. The
increasing focus on privacy is understandable considering the results of a 2013
poll regarding invasions of cyber-privacy:

- 21 percent of internet users have had an e-mail or social networking account compromised or taken over by someone else without permission.
- 12 percent have been stalked or harassed online.
- 11 percent have had important personal information stolen such as their
  Social Security number, credit card, or bank account information.
- 6 percent have been the victim of an online scam and lost money.
- 6 percent have had their reputation damaged because of something that
  happened online.
- 4 percent have been led into physical danger because of something that
  happened online.[81]

Those experiences are understandable when one recognizes just how much
information about an individual is available for free or little cost on the
Internet. Many "people search" websites contain not only identifying information such as age and address, but also known relatives and, for a small fee,
areas of interest, presumably based upon magazine subscriptions or other pur-
chasable data. A background check, available to private investigators for a few
dollars, contains that information plus—in this author's case—a photograph
of the subject, her education, her home value, her political party (presumably
from primary voting records), the make and model of her vehicle, her relatives

and known "associates," including those who had purchased the subject's former homes and vehicles, and photographs and the layout of the interior of her home drawn from prior real-estate listings on the Internet.[82] Indeed, when it was reported that the National Security Administration had used "sophisticated graphs of some Americans' social connections that can identify their associates,"[83] those who had had background checks done in recent years were likely unsettled but quite unimpressed; private detectives and other individuals who could pay for it have had ready access to such information for years.

Given all this, the Society of Professional Journalists would do well to consider the addition of privacy-related values even more significantly in any new version of its code.

We Are Not All Journalists

Jay Rosen, the New York University journalism professor, is a strong proponent of citizen journalism. He defined the term in 2008 with a focus on journalism's tools: "When the people formerly known as the audience employ the press tools they have in their possession to inform one another," he wrote, "that's citizen journalism."[84]

Five years after that blog entry, Rosen was featured in the James O'Keefe internet video noted earlier. In it, O'Keefe used the tools of journalism including a video camera, sound equipment, editing tools, and a voiceover script and attempted to interview Rosen by phone regarding O'Keefe's status within the journalism world. O'Keefe may have been inspired because, despite Rosen's earlier expansive definition for journalist, Rosen had labeled O'Keefe not a journalist at all, but a "right wing trickster."[85]

The argument that everyone is a journalist considers that the "press" mentioned within the First Amendment can no longer be simply the mainstream press but must necessarily encompass all who publish. Today, there are few barriers to publishing, given that the Internet is available to all at home or at a library. Therefore, the reasoning goes, all who publish information for others' consumption are journalists. Constitutional law scholar Mary-Rose Papandrea, for one, has argued that many who disseminate important information should be protected by a qualified reporter's privilege as would a journalist,[86] a change that would likely increase important, robust reporting.

By welcoming *all* into the journalism fold, however, journalists must necessarily welcome those quasi-journalists who today push the limits of First

Amendment protection into places where courts and legislators would presumably never go. External or even internal ethics considerations that bind
mainstream media are of no or little concern to some who publish. To ensure,
then, that others can differentiate between the two groups, and in an effort to
maintain some level of protection for the press and its news decisions, journalists must work against the perception—and, in some cases, the reality—that
the two have become one. Allowing all within journalism's protective First
Amendment bubble as "press" also denigrates the strong work many in mainstream journalism do to inform the public. First Amendment and media law
scholar Sonja West, who believes that some delineation between publishers is
necessary, has called this press exceptionalism.[87]

Those who assert instead that everyone is a journalist miss the opportunity
to join the important dialogue that legislators and courts must necessarily
confront today. Recall that in 2013 and 2014 alone, a number of courts necessarily struggled with the definition in cases involving reporter's privilege statutes.[88] They also struggled with laws that limit police searches of newsrooms,[89]
and laws that give news media special jurisdictional procedural protection in
First Amendment-related cases.[90] In each, courts were forced to consider
whether those who argued that they were journalists actually were: a blogger
covering county politics (yes), a labor union of janitors (no), and the author of
what the court called a "web gripe site" (no). One of those courts complained
that, without some sort of delineation, "today's world of blogs, tumblrs, and
tweets" would give anyone the ability to "claim the mantra of reporter."

In 2013, too, in a mostly procedural opinion, a federal court in New Jersey
was asked to classify those who had left comments on a website not as sources
but as members of the "news media."[91] The court decided that they were not.
"[T]he character and substance of the postings at issue are more akin to an
information message board and web forum," the court wrote, "not geared
toward the dissemination of news." In the court's eyes, the anonymous postings, in contrast with more typical news from a mainstream source, "amounted
to nothing more than vague allegations in an informal forum discussion
without any indicia of reliability or substantiation." Posters, therefore, were
not members of the news media even though they had left their messages on
a "current news" webpage.

Consider again the reporter's privilege. In Illinois, the law protecting
reporters from having to testify reads: "No court may compel any person to

disclose the source of any information obtained by a reporter" except under certain circumstances,[92] and the word "reporter" is defined this way:

> "Reporter" means any person regularly engaged in the business of collecting, writing or editing news for publication through a news medium on a full-time or part-time basis; and includes any person who was a reporter at the time the information sought was procured or obtained.[93]

That definition may be too limited for some, but those people who do not like it lose the opportunity to redefine the term when they argue that everyone deserves such protection. It is highly unlikely that any legislature would agree to a provision that exempts everyone from having to testify simply because they have access to the Internet and have published something. Such an "exception" would swallow the whole.

Consider, instead, the following attempt at a definition:

> A journalist is one who publishes reliable and substantiated news and information in context meant for multiple others so that those others may learn things of interest about the community in which they live or about the persons who comprise the community. A journalist is not one who simply publishes self-interested musings or the papers or the documents of another; he or she focuses on information of interest to the public, analyzes the information contained within those papers or documents, and publishes that analysis. A publisher who follows a well-accepted ethics code or an ethics code based upon well-accepted principles is presumptively a journalist. Not everyone is a journalist, however, and most random publishers—even publishers of truth—are not.

Sonja West instead focuses on a journalist's workaday habits: The press, she suggests, are "speakers [who] devote time, resources, and expertise to the vital constitutional tasks of informing the public on newsworthy matters and providing a check on the government and the powerful."[94]

The Electronic Frontier Foundation, certainly no wallflower in the debate over free expression, has argued instead that "journalism" be defined. It praised a definition proposed by the U.S. House of Representatives during the debate over a federal shield law: "The term journalism," the proposed definition read, "means the gathering, preparing, collecting, photographing, recording, writing, editing, reporting, or publishing of news or information that concerns local, national, or international events or other matters of public interest for dissemination to the public."[95] Without such definition, the EFF wrote, "the outcome looks pretty grim for bloggers, freelancers, and other non-salaried journalists." It specifically called out Senator Diane Feinstein as "misguided" for suggesting that the privilege is due only "real reporters."[96]

But an editorial writer for the *San Francisco Chronicle*, highly likely a journalist, but perhaps not, depending upon its definition, championed Feinstein's distinction and criticized those who looked critically upon those legislators who proposed that "real reporters" are limited to those who "regularly" engage in journalism.[97] She wrote that she was angered when her paper called a man imprisoned for contempt for refusing to release his video to government investigators "the longest imprisoned journalist" in America:

> He was a self-described artist, activist and anarchist who recorded a 2005 demonstration against the World Trade Organization at which a protester broke the skull of San Francisco police officer Peter Shields. [He] was not a real reporter; he had no confidential-source agreement. He was an activist and an amateur who later became a real journalist when he was hired by a newspaper and had to adhere to professional standards.

Just as there must be some line of demarcation for "newsworthiness" beyond simple public interest if privacy is to enjoy some legal protection, and just as not everyone who offers legal advice is a lawyer, then, not everyone who publishes information—even truthful information of some broad interest—is a journalist. A limited definition for journalist, one that looks more critically at the person behind the publication, helps protect First Amendment principles by ensuring that special constitutional privileges are extended only to those playing the distinctive societal role that warrants them.

Even Jay Rosen, the strong proponent of citizen journalism, suggests that some sort of line drawing is necessary for the health of the mainstream press:

> We need to keep the press from being absorbed into The Media. This means keeping the word press, which is antiquated. But included under its modern umbrella should be all who do the serious work in journalism, regardless of the technology used.[98]

Lee Bollinger suggests the same sort of delineation, albeit with a focus on professionalism: "For the press to flourish, it must be an *institution*, and it must have a culture of journalism as a *profession*."[99]

The First Amendment and Related Principles Must Be Taught to All Publishers

When one of the nation's top First Amendment lawyers wrote the article about his attempts to sell the First Amendment to a jury, he advised others who defend media to begin with the premise that jurors care less today about First Amendment protections for news organizations than they did before.[100]

But he further explained that jurors seemed to respond well to a message based upon something other than flag-waving: that the press works hard to inform the public. "[T]he polestar by which you should navigate through the trial is the right of the people to be informed," he wrote, "which is the ultimate interest that the press should strive to serve" and likely something that some jurors had not considered strongly before. When those who defend media address the jury during closing arguments, he suggested the same: that they simply teach jurors that "First Amendment freedoms are of critical importance to the people, not just the press."

In other words, he believes that jurors ultimately respond well to First Amendment arguments if they can be made to appreciate how First Amendment values and journalism's principles have worked to help them better understand the world. He ended his article with the constitutionally hopeful message that "to teach [such principles] is to touch lives forever."

Journalists can attempt to do that work themselves. Instead of a First Amendment-headstrong and strident tone, they can teach in editorials and in actions the potential jurors who are their readers and viewers about their important service to the public—and well before any trial outcome is at stake. Moreover, in doing so, they will necessarily differentiate themselves from the other publishers considered quasi-journalists here.

There is another avenue of education. Journalism schools are in a unique position to teach such principles at the college level, just as citizens are being called to jury service for the first time and just as individualized attitudes and beliefs toward media and constitutional principles are being shaped. A class that would be an introduction to journalism and designed for those students outside journalism schools would help do that.

There is another reason such education is critical at the college level. Today, while not everyone in college or otherwise is a journalist, many if not most are at least Twitter, Instagram, Snapchat, or Facebook publishers and require legal and ethical guidance in making decisions regarding what to post. To

learn in college that there are repercussions for a harmful publishing decision—one that could well bankrupt an individual blogger—will help protect
all media against judicial opinions written broadly enough to circumscribe
that blogger and all the mainstream press.

Journalism schools are already equipped to do this. A typical media law
course, for example, necessarily touches upon ethics and a fair number of texts
actually combine media law and journalism ethics.[101] Through such course-
based outreach, not only would journalism itself potentially benefit from fewer
court decisions against it, journalism departments would benefit from
increased revenue and more diverse voices in discussions regarding appropriate coverage.

In doing so, however, those who teach media law must recognize the
importance of incorporating lower court opinions or the ideas and holdings
within them into the syllabus and not be blinded by older Supreme Court
rhetoric. Today, the flowery language from the Justices lauding journalism is
at times drowned out by lower courts that condemn the profession explicitly
or implicitly. Young journalists and young publishers cannot leave school
emboldened with any mandate to defame; it is arguably this profound conflict
between idealism and reality that has helped expand the First Amendment to
its breaking point.

Newsrooms, too, must be more cognizant of both ethics and law and must
work to educate journalists at all levels. A young reporter who had not studied
journalism in college once explained to a law class that she had included
within her story information that its subjects had asked that she not include;
she reasoned that once they had told her something, she had permission to
print it because she knew it to be true. Courts have ruled against journalists in
similar cases[102] but she did not know that. Newsrooms would do well to call
upon media law professors and media law attorneys to update them regularly
on the law and to make such instruction mandatory for all in the newsroom.

A continuing review of ethics principles is also necessary so that young
reporters who have not been exposed to ethics principles in their undergraduate or graduate education will consider such things before they post or otherwise publish.

Those journalism professors and journalists might also wish to meet regularly with judges and attorneys within their communities to break down walls
between the two professions. Through education that explains journalism's
purpose and its news decisions and its ethical constraints, judges are more

likely to remember that sweeping condemnation of media brings even respectable journalism within its grip and that there is indeed a difference between journalism and quasi-journalistic publishers.

The need for education is strong, seen perhaps most profoundly on quasi-journalism websites that attempt to explain publishing liability to their readers. In 2013, a website calling itself The Deadbeat Link, one that invited readers to post identifying information about others they considered deadbeats and the reasons why, offered legal advice to those who worried about the potential for legal liability.[103] Its first two frequently asked questions and answers read this precise way:

> Q. Can I get in trouble for submitting a deadbeat?
> A. No! There are two types of defamation, "Slander," which is spoken defamation and "Libel," which is written defamation. The first amendment garuntees your right to free speech and you CANNOT get in trouble or be held accountable for any type of dafamation as long as it is is the truth. That being said, you are responsible for ensuring all submissions are truthfulness and accurate.
> Q. Will a deadbeat know who submitted him/her to the Deadbeat list?
> A. No! When you submit a deadbeat to the list, it will not have any information, other than your chosen user name, that will identify you as the submitter. Depending on what you choose to write in the body text, that person may guess who wrote it, but that person will not actually be able to tell.

Surely those behind The Deadbeat Link did not contact attorneys before helpfully asking and answering those questions for its contributors. The attorneys would have explained that, aside from defamation, privacy was an important legal consideration and that truth did not absolve posters from such liability. They would have also explained that, today, courts may well order websites such as The Deadbeat Link to reveal the identity of posters who defame or invade privacy. And, finally, they likely would have warned that it is possible that the Communications Decency Act may not protect those behind The Deadbeat Link if courts found that the website had encouraged defamatory or privacy-invading behavior.

To have educated those behind The Deadbeat Link well before they created the website would have potentially protected not only those persons who could one day be defamed, or find themselves liable for having defamed, but also the First Amendment itself by potentially warding off another boundary-pushing publisher whose breezy disregard for the rights of others invites a public and judicial backlash against media more generally.

The Communications Decency Act Needs Revision

The World Wide Web was a different place in 1996 when Congress passed the Communications Decency Act. Lawmakers' focus two decades ago was on the Internet's potential to provide both for economic growth and vibrant expression. Recall that under the statute "[n]o provider or user of an interactive computer service [is] treated as a publisher or speaker of any information provided by another content provider." By insuring no liability for websites or for internet service providers, Congress had hoped that expression would flourish, that web traffic would increase, and that the economy would strengthen. The CDA then would help and did help to create a literal marketplace of ideas.

What it also did and does, however, as revenge porn publisher Hunter Moore happily discovered, is protect many website owners from liability for others' posts; the owner of the website is, in most cases, not legally responsible for language, video, or photographs posted there by another. What that means is that, today, multiple websites like that which Moore created invade privacy and evade liability, courtesy of the CDA.

What's more, as philosopher and ethicist Martha Nussbaum has noted, "[m]uch of the damage done by the spread of gossip and slander on the Internet is damage to women,"[104] also courtesy of the CDA. The CDA has helped along the world of which media law scholar Lyrissa Lidsky precisely warned when she argued in 2000 that "the law cannot allow [the Internet's free-form] culture to degenerate into a realm where anything goes, where any embittered and malicious speaker can lash out randomly at innocent targets."[105] The world may be made richer literally and figuratively by social production on the Internet, as scholar Yochai Benkler, director of Harvard's Berkman Center for Internet and Society, has argued,[106] but individuals, a lot of them female, have been individually harmed by this "new information environment." Benkler's criticism of a newspaper that publishes only news that is palatable is well taken, yet embarrassing and emotionally harmful posts that pierce individual dignity surely should not be welcomed as a necessary part of the cure.

Recall that Moore, creator of the revenge porn-type website Is Anyone Up, initially removed nude photographs posted by others when women complained that those photos were not meant for public consumption and had invaded their privacy. When Moore learned of the CDA and its seeming blanket protection for websites, however, he changed his policy, returned those he had removed to the website, and thereafter refused to remove similar nude photos.

If Congress amended the CDA to include a provision carving out from protection those websites that have a plaintiff-proved intent to invade privacy or to defame or to inflict severe emotional distress, many people would be protected from emotional harm. Consider Is Anyone Up and the effect an amendment to the CDA would have on it and similar websites. A website owner like Moore would be liable for material that others posted as long as the plaintiff could prove that the website or that a particular section of a website was created for the purpose of harming others through privacy invasions, intentional emotional distress, or otherwise. This is the targeted harmful internet speech that the Supreme Court seemed to suggest could well be the basis for liability even as it embraced funeral protests in *Snyder*. Privacy scholar Danielle Citron, for one, has argued that the CDA should not give blanket immunity to websites like Moore's that offend what she has called "cyber civil rights."[107]

Moreover, to prevent immediate harm, as others including Daniel Solove have suggested,[108] the CDA could well incorporate a takedown provision in line with current federal intellectual property law, one that, in sharp contrast to the strong protection within the CDA, mandates an expeditious response to intellectual property infringements.[109] There is preexisting privacy-related liability that exists for commercial use of another's image, name, or identity, after all; misappropriation is one privacy tort that some courts have specifically linked with "dignity and peace of mind."[110] Curiously, and infuriatingly for those whose images remain on revenge or other humiliation websites, however, intellectual property law requires an expeditious takedown of any copyrighted or trademarked image that a website learns about—even if posted by another—or the website operator can be liable,[111] whereas privacy law does not. If the CDA were amended to mimic copyright law, those websites that failed to take images down expeditiously upon notification could be sued. Such limitations on publication, of course, already exist in other countries.[112]

These fixes would most likely have the most significant negative effect on quasi-journalism and other publishers of truth that do not often abide by an ethics code and would have a profoundly supportive effect on privacy rights. Suddenly, push-the-envelope websites within the jurisdiction of the United States would face significant financial liability and would very likely shut down—or, even more importantly, never begin. Revenge porn websites would be particularly affected, but so would websites that serve as conduits for defamatory or privacy-invading rumors or images and do so intentionally, with a seeming purpose to inflict emotional harm. Moreover, the limitation on speech would be appropriate. As media law scholar Eric Barendt has noted, in libel cases the marketplace-of-ideas argument for more speech to drown out incorrect speech has validity, "but this medicine can obviously not cure a loss of privacy."[113]

Finally, because proof of intent or proof of targeted emotional harm, either in an individual or collective sense, would be necessary to most claims, websites owned by mainstream news organizations and other similar publishers would continue to be protected by the CDA and would not be held liable for others' posts after most news stories or other more innocuous publications.

There are indications that such an amendment to the Communications Decency Act would be feasible and would also produce results. Not only did Hunter Moore originally remove offending photographs when he feared liability, Nik Richie settled one of the two cases that had been initially decided against him.

Today's Older Publishers Need Education Too

Recall that The Deadbeat Link developers, considered quasi-journalists here for their website that asked others to post information on alleged deadbeats, apparently did not understand the law as well as they could have. In their FAQ, they seemed focused on defamation, the tort that has truth as its powerful defense, but neglected the privacy-related torts, most of which have truth as a necessary element. Not all internet publishers write for websites that are potentially harmful, but even those with more mainstream blogs and websites need to know the law. If some bloggers reject mainstream journalism's grammar rules and other guidelines as too restrictive and old-fashioned, they still must understand that the laws of liability that apply to mainstream journalism also apply to them.

After a talk on defamation given to a group of law students, for example, one older blogger approached with concern to ask whether, in fact, his blog posts could be the basis for a defamation action. It is not clear why he would have believed otherwise, but before the talk, he had published freely under the mistaken belief that anything he published on the Internet would be exempt from legal consequence. In a world in which style rules mandate that we capitalize the word Internet, one in which news outlets publish headlines relaying the apparently still newsworthy information that a poster had been sued for a negative review on the Internet,[114] and one in which commentators begin buzzing with incredulity that a store that tweets a photograph of a celebrity shopping there might be liable for the commercial use of her identity,[115] perhaps such a misguided belief is to be expected.

Once non-nefarious publishers such as that student and others learn that the law applies to them, they will likely become more aware of the potential for harm within their posts, thereby making their posts less harmful to others.

Ethics, too, should be a consideration for such publishers and could well protect them legally. If some courts today seem inclined to use journalism's codes of ethics against mainstream journalism, quasi-journalists, especially those who publish on journalism-like websites, may wish to familiarize themselves with those provisions.

As should be clear by now, quasi-journalists do not have an all-encompassing ethics code. But neither apparently do many more mainstream bloggers, including those who would presumably be more closely aligned with traditional journalism. In 2008, NYU professor Jay Rosen developed several blogging ethics provisions he pointed to as "the codification in rules of the practices" that had led others to trust internet-published work, a more powerful guiding force for bloggers, he suggested, than old-journalism's ethics codes. But Rosen's provisions lack the more forceful, contemplative, at times compassionate, language of journalism's models:

Good bloggers observe the ethic of the link.

They correct themselves early, easily and often.

They don't claim neutrality but they do practice transparency.

They aren't remote, they habitually converse.

They give you their site, but also other sites as a proper frame of reference. (As with the blogroll.)

When they grab on to something they don't let go; they "track" it.[116]

As dense as those provisions may be for the blog illiterate, Rosen could well be correct that bloggers' ethics must necessarily be different from those in mainstream journalism, if only to have bloggers find the mere suggestion of adherence to a code of ethics acceptable. One blogging code of ethics proposed in 2003 reflected the SPJ code: Be honest and fair, minimize harm, and be accountable.[117] It did not catch on.

Another code that seemed even more benign—one that "called on bloggers to not post material that harasses others, is libelous or is knowingly false"— was also met with tremendous resistance in the blogosphere in 2007.[118] Even though such seemingly sensible suggestions would have been merely voluntary in an ethics sense, bloggers and others fought against them as a restriction on their speech freedoms: the *San Francisco Chronicle* reported that the proposal created a "firestorm" of "intense resistance" and that bloggers complained that the proposed code of conduct was "excessive, unworkable, and an open door to censorship." One blogger told the *Chronicle* that he was "rather resentful of someone who has the temerity to tell me how they think I should behave."

The trouble is, of course, that if bloggers and quasi-journalists do not behave, the courts will be the ones to step in with such temerity. And all of journalism could well be affected.

In the End, Judges Must Recognize the Danger in Condemning Media

The one with the final word in all these law-based determinations is the judge. For every media-based privacy or intentional-infliction-of-emotional-distress case that makes its way to a courtroom or chambers, a judge will be challenged to decide whether it moves to a jury or is stopped by a motion to dismiss or a motion for summary judgment filed by the defense.

The stakes are extraordinary. A Florida jury deciding a false light case against a newspaper in 2006, for example, awarded the plaintiff nearly nineteen million dollars; the plaintiff had argued that an article had implied that he had murdered his wife and had gotten away with it.[119] In the misappropriation case brought against *Hustler* magazine by Nancy Benoit's mother, too, the jury had initially awarded twenty million dollars in punitive damages. And the jury that had decided the case against The Dirty decided that Nik Richie should pay more than three hundred thousand dollars in damages for the harm done to the once-teacher on his website. The Reporters Committee for Freedom of the Press website contains numerous other examples of high damage awards against media.[120] This is why media defense attorneys worry about bringing cases before juries.

Moreover, these examples fail to include the price of litigation itself. The initial costs stemming from one lawsuit on appeal were said to be nine million dollars. One insurer suggested that the money paid to try a case bested by ten to one the amounts paid in settlement to plaintiffs. It is no wonder, then, that one study suggested that 80 percent to 90 percent of libel cases filed against the press usually settle before trial.[121]

The costs of litigation are financially significant because so many must be paid. The newspaper must hire attorneys and pay them by the hour at the extraordinary rates that make good sense in a particularly important First Amendment case. In 2013, the average prices for top law firms, those most likely to have the expertise to handle First Amendment cases, were $536 per hour for partners and $370 per hour for associates; New York law firm partners' rates averaged $756 per hour.[122] The deposition costs alone in one intentional-infliction-of-emotional-distress case involving media came to more than $132,000.[123]

As news media face what appears to be an even more perilous economic future, the potential for these sorts of awards could well help journalists determine what becomes news and what does not. The greater the potential for liability springing from a news story, the less of a chance that media will take the risk. Even smaller awards could well have a chilling effect. And, many times, those stories that are most important—involving criminal activity by a politician, for example—are those that have the greatest potential for a lawsuit.

Moreover, as suggested earlier, those numbers serve as a potential deterrent not only for the media defendant facing suit, but for other news organizations that must decide whether to publish a particular difficult story themselves. The problem with an outcome like the one in the *To Catch a Predator* case involving the arrest of the prosecutor who seemingly solicited a child for sex, therefore, is not only what it does to that particular program (many were delighted when it ceased production), but also what it does to all future news-gathering and coverage. After that decision, more timid journalists could well withhold stories regarding arrests of prosecutors for child sex crimes or other illegal behavior even though the information is decidedly newsworthy: the arrestee public official, one who had pledged to uphold the law, would also be one who had decided the viability of others' arrests for similar heinous crimes.

It is possible, some might say obvious, that some judges are fully aware of such repercussions and use language specifically and fully intending that they limit media in the future. But there may be other judges who are not aware. Those judges should recognize that what harms The Dirty could, in fact, also harm the *New York Times*—that "media" is often too broad a word—and should write their opinions accordingly.

It might also help courts to recognize that the most helpful experts on the subject of newsworthiness may not necessarily be the scholars they would look to in other types of cases. One expert, who testified for the plaintiff in a case in which the jury later awarded the plaintiff two million dollars, was said to have counseled the jury that a journalist must "never" alter quotes within a story and that a potentially explosive revelation must be confirmed by two separate sources.[124] The court thereafter called those "principles" of journalism. And yet they are but two suggestions—neither of which is found in the current SPJ code—and are not strongly adhered to in cases in which sources misspeak or in which a single source is well-trusted.

Instead, when allowed under rules of evidence, a court may wish to rely upon guidance from practicing journalists within that community who follow an ethics code as independent, court-appointed experts when the judge's sense is that the case before the court is the exceptional one in which human dignity trumps news value. As ethical journalists who must make such decisions daily and must decide to publish or not to publish, these experts would not blindly accept the news judgment put before them but would necessarily objectively explain the ethical appropriateness—or lack thereof—of their peer's decision.

That the experts be practicing local journalists is important. Just as law professors who have never practiced law or who have never taken a bar exam would likely not be the best experts in legal malpractice cases, so too should judges hesitate to rely solely on newsworthiness experts whose experience is mostly if not exclusively in the classroom. In classrooms is where much more theoretical decisions regarding newsworthiness are made by those who often have never worked in a fast-paced newsroom necessarily publishing the news it believes will be of interest to the people it serves balanced against competing ethics considerations.

Without such understanding and without such action by courts, news media will face even greater pressures to not publish, leading to fewer news stories of substance and, if the Supreme Court is correct, ultimately failing democracy.

Conclusion

These suggestions for changes in courtrooms, newsrooms, classrooms, and Congress are meant ultimately to stem the chilling tide of lawsuits brought by litigants against media. They also are meant to suggest that some claims brought by plaintiffs are—and should be—viable. Finally, they attempt to draw the difficult lines that could well move all media toward more legally and ethically sound newsworthiness determinations.

The hope is that such changes will lessen the pressure on an already at-risk First Amendment. Or, to put it in the language of this chapter's start, the hope is that by drawing difficult lines, we can provide a manageable outlet for the enormity of the outrage that otherwise might overthrow the media-protective disposition of the First Amendment more broadly.

After all, another important right—the right to privacy—is often at stake. And privacy, too, has a rich history of protection for its own essential reasons.

In the 1920s, photographer and filmmaker Dziga Vertov traversed the streets of multiple Soviet cities, recording daily activities with his movie camera. He called the hour-long film that he put together from these vignettes *Man with the Movie Camera*. The film (and its camera) "shows[s] us the spectacle of life, both intimate and public, and it also invites us to marvel at its power to show," *New York Times* film critic A. O. Scott wrote of Vertov's work.[125]

Scott also noted *Man with the Movie Camera*'s ability to communicate truth: the truthfulness of everyday life. In that way, it is one of the very earliest reality productions, created at just around the time that the U.S. Supreme Court called such real-life moving pictures potentially "evil."

What is noteworthy about the film is that, even at the dawn of documentary cinema, people shield themselves from the camera throughout. Homeless people lying on the streets, people in carriages, and, perhaps in the most poignantly private scene, a woman at the divorce office who hides her face with her hand in a seemingly desperate attempt to regain privacy once she recognizes that she is being filmed.

Man with the Movie Camera is not a sex tape. It does not feature nudity. It does not even record everyday images within the privacy of homes. But it captures moments those people consider private, even though they are in public and even though the camera is interested in them. Those people do, in fact, recognize the power of the camera to show, as A. O. Scott suggested.

Vertov, then, is one of the earliest moving picture publishers to show us what the world is like—and then to push for more.

Freedom of expression's "central idea is that the reader, listener, and watcher is free to decide for himself what interests him,"[126] that federal court in Texas once wrote. Yet, clearly there must be some law to protect the watched as well: today's people in the divorce office or on the street or in cars who wish to shield themselves from media that they feel will reveal too much about them. Sometimes we will agree with them in a legal sense and sometimes we will not.

Where to draw that line in the newsroom and in the courtroom is a difficult task, but one that is absolutely necessary, both for the protection of privacy and for the protection of First Amendment freedoms.

Notes
Acknowledgments
Index

Notes

1. An Introduction

1. A. J. Daulerio, "Even for a Minute, Watching Hulk Hogan Have Sex in a Canopy Bed is Not Safe For Work but Watch it Anyway," www.Gawker .com (Oct. 4, 2012).
2. John Cook, "A Judge Told Us to Take Down Our Hulk Hogan Sex Tape Post. We Won't," www.Gawker.com (Apr. 25, 2013). The Gawker website used the profanity.
3. Restatement (Second) of Torts, § 652D, cmts. g, h (1977).
4. Hashtag Nation, "The Stir About Hulk," *N.Y. Times* and www.nytimes.com (Oct. 11, 2012).
5. Abner J. Mikva, "In My Opinion, Those are Not Facts," 11 *Ga. St. U.L. Rev.* 291 (1995).
6. Bollea v. Gawker Media, 40 Media L. Rep. 2601 (M.D. Fla. 2012).
7. Bollea v. Gawker Media, 913 F. Supp. 2d 1325 (M.D. Fla. 2012).
8. John Cook, "A Judge Told Us to Take Down Our Hulk Hogan Sex Tape Post. We Won't," www.Gawker.com (Apr. 25, 2013).
9. Gawker Media v. Bollea, 129 So. 3d 1196 (Fla. App. 2014).
10. Jeff Bercovici, "A Candid Conversation with Gawker's Nick Denton," *Playboy* (March 2014).
11. Sonia Sotomayor, *My Beloved World* (New York: Random House 2013).
12. Anne Stolley Persky, "50 Years after New York Times v. Sullivan, Do Courts Still Value Journalists' Watchdog Role?" *ABA Journal* (Mar. 7, 2014).
13. Ann Oldenburg, "Hulk Hogan Apologizes for Gory Photos," www.freep .com (May 27, 2013).

14. Gael Fashingbauer Cooper, "Geraldo Rivera Tweets Half-naked Photo of Himself," www.today.com (July 22, 2013).

15. Anita L. Allen, "What Must We Hide: The Ethics of Privacy and the Ethos of Disclosure," 25 *St. Thomas L. Rev.* 1 (2012).

16. Jeffrey Rosen, "The Right to Be Forgotten," 64 *Stan. L. Rev. Online* 88 (2012).

17. Teens, Media, and Social Privacy, Pew Internet and American Life Project Poll, May 2013, www.pewinternet.org.

18. Posts from 2010–2011 on www.collegeconfidential.com; poster's name and screen name not included for privacy reasons.

19. http://hellothereracists.tumblr.com/.

20. Emily Bazelon, "Hey Internet, Stop Outing Kids for Racism," Slate.com (Nov. 16, 2012).

21. "Is Anybody Down?", www.onthemedia.org (Nov. 16, 2012). Interestingly, in comments on the webpage, a mother asks that her fifteen-year-old daughter's photographs be taken down from Is Anybody Down and names the girl. As of 2014, On the Media had not removed the mother's comment, apparently meant for the Is Anybody Down website, though it is not clear if the post itself is a prank.

22. Linda McDonald, *Vanity Fair*, September 2012, p. 152.

23. 2013 First Amendment Survey, First Amendment Center, Newseum Institute, Washington, D.C., www.newseum.org.

24. Ibid.

25. Pew Research Center's Project for Excellence in Journalism, "The State of the News Media 2013," www.stateofthemedia.org.

26. Emily Guskin, "Newspaper Newsrooms Suffer Large Staffing Decreases," Pew Research Center, www.pewresearch.org (June 25, 2013).

27. Matthew Jacobs, "Celebrities Insulted By The Media: When Criticism Goes Too Far," www.huffpost.com (Mar. 1, 2013).

28. Anna Stolley Persky, "Coverage or Crime? When Journalism Crosses the Line," *Washington Lawyer* (Dec. 2011).

29. Ashley Anderson, Dominique Brossard, Dietram A. Scheufele, Michael A. Xenos, Peter Ladwig, "The 'Nasty Effect:' Online Incivility and Risk Perceptions of Emerging Technologies," Journal of Computer-Mediated Communication, www.onlinelibrary.wiley.com (2013).

30. Readers' Comments, "Woods Apologizes for 'Personal Failings,'" NYTimes.com (Dec. 2, 2009). The comment remained up as late as 2013.

31. The transcript of the chats is available on the Perverted Justice website, www.perverted-justice.com.

32. www.perverted-justice.com

33. Bill Lodge, "Ex-Mabank Teacher Is Named in Abuse Suit," *Dallas Morning News* (Sept. 22, 1993).

34. Near v. Minnesota, 283 U.S. 697 (1931), citing 1774 language from Journals of the Continental Congress.

35. Restatement (Second) of Torts, § 652D, cmt. g (1977).

36. Conradt v. NBC, 536 F. Supp. 2d 380 (S.D.N.Y. 2008).

37. Society of Professional Journalists Code of Ethics, www.spj.org.

38. Kelly McBride, "What's Wrong With To Catch a Predator," www.poynter .org (Aug. 7, 2007, Mar. 3, 2011).

39. Tiwari v. NBC, 2011 WL 5079505 (N.D. Cal. Oct. 25, 2011); Armstrong v. NBC, 2011 WL 2193379 (W.D. Ky. June 6, 2011); Patterson v. NBC, 2011 WL 3163239 (W.D. Ky. July 26, 2011). The latter two cases were eventually dismissed on motions for summary judgment.

40. Sprague v. Walter, 22 Pa. D. & C.3d 564 (1982).

41. United States v. Blagojevich, 743 F. Supp. 2d 794 (N.D. Ill. 2010).

2. Legal Protections for News and Truthful Information: The Past

1. People v. Winters, 48 N.Y.S.2d 230 (N.Y. App. Div. 1944).

2. People v. Winters, 63 N.E.2d 98 (N.Y. 1945).

3. Winters v. New York, 333 U.S. 507 (1948).

4. "Scores Yellow Press," *Washington Post* (Jan. 17, 1900).

5. Nicholson Baker and Margaret Brentano, *The World on Sunday: Graphic Art in Joseph Pulitzer's Newspaper* (New York: Bulfinch Press 2005).

6. See Amy Gajda, "Scandal! The Lasting Effects of Early Supreme Court News Coverage," 48 *Georgia Law Review* 781 (2014).

7. Samuel D. Warren & Louis Brandeis, "The Right to Privacy," 4 *Harv. L. Rev.* 193 (1890).

8. See Amy Gajda, "What If Samuel D. Warren Hadn't Married a Senator's Daughter?: Uncovering the Press Coverage That Led to 'The Right to Privacy,'" 2008 *Mich. St. L. Rev.* 35 (2008).

9. Amy Gajda, "Privacy Before 'The Right to Privacy,'" manuscript on file with author.

10. William Prosser, "Privacy," 48 *Calif. L. Rev.* 383 (1960).

11. Restatement of the Law of Torts, American Law Institute §867 (1939).

12. Restatement (Second) of Torts, American Law Institute §652D (1977)

13. Neil Richards, "Reconciling Data Privacy and the First Amendment," 52 *U.C.L.A. L. Rev.* 1149 (2005).

14. 376 U.S. 254 (1964).

15. Garrison v. Louisiana, 379 U.S. 64 (1964).

16. 385 U.S. 374 (1967).

17. Time, Inc. v. Pape, 401 U.S. 279 (1971).

18. Miami Herald Publ'g v. Tornillo, 418 U.S. 241 (1974).

19. 403 U.S. 713 (1971).

20. 427 U.S. 539 (1976).

21. Oklahoma Publ'g Co. v. District Court, 430 U.S. 308 (1977).

22. Smith v. Daily Mail Publ'g Co., 443 U.S. 97 (1979).

23. Landmark Communications, Inc. v. Virginia, 435 U.S. 829 (1978)

24. Smith v. Daily Mail, 443 U.S. at 102.

25. Harte-Hanks Communications v. Connaughton, 491 U.S. 657 (1989).

26. Hustler Magazine v. Falwell, 485 U.S. 46 (1988).

27. 418 U.S. 323 (1974).

28. Regan v. Time, Inc. 468 U.S. 641 (1984).

29. Nixon v. Warner Communications, Inc., 435 U.S. 589 (1978).

30. Richmond Newspapers v. Virginia, 448 U.S. 555 (1980).

31. 420 U.S. 469 (1975).

32. 491 U.S. 524 (1989).

33. 68 Cornell L. Rev. 291 (1983).

34. New Jersey State Lottery Comm'n v. United States, 491 F.2d 219 (3d Cir. 1974).

35. Greg B. Smith, "'Trashed' Model Wins: Mag to Cough up $100,000," *New York Daily News* (March 28, 1998).

36. Messenger v. Gruner + Jahr USA Publ'g, 994 F. Supp. 525 (1998).

37. Messenger v. Gruner + Jahr Printing and Publ'g, 727 N.E.2d 549 (N.Y. 2000).

38. Howell v. New York Post Co., Inc., 596 N.Y.S.2d 350 (N.Y. 1993). See also Gilbert v. Medical Economics Co., 665 F.2d 305 (10th Cir. 1981), in which the court refused to find liability for a news story that included information regarding a woman's psychiatric history and other private facts.

39. Sipple v. Chronicle Publ'g Co., 201 Cal. Rptr. 665 (Cal. Ct. App. 1984).

40. Shulman v. Group W Productions, 18 Cal. 4th 200 (Cal. 1998).

41. Bernstein v. National Broad. Co., 129 F. Supp. 817 (D.D.C. 1955).

42. Jenkins v. Dell Publ'g Co., 251 F.2d 447 (3d Cir. 1958).

43. Frith v. Associated Press, 176 F. Supp. 671 (E.D.S.C. 1959).

44. Travers v. Paton, 261 F. Supp. 110 (D. Conn. 1966).

45. Williams v. KCMO Broad., 472 S.W.2d 1 (Mo. App. 1971).

46. Cantrell v. Forest City Publ'g, 484 F.2d 150 (6th Cir. 1973); reversed on other grounds, 419 U.S. 245 (1974).

47. New Jersey State Lottery Comm'n v. United States, 491 F.2d 219 (3d Cir. 1974).

48. Neff v. Time, Inc., 406 F. Supp. 858 (W.D. Pa. 1976).

49. Howard v. Des Moines Register, 283 N.W.2d 289 (Iowa 1979).

50. Dresbach v. Doubleday & Co., 518 F. Supp. 1285 (D.D.C. 1981).

51. Pierson v. News Group Publications, 549 F. Supp. 635 (S.D. Ga. 1982).

52. Cape Publications v. Bridges, 423 So. 2d 436 (Fla. Dist. Ct. App. 1982).

53. Roshto v. Hebert, 439 So. 2d 428 (La. 1983).

54. Lerman v. Flynt Distrib. Co., 745 F.2d 123 (2d Cir. 1984).

55. Gaeta v. New York News, 62 N.Y.2d 340 (N.Y. 1984).

56. Ross v. Midwest Communications, 870 F.2d 271 (5th Cir. 1989).

57. Anderson v. Fisher Broad., 712 P. 2d 803 (Or. 1986).
58. Scheetz v. Morning Call, 747 F. Supp. 1515 (E.D. Pa. 1990).
59. Desnick v. American Broad. Companies, Inc., 44 F.3d 1345 (7th Cir. 1995).
60. Eagle v. Morgan, 88 F.3d 620 (8th Cir. 1996).
61. Detroit Free Press v. Dep't of Justice, 73 F.3d 93 (6th Cir. 1996).
62. Huggins v. Moore, 94 N.Y.2d 296 (N.Y. 1999).
63. 532 U.S. 514 (2001).
64. Ibid. at 540.

3. Legal Protections for News and Truthful Information: The Present

1. Erin Coyle, *The Press and Rights to Privacy* (El Paso: LFB Scholarly Publishing 2012), p. 173.
2. Denver Publishing Co. v. Bueno, 54 P.3d 893 (Colo. 2002).
3. Welling v. Weinfeld, 866 N.E.2d 1051 (Ohio 2007).
4. Peterson v. Moldofsky, 2009 U.S. Dist. LEXIS 90633 (D. Kan. Sept. 29, 2009).
5. Meyerkord v. Zipatoni Co., 276 S.W.3d 319 (Mo. Ct. App. 2008).
6. National Archives and Records Administration v. Favish, 541 U.S. 157 (2004).
7. Catsouras v. Department of California Highway Patrol, 104 Cal. Rptr. 3d 352 (Cal. Ct. App. 2010).
8. The cases discussed here, and throughout the book, were mostly identified through ongoing searches of the Lexis and Westlaw databases for court opinions including terms such as "privacy," "journalism," and "newsworthiness." The Lexis and Westlaw databases provide the most comprehensive available catalog of published and unpublished court decisions by state and federal courts in the United States, dating from around the time of the nation's founding to the present and updated continuously.
9. Renwick v. News and Observer Publishing, 312 S.E.2d 405 (N.C. 1984).
10. Haas v. Gill, 531 So. 2d 457 (La. 1988) (Cole, J., dissenting).
11. Hawkins v. Multimedia, Inc., 344 S.E.2d 145 (S.C. 1986).
12. Times-Mirror Co. v. Superior Court of San Diego County, 244 Cal. Rptr. 556 (Cal. Ct. App. 1988).
13. Raffery v. Harford Courant Co., 416 A.2d 1215 (Conn. Super. 1980).
14. Y.G. v. Jewish Hospital of St. Louis, 795 S.W.2d 488 (Mo. Ct. App. 1990).
15. Armstrong v. H & C Communications, Inc., 575 So. 2d 280 (Fla. Dist. Ct. App. 1991).
16. Sharrif v. American Broadcasting Co., 613 So. 2d 768 (La. Ct. App. 1993).
17. Weinstein v. Bullick, 827 F. Supp. 1193 (E.D. Pa. 1993).
18. Baugh v. CBS, Inc., 828 F. Supp. 745 (N.D. Cal. 1993).
19. Multimedia WMAZ, Inc. v. Kubach, 443 S.E.2d 491 (Ga. Ct. App. 1994).
20. Winstead v. Sweeney, 517 N.W.2d 874 (Mich. Ct. App. 1994).

21. Manocchia v. Narragansett Television, 1996 R.I. Super. LEXIS 77 (R.I. Super. Ct. Dec. 12, 1996).
22. Clift v. Narragansett Television L.P., 688 A.2d 805 (R.I. 1996).
23. Michaels v. Internet Entertainment Group, 5 F. Supp. 2d 823 (C.D. Cal. 1998).
24. Doe v. Univision Television Group, 717 So. 2d 63 (Fla. Dist. Ct. App. 1998).
25. Sanders v. American Broadcasting Companies, Inc., 978 P. 2d 67 (Cal. 1999).
26. Rogers v. Home Shopping Network, Inc., 57 F. Supp. 2d 973 (C.D. Cal. 1999).
27. David Anderson, "Freedom of the Press," 80 *Tex. L. Rev.* 429 (2002).
28. Barry McDonald, "The First Amendment and the Free Flow of Information," 65 *Ohio St. L.J.* 249 (2004).
29. Persky, "50 years after New York Times v. Sullivan."
30. Albanese v. Menounos, 218 Cal. App. 4th 923 (Cal. App. 2013).
31. Electronic Privacy Information Center v. Department of Defense, 355 F. Supp. 2d 98 (D.D.C. 2004).
32. American Civil Liberties Union of Northern California v. Department of Justice, 2005 U.S. Dist. LEXIS 3763 (N.D. Cal. Mar. 11, 2005).
33. Lowe v. Winter, 2007 U.S. Dist. LEXIS 49962 (D.D.C. July 12, 2007).
34. Wadelton v. Dep't of State, 941 F. Supp. 2d 120 (D.D.C. 2013)
35. Al-Fayed v. CIA, 254 F.3d 300 (D.C. Cir. 2001).
36. McClatchy v. Associated Press, 35 Media L. Rep. 1513 (W.D. Pa. 2007).
37. Tillman v. Freedom of Information Commission, 2008 Conn. Super. LEXIS 2120 (Conn. Super. Ct. Aug. 15, 2008).
38. Castillon v. Correctional Corporation of America, 41 Media L. Rep. 2507 (D. Idaho 2013). The complaint with allegations is available at www.angstman.com.
39. Calderone v. Fitzgerald, 2007 Conn. Super. LEXIS 1637 (Conn. Super. Ct. June 25, 2007).
40. Rossbach v. Rundle, 128 F. Supp. 2d 1348 (S.D. Fla. 2000).
41. Anaya v. CBS Broadcasting Inc., 626 F. Supp. 2d 1158 (D.N.M. 2008).
42. Burns v. Chapman, 2008 Conn. Super. LEXIS 3228 (Conn. Super. Ct. Dec. 12, 2008).
43. Klentzman v. Brady, 312 S.W.3d 886 (Tex. App. 2009).
44. Freedom Communications, Inc. v. Coronado, 296 S.W.3d 790 (Tex. App. 2009). This decision was vacated and remanded in June 2012 because the trial court judge was accused of accepting a bribe in the underlying case.
45. Tiwari v. NBC Universal, Inc., 2011 U.S. Dist. LEXIS 123362 (N.D. Cal. Oct. 25, 2011).
46. Turnbull v. American Broadcasting Co., 32 Media L. Rep. 2442 (C.D. Cal. 2004).
47. Stratton v. Krywko, 33 Media L. Rep. 2265 (Mich. Ct. App. 2005).

48. Kinsella v. Welch, 827 A.2d 325 (N.J. Super. Ct. App. Div. 2003). See also Castro v. NYT Television, 895 A.2d 1173 (N.J. Super. Ct. App. Div. 2006), Carter v. Superior Court of San Diego County, 2002 Cal. App. Unpub. LEXIS 5017 (Cal. Ct. App. Jan. 10, 2002).
49. Chavez v. City of Oakland, 37 Media L. Rep. 1905 (N.D. Cal. 2009).
50. Santini v. American Media, Inc., 35 Media L. Rep. 1699 (Cal. Ct. App. 2005).
51. Chapman v. Journal Concepts, Inc., 528 F. Supp. 2d 1081 (D. Haw. 2007).
52. Hood v. National Enquirer, 17 No. 9 Ent. L. Rep. 3, 4 n.2 (Cal. Ct. App. 1995).
53. Gallon v. Hustler Magazine, Inc., 732 F. Supp. 322 (N.D.N.Y. 1990).
54. Padilla v. MRA Holding, Inc., 2004 WL 2988172 (Cal. Ct. App. Dec. 28, 2004).
55. Whitney v. Playboy Entertainment Group, 34 Media L. Rep. 2404 (Cal. Ct. App. 2006).
56. Prince v. Viacom, 2008 U.S. Dist. LEXIS 32092 (S.D. Tex. April 18, 2008).
57. Ignat v. Yum! Brands, Inc., 154 Cal. Rptr. 3d 275 (Cal. Ct. App. 2013).
58. Sharp v. Whitman Council, Inc., 2007 WL 2874058 (E.D. Pa. October 1, 2007).
59. Gettner v. Fitzgerald, 677 S.E.2d 149 (Ga. Ct. App. 2009).
60. Thomas v. Telegraph Publishing, 2007 N.H. LEXIS 240 (N.H. May 1, 2007).
61. Englert v. MacDonell, 2006 U.S. Dist. LEXIS 29361 (D. Or. May 10, 2006).
62. William Nack, Don Yaeger, "Every Parent's Nightmare," *Sports Illustrated* (Sept. 13, 1999).
63. M.G. v. Time Warner, Inc., 107 Cal. Rptr. 2d 504 (Cal. Ct. App. 2001).
64. Green v. Chicago Tribune Co., 675 N.E.2d 249 (Ill. App. Ct. 1996).
65. William Recktenwald, Colin McMahon, "Deadly End to a Deadly Year: 934th Victim Part of Homicide Record," *Chicago Tribune* (Jan. 1, 1993).
66. Benz v. Washington Newspaper Publishing Co., 2006 WL 28944896 (D.D.C. Sept. 29, 2006).
67. Macklin v. Cosmos Broadcasting, Inc., 2008 WL 2152188 (W.D. Ky. May 21, 2008).
68. Snyder v. Phelps, 131 S. Ct. 1207 (2011).
69. Holloway v. Am. Media, Inc., 41 Media L. Rep. 1921 (N.D. Ala. 2013).
70. Araya v. Deep Dive Media, 966 F. Supp. 2d 582 (W.D.N.C. 2013).
71. Jennifer Garcia, "Justin and Jessica's Wedding," *People* (Oct. 25, 2012).
72. John Cook, "Justin Timberlake's $6.5 Million Italian Wedding Featured a Video of Sad L.A. Vagrants Wishing Him Well," www.gawker.com (Oct. 24, 2012).

73. "Justin Timberlake Responds to 'Distasteful' Wedding Video," *People* (Oct. 26, 2012).

74. 17 U.S.C. § 107 (2013).

75. Harper & Row Publishers v. Nation Enterprises, 471 U.S. 539 (1985).

76. Toffoloni v. LFB Publishing Group, 572 F.3d 1201 (11th Cir. 2009).

77. Toffoloni v. LFB Publishing Group, 483 Fed. Appx. 561 (11th Cir. 2012).

78. Monge v. Maya Magazines, Inc., 688 F.3d 1164 (9th Cir. 2012).

79. Kyu Ho Youm, "'Actual Malice' in U.S. Defamation Law: The Minority of One Doctrine in the World?" 4 *Journal of International & Entertainment Law* 1 (2011–2012).

80. Archdiocese of Cincinnati, http://www.catholiccincinnati.org.

81. Bahen v. Diocese of Steubenville, 42 Media L. Rep. 1471 (Ohio Ct. App. 2013)

82. Trover v. Kluger, 37 Media L. Rep. 1165 (W.D. Ky. 2007).

83. As described by the trial court in 2007. All facts are as reported by the court in 2005, 2007, and 2008.

84. Trover v. Kluger, 37 Media L. Rep. 1174 (W.D. Ky. 2008).

85. In 2011, a jury found the doctor not negligent in one of the malpractice cases brought against him, but a state appeals court overturned that decision because the plaintiff had not been allowed to cross-examine the doctor about the suspension of his medical license. And in 2013, a state court dismissed several lawsuits brought against the doctor because the statute of limitations had run. The attorney for the plaintiffs promised an appeal.

86. Trover v. Kluger, 2005 WL 2372043 (W.D. Ky. Sept. 26, 2005).

87. Trey Iles, "Former San Francisco 49ers Owner Eddie DeBartolo Jr. among 15 Hall of Fame Finalists," *Times-Picayune* (Jan. 28, 2013).

88. A Lexis search in the News database shows approximately 300 hits for "Reese Witherspoon" and "mug shot."

89. Department of the Air Force v. Rose, 425 U.S. 352 (1976).

90. 5 U.S.C. § 552 (2013), emphasis added.

91. Chicago Police, http://www.chicagopolice.org/ps/list.aspx.

92. Detroit Free Press v. Department of Justice, 73 F.3d 93 (6th Cir. 1996).

93. Steve Helling, "Reese Witherspoon's Mug shot: Why She's Looking Down," *People* (Apr. 23, 2013).

94. Times-Picayune Publishing v. United States, 37 F. Supp. 2d 472 (E.D. La. 1999).

95. A&E Shows: *Manhunters*, http://www.aetv.com/manhunters/.

96. World Publishing Co. v. United States Department of Justice, 672 F.3d 825 (10th Cir. 2012).

97. Apple, Inc., v. Samsung Electronics Co., 727 F.3d 1214 (Fed. Cir. 2013).

4. The Devolution of Mainstream Journalism

1. www.chicagotribune.com
2. Some high-profile examples include the incorrect suggestion by some media that security guard Richard Jewell was Atlanta's Olympic Park bomber and the created profile of Jimmy, an eight-year-old heroin addict, by Janet Cooke of the *Washington Post*. This chapter is intentionally designed to address the much more prevalent everyday ethics decisions that help to create a negative impression of mainstream media in some minds.
3. www.wdsu.com.
4. www.tampabay.com.
5. www.newyorkdailynews.com
6. "Sigma Delta Chi's First Code of Ethics Was Borrowed from the American Society of Newspapers Editors in 1926." "Ethics Answers: Frequently Asked Questions," www.spj.org.
7. Barrett v. Outlet Broadcasting, 22 F. Supp. 2d 726 (S.D. Ohio 1997).
8. Herbert Gans, *Deciding What's News: A Study of CBS Evening News, NBC Nightly News, Newsweek, and Time* (Evanston: Northwestern University Press 2004) p. 79.
9. Barbara Starr, Chris Lawrence and Tom Cohen, "Intercepted al Qaeda message led to shuttering embassies, consulates," www.cnn.com (Aug. 4, 2013).
10. Paul Farhi, "Publication of Hacked George W. Bush's E-mails Raises Journalism Ethics Questions," *Washington Post* (Feb. 8, 2013).
11. Ibid.
12. United States v. Sterling, 724 F.3d 482 (4th Cir. 2013).
13. Dylan Byers, "Pulitzer Prize-Winning Photographer Banned by AP after Photo Alteration," *Politico* (Jan. 22, 2014).
14. Oralandar Brand-Williams, "Lawyer for Family of Detroit Woman Slain on Dearborn Heights Porch Says Shooting Wasn't Accidental," *Detroit News* (Nov. 8, 2013).
15. Dominic Massa, "The Rault Center Fire 40 Years Later," www.wwltv.com (Jan. 7, 2014).
16. See also Rich Martin, *Living Journalism: Principles and Practices for an Essential Profession* (Scottsdale, Arizona: Halcomb Hathaway, 2011) ("You must . . . learn to make sound decisions about what you choose to report and what you choose not to report.").
17. Philip Patterson and Lee Wilkins, *Media Ethics: Issues and Cases* (Boston: McGraw Hill, 2008).
18. Postscript, "Stevens' Photo on the Front Page," *Los Angeles Times* (Sept. 15, 2012).
19. Transcript, *Anderson Cooper 360°* (Sept. 24, 2012); Snejana Farberov, "Anderson Cooper Admits that CNN Found Slain American Ambassador's

Journal Inside U.S. Consulate in Libya and 'Secretly' Used It in Reporting," *Daily Mail* (Sept. 22, 2012).

20. Erik Wemple, "CNN vs. The State Department: A Long Story," *Washington Post* (Sept. 23, 2012).

21. See, e.g., comment from iseegreyhounds, "Was CNN Right to Use Ambassador Stevens' Diary for Stories," www.theatlanticwire.com (Sept. 23, 2012).

22. See, e.g., comment from DocScience, "CNN Finds, Returns Journal Belonging to Late Ambassador," www.cnn.com (Sept. 23, 2012).

23. Kevin Allman, "Dark Days at *The Times-Picayune*," www.gambit.com (June 18, 2012).

24. Ibid.

25. Jim Romenesko, "Times-Picayune Reporter: I Can't Keep My Mouth Shut and Pretend that Everything Is Okay," www.jimromenesko.com (July 8, 2012).

26. Robert Channick, "Chicago Sun-Times Lays Off Its Photo Staff," *Chicago Tribune* (May 30, 2013). In March 2014, the newspaper rehired four of them.

27. Bryan Smith, "Michael Ferro Isn't Worried," *Chicago Magazine* (Oct. 2013).

28. David J. Krajicek and Debora Wenger, "Crime Coverage Now Requires Constantly 'Feeding the Beast,'" www.poynter.org (Mar. 5, 2013).

29. Pew Research Center, "The State of the News Media 2013," www.journalism.org.

30. Emails on file with author.

31. Chris Johanesen, "Why Publishers Should Ban Slideshows," www.buzzfeed.com (June 17, 2013).

32. "Top Ten Cannabis Strains of 2012," www.sfgate.com (December 31, 2012).

33. "Top Ten Most-Stolen Vehicles," www.washingtonpost.com (Dec. 4, 2012).

34. Ibid. Comment from lokinator.

35. *New York Post* cover (Dec. 4, 2012).

36. www.nypost.com (Dec. 4, 2012).

37. R. Umar Abbasi, "Anguished Photog: Critics Are Unfair to Condemn Me," *New York Post* (Dec. 5, 2012).

38. Kate Sheehy, "Experts Split on Getting Involved," *New York Post* (Dec. 5, 2012).

39. Howard Kurtz, "Why the Outrage Over Photo in Subway Death," www.cnn.com (Dec. 5, 2012).

40. Jeff Sonderman, "New York Post Faces Backlash Over Front-Page Photo of Man 'about to Die' on Subway Track," www.poynter.org (Dec. 5, 2012).

41. Jodi S. Cohen, Stacy St. Clare, Tara Malone "Clout Goes to College," *Chicago Tribune* (May 29, 2009).

42. Jodi S. Cohen, Stacy St. Clare, "Squeeze on Law School," *Chicago Tribune* (July 9, 2009).

43. Original news item and posts on file with author.
44. Neetzan Zimmerman, "Man Records Final Fight with Soon-to-Be-Ex-Wife, Uploads It to YouTube," www.gawker.com (July 22, 2013).
45. Paul Thompson, "Temper Tantrum Wife's Mother Says Her 'Shattered' Daughter Has Been 'Betrayed' by Husband Who Posted Humiliating YouTube Video of Her Meltdown," www.dailymail.co.uk (July 26, 2013).
46. Paul Farhi, "On Live Air, Fox News Shows Suicide of a Driver Chased by Police," *Washington Post* (September 28, 2012).
47. Steve Schmadeke, "Brother Says He Killed Sister to Save Her," *Chicago Tribune* (Jan. 26, 2011).
48. Lee Moran, "Terminally Ill Woman Jumps to Her Death from Argentina's Iguazu Falls in Front of Horrified Tourists," www.nydailynews.com (Mar. 14, 2013).
49. Liz Sadler, "Husband of Tossed Cart Woman Says Family Is Going through 'Very Difficult Time,'" www.nypost.com (Nov. 1, 2011).
50. Eric D. Lawrence, "Girl, 15, 'Humiliated' by Relationship with Robert Messer, Her Mom Says," *Detroit Free Press* (Nov. 8, 2013).
51. David Jesse, "Students across Michigan Sign Up for 'Sugar Daddies' to Help Pay for College," *Detroit Free Press* (Jan. 15, 2013).
52. Ibid.
53. Ibid.
54. Breaking News Desk, "Website: Temple Women Near Top in Seeking 'Sugar Daddies,'" *Philadelphia Inquirer,* (January 14, 2013).
55. Jane Roberts, "Website Touts Rise in College Girls Seeking 'Sugar Daddies,'" *Commercial Appeal* (Jan. 15, 2013).
56. Paul Purpura, "Rev. Grant Storms, Critic of Southern Decadence, Convicted of Obscenity for Public Masturbation," www.nola.com (Aug. 22, 2012).
57. Ethan Sacks, "Suri Cruise Called a 'Little Brat' and 'B—h' by Paparazzo as She's Photographed with Mom Katie Holmes," *New York Daily News* (July 12, 2013).
58. Shashank Bengali, David S. Cloud and Joseph Tanfani, "Jill Kelley, Key Figure in David Petraeus Scandal, Led Lavish Life," *Los Angeles Times* (November 14, 2012). The information, of course, could be untrue.
59. Jenniver Steinhauer, "From Petraeus Scandal, an Apostle for Privacy," *N.Y. Times* (Jan. 5, 2014).
60. Christine Roberts, "Shocker! Honey Boo Boo's Momma Had 2008 Run-in with the Law," *New York Daily News* (Aug. 16, 2012).
61. Leonora LaPeter Anton, "Woman Featured in Times Story about Sexual Disorder Commits Suicide," *Tampa Bay Times* (Dec. 4. 2012).
62. Brian Solis, "Extra Extra, Read All about It! Newspapers Respond to the Social Web," www.briansolis.com (Dec. 19, 2008).
63. The firm is now known as The Brick Factory.

64. The Bivings Group, "American Newspapers and the Internet: Threat or Opportunity?," www.thebrickfactory.com (July 19, 2007).

65. Jeff Sonderman, "News Sites Using Facebook Comments See Higher Quality Discussion, More Referrals," www.poynter.org (Aug. 19, 2011).

66. Jim Witt, "Star-Telegram Changing Method for Reader Comments on Stories, Columns, Editorials," *Ft. Worth Star-Telegram* (Sept. 10, 2013).

67. Comment left by T V-W after story by Leon Hendrix, "Video of Van in Jessica Heeringa Case," www.woodtv.com (Apr. 29, 2013).

68. Lindsay Wise, Paige Hewitt, "Search Continues for Missing 12-Year-Old," www.chron.com (Dec. 28, 2010), comment by Phoenix is Rising.

69. See, e.g., Mitchell Byars, "Released Indictment Names John and Patsy Ramsey on Two Charges in JonBenet Death," *Daily Camera* (Oct. 25, 2013).

70. Keith L. Alexander, "At Conspiracy Trial in Robert Wone Killing: 911 Call is Played," www.washingtonpost.com (May 19, 2010), posts by logan9, SoCali, and beaupre33, among others.

71. Serena Maria Daniels, "U-M Freshman Found Dead Excelled in Theater," *Detroit News* (Nov. 19, 2013).

72. Comments by Roosterchicky, emergaldcateyez, and TexAugMan after story by Paul Purpura, "Former Archbishop Chapelle High School Teacher Pleads Guilty to Sexual Relationship with Student," www.nola.com (July 11, 2013).

73. Miles v. Raycom Media, Inc., 38 Media L. Rep. 2374 (S.D. Miss. 2010).

74. Maureen O'Connor, "Married GOP Congressman Sent Sexy Pictures to Craigslist Babe," www.gawker.com (Feb. 9, 2011).

75. David Harding, "Married Christian Teacher Arrested for Lying to Police over Online Naked Photos," *N.Y. Daily News* (Feb. 1, 2014).

76. Saeed Ahmed, "That 'Worst Twerk Fail EVER' Video? Fake!," www.cnn .com (Sept. 10, 2013).

77. Doug Gross, "Man Faces Fallout for Spreading False Sandy Reports on Twitter," www.cnn.com (Oct. 31, 2013).

78. Doug Gross, "How a Fake Google News Story Spread Online," www.cnn .com (Nov. 28, 2012).

79. Rocco Parascandola, Vera Chinese, Ginger Adams Otis, "9-Year-Old Bronx Girl Discovered by Mother Hanging from Shower Curtain in Horrific Suicide," *New York Daily News* (Apr. 8, 2013).

80. Comments from tnxbutterfly97 and NY2VA11412.

81. Alia E. Dastagir, "Dark Picture of Castro Family Emerges," www.freep.com (May 8, 2013), still available online without apparent correction in July 2014.

82. iReport 101, "About," www.ireport.cnn.com.

83. "Community Guidelines," www.ireport.cnn.com.

84. "Community Guidelines," www.ireport.cnn.com.

85. Burrill v. Nair, 217 Cal. App. 4th 357 (Cal. Ct. App. 2013).

86. BruddahRod, "Halloween Scares from Texas!," www.ireport.cnn.com (Oct. 25, 2012).

87. www.cnnphotos.blogs.cnn.com (Mar. 1, 2013).

88. Brian Solis, "Extra Extra, Read All About It! Newspapers Respond to the Social Web," www.briansolis.com (Dec. 19, 2008).

89. www.imdb.com.

90. www.cnn.com (Dec. 16, 2013).

91. Edward Wyatt, "As Online Ads Look More Like News Articles, F.T.C. Warns Against Deception," *N.Y. Times* (Dec. 5, 2013).

92. www.cnn.com (March 26, 2013).

93. KOVR-TV, Inc. v. Superior Court of Sacramento County, 31 Cal. App. 4th 1023 (Cal. Ct. App. 1995).

94. Utah v. Krueger, 975 P. 2d 489 (Utah Ct. App. 1999).

95. United States v. Calabrese, 515 F. Supp. 2d 880 (N.D. Ill. Oct. 5, 2007).

96. Kathleen Parker, "The Double Standard in Affairs," *Washington Post* (Nov. 27, 2012).

97. Kathleen O'Toole, "Journalists Discuss Clash of Ideals, Reality in Their Business," *Stanford News Service* (July 2, 1997).

98. The State of the News Media 2013, Pew Center's Project for Excellence in Journalism, available at www.stateofthemedia.org.

99. Clarence Williams, Martin Well, "Car Plunges from Chesapeake Bay Bridge, Woman Lives," www.washingtonpost.com (July 19, 2013).

100. Comments from JimG-AlexandriaVA, bailinnumberguy, whistling, and ViennaDude.

101. Paul Farhi, "Jeffrey Bezos, Washington Post's Next Owner, Aims for a New 'Golden Era' at the Newspaper," *Washington Post* (Sept. 2, 2013).

102. C. W. Anderson, Emily Bell, Clay Shirky, "Post Industrial Journalism: Adapting to the Present," Tow Center for Digital Journalism, Columbia University (2012).

103. Erik Sass, "Public Trust in Newspapers Dips Again," www.mediapost.com (June 17, 2013).

104. The State of the News Media 2013, Pew Center's Project for Excellence in Journalism, available at www.stateofthemedia.org.

105. David Carr, "Storytelling Ads May Be Journalism's New Peril," *N.Y. Times* (Sept. 16, 2013).

106. Josh Sternberg, "How Top Publishers Handle 'Sponsored Content,'" www.digiday.com (June 14, 2013).

107. Carr, "Storytelling Ads May Be Journalism's New Peril."

108. Paul Farhi, "You'll Never Believe How Recommended Stories Are Generated on Otherwise Serious News Sites," *Washington Post* (Jan. 9, 2014).

109. Richard Morgan, "The (Robot) Creative Class," *New York* (June 17, 2013).

110. Sean O'Neal, "Algorithms Can't Replace Editorial Judgment," www.digiday.com (Mar. 11, 2013).

111. Lili Levi, "Social Media and the Press," 90 N.C.L. Rev. 1531 (2012).

5. The Rise, and Lows, of Quasi-Journalism

1. Amy Gajda, "Judging Journalism," 97 *Cal. L. Rev.* 1039 (2009), quoting Tim Harrower, *Inside Reporting* (2006).
2. Philip Patterson, Lee Wilkins, *Media Ethics: Issues and Cases* (Boston: McGraw Hill 2008) p. 35.
3. Randall P. Bezanson, *How Free Can the Press Be?* (Urbana: University of Illinois Press 2003) p. 251.
4. Randall Bezanson, "The Right to Privacy Revisited: Privacy, News, and Social Change, 1890–1990," 80 *Calif. L. Rev.* 1133 (1992).
5. See, e.g., Nik Richie, who considers himself merely a blogger who posts information from "citizen paparazzi" on a "reality-based blog." Chris Cole, "Website The Dirty Flourishing with New Scandals," *The Arizona Republic* (Aug. 2, 2013).
6. "No One Invited Her," www.thedirty.com (Jan. 20, 2011).
7. Cole, "Website The Dirty Flourishing with New Scandals."
8. 47 U.S.C. § 230(c)(1) (1996).
9. Gavra v. Google, Inc., 2013 U.S. Dist. LEXIS 100127 (N.D. Cal. July 17, 2013), rev'd 2014 WL 2694184 (6th Cir. June 16, 2014).
10. Jones pleaded guilty to having sex with a student in 2012. Amanda Lee Myers, "Ex-NFL Cheerleader Pleads Guilty to Student Sex," *Associated Press* (Oct. 8, 2012).
11. Jones v. Dirty World Entertainment, 840 F. Supp. 2d 1008 (E.D. Ky. 2012).
12. Kashmir Hill, "Big Deal for Internet Law: Ex-Bengals Cheerleader Sarah Jones Wins Suit against The Dirty Over 'Reputation-Ruining' Comments," *Forbes* (July 11, 2013).
13. Jones v. Dirty World Entertainment Recordings, 965 F. Supp. 2d 818 (E.D. Ky. 2013), rev'd 2014 WL 2694184 (6th Cir. June 16, 2014).
14. Hare v. Richie, 2012 U.S. Dist. LEXIS 122893 (D. Md. 2012).
15. Beth Moszkowicz, "Settlement Deal Leads to Removal of Posts about Maryland Man from www.thedirty.com," *Daily Record* (Feb. 28, 2013).
16. Victor Li, "Gossip Website's Appeal of Ex-cheerleader's Defamation Verdict Watched Closely by Internet Giants," *ABA Journal* (May 2, 2014).
17. Robert L. Rogers, "The 'Dirt' on Revocation of Immunity for Websites that 'Encourage' Defamatory Posts," *Communications Lawyer,* American Bar Association (Feb. 2013).
18. Prall v. New York City Department of Corrections, 40 Misc. 3d 940 (N.Y. Sup. Ct. 2013)
19. Capitol Resource Corp. v. Department of State Police, 2007 Ky. App. Unpub. LEXIS 355 (Ky. Ct. App. Aug. 3, 2007)
20. Prison Legal News v. Executive Office for United States Attorneys, 628 F.3d 1243 (10th Cir. 2011).

21. Ricardo Lopez, "Lawsuit Targets Website that Posts Mug Shots," *Los Angeles Times* (Jan. 22, 2014).

22. Bilotta v. Citizens Information Associates, 42 Media L. Rep. 1130 (M.D. Fla. 2014).

23. Elvis Presley Enterprises v. Passport Video, 357 F.3d 896 (9th Cir. 2003).

24. Obsidian Finance Group v. Cox, 812 F. Supp. 2d 1220 (D. Or. 2011).

25. Roe v. McClellan, 2009 Cal. App. Unpub. LEXIS 335 (Cal. Ct. App. Jan. 15, 2009).

26. U.S. v. Petrovic, 701 F.3d 849 (8th Cir. 2012).

27. Trummel v. Mitchell, 121 Wash. App. 1078 (Wash. Ct. App. 2004), reversed on other grounds, 131 P.3d 305 (Wash. 2006).

28. Backlund v. Stone, 2012 Cal. App. Unpub. LEXIS 6467 (Cal. Ct. App. Sept. 4, 2012).

29. Condit v. National Enquirer, 248 F. Supp. 2d 945 (E.D. Cal. 2002).

30. Meyers v. Tempesta, 2013 Cal. App. Unpub. LEXIS 173 (Cal. Ct. App. Jan. 9, 2013).

31. Camille Dodero, "Hunter Moore Makes a Living Screwing You," *Village Voice* (Apr. 4, 2012).

32. Carol Kuruvilla, "Revenge Porn Curators Defend Their X-rated Websites," *New York Daily News* (Feb. 8, 2013).

33. Carol Kuruvilla, "Revenge Porn? Women Sue Website Charging X-rated Pics of Them Were Uploaded on Site and Rated without Their Knowledge," *New York Daily News* (Jan. 27, 2013).

34. www.boards.4chan.org/b/1

35. Consider, for example, the comments posted following a woman's photograph: "Is it normal to fantasize about rape?" "Nope, I would do it to her too." "Would love to sodomized [*sic*] me a young teen girl. Then kill her." Comments by anonymous posters on 4chan's /b/-Random on April 18, 2012.

36. www.myex.com (Feb. 9, 2014).

37. www.removemanager.com/payment/ (May 14, 2014).

38. Lateef Mungin, "Man Once Called the 'Revenge Porn King' Indicted," www.cnn.com (Jan. 24, 2014).

39. www.collegeacb.com (Jan. 26, 2011).

40. www.collegeacb.com (Feb. 16, 2011).

41. www.collegeleak.com (Aug. 30, 2013).

42. www.collegiateacb.com (Apr. 17, 2014).

43. www.collegewallofshame.com (May 14, 2014).

44. www.peopleofwalmart.com

45. www.dirtyphonebook.com (May 14, 2014).

46. www.exposed.su/ (Mar. 12, 2013).

47. www.whosarat.com/aboutus (Sept. 15, 2013).

48. www.whosarat.com (May 14, 2014).
49. www.fairfaxunderground.com.
50. Tom Jackman, "Fairfax Underground Exposes Teen Sex Tape Scandal and Other Juicy Topics," *Washington Post* (Feb.8, 2013).
51. Connor Adams Sheets, "10 Boston Marathon Bombing 'Suspects' 4chan and Reddit Found [Photos]," www.ibtimes.com (Apr. 17, 2013).
52. Shahriar Rahmanzadeh, Jennifer Leong, Samantha Riley, Santina Leuci, and Rhonda Schwartz, "Teen: I Am Not the Marathon Bomber," www.abcnews.com (Apr. 19, 2013).
53. Michael Walsh, "Reddit Apologizes for Online 'Witch Hunt' for Boston Marathon Bombers," *New York Daily News* (Apr. 24, 2013).
54. Bullard v. MRA Holdings, 890 F. Supp. 2d 1323 (N.D. Ga. 2012).
55. Padilla v. Holding, 2004 Cal. App. Unpub. LEXIS 11772 (Cal. Ct. App. Dec. 28, 2004).
56. Glaze v. M.R.A. Holding, 2003 U.S. Dist. LEXIS 25572 (M.D. Fla. July 11, 2003).
57. Capdeboscq v. Francis, 98 Fed. Appx. 988 (5th Cir. 2004).
58. Ibid.
59. Plaintiff B v. Francis, 38 Media L. Rep. 1925 (N.D. Fla. 2010).
60. Gritzke v. M.R.A. Holding, 2002 U.S. Dist. LEXIS 28085 (N.D. Fla. Mar. 16, 2002).
61. Padilla v. Holding, 2004 Cal. App. Unpub. LEXIS 11772 (Cal. Ct. App. Dec. 28, 2004).
62. Capdeboscq v. Francis, 2004 U.S. Dist. LEXIS 3790 (E.D. La. Mar. 10, 2004).
63. Ibid.
64. Lane v. MRA Holdings, 242 F. Supp. 2d 1205 (M.D. Fla. 2002).
65. Gritzke v. M.R.A. Holding, 2002 U.S. Dist. LEXIS 28085 (N.D. Fla. Mar. 16, 2002).
66. Bullard v. MRA Holding, 740 S.E.2d 622 (Ga. 2013).
67. Padilla v. Holding, 2004 Cal. App. Unpub. LEXIS 11722 (Cal. Ct. App. Dec. 28, 2004).
68. Capdeboscq v. Francis, 2004 U.S. Dist. LEXIS 3790 (E.D. La. Mar. 10, 2004).
69. Padilla v. Holding, 2004 Cal. App. Unpub. LEXIS 11722 (Cal. Ct. App. Dec. 28, 2004).
70. Plaintiff B v. Francis, 631 F.3d 1310 (11th Cir. 2011).
71. See Ibid.
72. Ex parte Cohen, 988 So. 2d 508 (Ala. 2008).
73. Lemerond v. Twentieth Century Fox Film Corp., 36 Media L. Rep. 1743 (S.D.N.Y. 2008).
74. Johnston v. One America Productions, 2007 U.S. Dist. LEXIS 62029 (N.D. Miss. Aug. 22, 2007).
75. Ibid.

76. http://www.projectveritas.com (Apr. 10, 2014).

77. "4 Charged in U.S. Senate Office Infiltration in New Orleans," www.cnn
.com (Jan. 26, 2010).

78. "Debate Over Activists' Actions in Senator's Office," National Public Radio:
"All Things Considered" transcript (Feb. 4, 2010).

79. Ibid.

80. Ramon Antonio Vargas, "James O'Keefe and Friends Plead Guilty in Mary
Landrieu Office Caper," *Times-Picayune* (May 26, 2010).

81. Conor Friedersdorf, "Andrew Breitbart and James O'Keefe Ruined Him,
and Now He Gets $100,000," *Atlantic* (Mar. 2013).

82. Vera v. O'Keefe, 40 Media L. Rep. 2564 (S.D. Cal. 2012).

83. Vera v. O'Keefe, 2011 U.S. Dist. LEXIS 108908 (S.D. Cal. Sept. 23, 2011).

84. Vera v. O'Keefe, 791 F. Supp. 2d 959 (S.D. Cal. 2011).

85. News release, "Hannah Giles Sued by Third ACORN Employee" (Feb. 2,
2010).

86. "O'Keefe's Latest: Voter Fraud Investigation Lands on Eric Holder's
Doorstep," www.breitbart.com (Apr. 9, 2012).

87. PG Publishing Co. v. Aichele, 705 F.3d 91 (3d Cir. 2013).

88. www.aetv.com.

89. www.amazing911calls.com (Apr. 2, 2014).

90. Carter v. Superior Court of San Diego County, 2002 Cal. App. Unpub.
LEXIS 5017 (Cal. Ct. App. Jan. 10, 2002).

91. Beall v. Turner Broadcasting Systems, 2012 U.S. Dist. LEXIS 179383 (D.
Nev. Dec. 19, 2012).

92. Tammy Stables Battaglia, "WWJ Reporter Fired for Wearing Obama
T-shirt," *Detroit Free Press* (Oct. 2, 2008).

93. Joe Holleman, "Fired KMOV Anchor Larry Conners Defends Facebook
Comments about IRS," *St. Louis Post-Dispatch* (May 23, 2013).

94. Doe v. Gangland Productions, 730 F.3d 946 (9th Cir. 2013).

95. Battle v. A&E TV Networks, 837 F. Supp. 2d 767 (M.D. Tenn. 2011).

96. Burke v. Gregg, 2011 R.I. Super. LEXIS 15 (R.I. Super. Feb. 4, 2011).

97. Klapper v. Graziano, 970 N.Y.S.2d 355 (N.Y. Sup. 2013).

98. Zimmerman v. Board of Trustees of Ball State University, 940 F. Supp. 2d
875 (S.D. Ind. 2013).

99. United States v. Spann, 963 F. Supp. 2d 1198 (D. Kan. 2013).

100. www.houston.craigslist.org (June 12, 2013).

101. James Taranto, "Best of the Web: The Prurience of the Idaho Press," *Wall
Street Journal* (Dec. 3, 2007).

102. James Taranto, "Unstatesmanlike Conduct," *American Spectator* (Nov. 2007).

103. John Cook, "We Are Raising $200,000 to Buy and Publish the Rob Ford
Crack Tape," www.gawker.com (May 17, 2013).

104. John Cook, "The Rob Ford Crack Video Might Be Gone," www.gawker
.com (June 4, 2013).

105. David Carr, "For Journalists, More Firepower to Protect Sources and Secrets," *N.Y. Times* (Sept. 29, 2013).
106. SEIU v. Professional Janitorial Service of Houston, 415 S.W.3d 387 (Tex. Ct. App. 2013).
107. In re January 11, 2013 Subpoena, 75 A.3d 1260 (N.J. Super. 2013).
108. Charles D. Tobin, "First Amendment Caste System," *Communications Lawyer* (Jan. 2012).
109. Five for Entertainment v. Rodriguez, 877 F. Supp. 2d 1321 (S.D. Fla. 2012).
110. Bailey v. Maine Com'n on Governmental Ethics and Election Practices, 900 F. Supp. 2d 75 (D. Maine 2012).
111. www.mediatakeout.com
112. Edme v. Internet Brands, Inc., 968 F. Supp. 2d 519 (E.D.N.Y. 2013).

6. The New Old Legal Call for Privacy

1. Ignat v. Yum! Brands, 214 Cal. App. 4th 808 (Cal. Ct. App. 2013).
2. Denis v. LeClerc, 1 Mart. 297 (La. Sup. Ct. 1811).
3. Jeremy Fogel, "From the Bench: A Reasonable Expectation of Privacy," *Litigation* (Spring 2014).
4. Remarks by the chair of the American Psychiatric Association Committee on Confidentiality, as reported in Beverly Beyette, "The Human Condition: The Need for Privacy," *Los Angeles Times* (Mar. 17, 1992).
5. Charles Fried, Privacy, 77 *Yale L.J.* 475 (1968).
6. Julie Cohen, "What Privacy Is for," 126 *Harv. L. Rev.* 1904 (2013).
7. Joe Nocera, "'The Wild West of Privacy,'" *New York Times* (Feb. 24, 2014).
8. Sheridan Newspapers v. Sheridan, 660 P. 2d 785 (Wyo. 1983), (citing Nebraska Press Association v. Stuart, 427 U.S. 539, 613 (1976) (Brennan, J., concurring).
9. Commonwealth v. Winfield, 985 N.E.2d 86 (Mass. 2013).
10. In re Thow, 392 B.R. 860 (W.D. Wash. 2007).
11. Arenas v. Shed Media, 881 F. Supp. 2d 1181 (C.D. Cal. 2011).
12. Thomas v. McKee, 205 F. Supp. 2d 1275 (M.D. Ala. 2002).
13. In re Application for a Search Warrant, 71 A.3d 1158 (Vt. 2012), quoting dissent from United States v. Gourde, 440 F.3d 1065 (9th Cir. 2006).
14. Ronald Brownstein, "Americans Know They've Already Lost Their Privacy," *National Journal* (June 13, 2013).
15. Clay Calvert, "Dying for Privacy: Pitting Public Access against Familial Interests in the Era of the Internet," 105 *Nw. U.L. Rev. Colloquy* 18 (2010).
16. Laura Ly, "Bill to Withhold Newtown Photos, Records Gets Strong OK in Connecticut Legislature," www.cnn.com (June 6, 2013).
17. Jenny Wilson, "Panel Proposes Limiting Access to Public Records," *Hartford Courant* (Jan. 24, 2014).

18. Anna Stolley Persky, "Coverage or Crime: When Journalism Crosses the Line," *Washington Lawyer* (Dec. 2011).
19. The cover featured a glasses-wearing man with the bold headline: "Heads Up: Why Wearable Tech Will Be as Big as the Smartphone," *Wired* (Jan. 2014).
20. Dan Gillmore, "Prepare for the New Cameras-Everywhere World," www.slate.com (Dec. 12, 2012).
21. Wolfson v. Lewis, 924 F. Supp. 1413 (E.D. Penn. 1996).
22. Craig Timberg, "License Plate Cameras Track Millions of Americans," *Washington Post* (July 17, 2013).
23. Craig Timberg, "Blimplike Surveillance Craft Set to Deploy over Maryland Heighten Privacy Concerns," *Washington Post* (Jan. 22, 2014).
24. See, e.g., Carolyn P. Smith, "Suit filed over ESL speed cameras; two plaintiffs get tickets voided," *News Democrat* (June 11, 2014); Note 25.
25. "Ohio Supreme Court Denies Village's Speed Camera Appeal," www.wlwt.com (Aug. 7, 2013).
26. Birgitta Forsberg, "Restrictions Placed on Camera Phones / More Places Say They May Violate Privacy, Security," *San Francisco Chronicle* (May 23, 2005).
27. Lori Obert & Jeremy Jojola, "Upskirting Cases on the Rise," www.9news.com (Sept. 16, 2011).
28. Chris Matyszczyk, "Survey: 50% of Americans Are Cell Phone Video Spies," www.cnet.org (Oct. 11, 2011).
29. State v. Earls, 70 A.3d 630 (N.J. 2013).
30. Sam Biddle, "iSpy Conspiracy: Your iPhone Is Secretly Tracking Everywhere You've Been, All The Time," www.gizmodo.com (Apr. 20, 2011).
31. "Michigan: Police Search Cell Phones During Traffic Stops," www.thenewspaper.com (Apr. 19, 2011).
32. A. J. Daulerio, "The Full Duke University "F—List" Thesis From a Former Female Student," www.deadspin.com (Sept. 30, 2010).
33. Brian Stelter, "Company Parts Ways with PR Exec after AIDS in Africa Tweet," www.cnn.com (Dec. 21, 2013).
34. Barket v. Clark, 2013 U.S. Dist. LEXIS 24365 (D. Nev. Feb. 21, 2013).
35. U.S. v. Gourde, 440 F.3d 1065 (9th Cir. 2006).
36. Bursac v. Suozzi, 868 N.Y.S.2d 470 (N.Y. Sup. Ct. 2008).
37. Bierman v. Weier, 826 N.W.2d 436 (Iowa 2013).
38. W.J.A. v. D.A., 43 A.3d 1148 (N.J. 2012).
39. Heather Kelly, "California Weighs Making 'Revenge Porn' Illegal," www.cnn.com (Aug. 30, 2013).
40. Erica Goode, "Victims Push Laws to End Online Revenge Posts," *New York Times* (Sept. 23, 2013).
41. Ibid.
42. David Kravets, "Lawsuit by 19 Groups Seeks to Halt NSA Snooping," www.cnn.com (July 17, 2013).

43. Bruce Schneier, "The Internet Is a Surveillance State," www.cnn.com (Mar. 16, 2013).

44. Julia Angwin, Steve Stecklow, "'Scrapers' Dig Deep for Data on Web," *Wall Street Journal* (Oct. 12, 2010).

45. Anthony J. Dreyer and Jamie Stockton, "Internet 'Data Scraping': A Primer for Counseling Clients," *New York Law Journal* (July 23, 2013).

46. Melanie Hicken, "Data Brokers Selling Lists of Rape Victims, AIDS Patients," www.cnn.com (Dec. 19, 2013).

47. 42 USCS § 2000ee-3 (2007).

48. Jack Gillum, "AP Exclusive: Romney Uses Secretive Data-Mining," *Associated Press* (Aug. 24, 2012).

49. "California High Court: Retailers Can't Request Cardholders' ZIP Code," www.cnn.com (Feb. 15, 2011).

50. Costas Pitas, "Snowden Warns of Loss of Privacy in Christmas Message," *Reuters* (Dec. 25, 2013).

51. Matt Waite, "The Drone Age Is Here, and So Are the Lawyers," www.niemanlab.org (Dec. 2013).

52. Joel Landau, "FAA Bans Outdoor Drone Use at University of Missouri," *New York Daily News* (Apr. 27, 2014).

53. *Popular Mechanics* (Feb. 2014).

54. 18 U.S.C. § 2721 (1994); Senne v. Village of Palatine, 695 F.3d 597 (7th Cir. 2012).

55. Eisenstein v. WTVF-TV, 389 S.W.3d 313, 329 (Tenn. Ct. App. 2012).

56. West v. Media General Convergence, 53 S.W.3d 640 (Tenn. 2001).

57. Tacoma News v. Cayce, 26 P. 3d 1179 (Wash. 2011).

58. Ryan v. Fox Television, 979 N.E.2d 954 (Ill. App. Ct. 2012).

59. www.99rise.com (May 16, 2014).

60. Eileen Shim, "A Protester Smuggled a Camera in and Secretly Recorded This Video of the Supreme Court," www.policymic.com (Feb. 28, 2014).

61. Robert Barnes, "At Supreme Court, Tradition Trumps Technology, and Transparency," *Washington Post* (Oct. 27, 2013).

62. www.pen.org; "Sonia Sotomayor Freedom to Write Lecture," www.cspan .org (May 5, 2013). Interestingly, Justice Sotomayor suggested that she had used intimate stories in her memoir to help the reader imagine themself in another's shoes. When asked about the potential privacy invasions in her own memoir's revelations, she suggested that she had shared her manuscript with a family member before publication and that, ultimately, her mother appreciated the personal stories that she had shared.

63. Derek Paulson, "Wrong Side of the Tracks: Exploring the Role of Newspaper Coverage of Homicide in Socially Constructing Dangerous Places," *Journal of Criminal Justice and Popular Culture* 9-113 (2002).

64. United States v. Kravetz, 706 F.3d 47 (1st Cir. 2013).

65. Karantsalis v. U.S. Department of Justice, 635 F.3d 497 (11th Cir. 2011).

66. Marsh v. County of San Diego, 680 F.3d 1148 (9th Cir. 2012).

67. Doe v. Idaho, 290 P. 3d 1277 (Idaho 2012).

68. Rush v. Chronicle Telegram, 1980 Ohio App. LEXIS 12249 (Ohio Ct. App. May 30, 1980).

69. Roshto v. Hebert, 439 So. 2d 428 (La. 1983)

70. Connecticut Judicial-Media Committee, "Results of Judges' and Journalists' Surveys Conducted October 2007," available at www.jud.ct.gov.

71. Restatement of Torts, Second § 652D, cmt. k (1977).

72. 48 *Cal. L. Rev.* 417 (1960).

73. Archibald v. United States Department of Justice, 950 F. Supp. 2d 80 (D.D.C. 2013).

74. Cook v. National Archives and Records Administration, 921 F. Supp. 2d 148 (S.D.N.Y. 2013).

75. Journal News v. City of White Plains, 40 Media L. Rep. 1618 (N.Y. Sup. 2012).

76. Stephens v. Dolcefino, 126 S.W.3d 120 (Tex. Ct. App. 2003).

77. Dorsett v. County of Nassau, 289 F.R.D. 54 (E.D.N.Y. 2012).

78. Billings Gazette v. City of Billings, 313 P.3d 129 (Mont. 2013) (McKinnon, J., dissenting).

79. Press release, "Paparazzi Harassment Deterrent Bill Signed by the Governor—Increases Penalties & Allows for Civil Action to Protect Children," www.sd22.senate.ca.gov.

80. Gloria Goodale, "Is California Going too Far to Protect Celebrity Kids from Paparazzi?," *Christian Science Monitor* (Sept. 25, 2013).

81. *OK! USA* (Jan. 6, 2014).

82. Nardine Saad, "JustJared, People Tout 'No Kids' Photo Policies after Stars' Pleas," *L.A. Times* (Feb. 25, 2014).

83. Cal. Civ. Code § 1708.8

84. Mireya Navarro, "Everyone Wants to Be Taking Pictures," *New York Times* (Nov. 18, 2007).

85. Brandi Fowler, "'Steven Tyler Act': Hawaii Proposes to Protect Celebs from Paparazzi," www.eonline.com (Feb. 4, 2013).

86. Michael Cieply, "Actress's Suit Against IMDb for Publishing Her Actual Age Can Go to Trial," *N.Y. Times,* Mar. 19, 2013.

87. Ventura v. Kyle, 2012 U.S. Dist. LEXIS 179929 (D. Minn. Dec. 20, 2012).

88. Tripp v. United States of America, 257 F. Supp. 2d 37 (D.D.C. 2003)

89. See, e.g., Vasquez v. Lopez, 2012 Cal. App. Unpub. LEXIS 6908 (Cal. Ct. App. Sept. 24, 2012); Coady v. Harpo, Inc., 308 Ill. App. 3d 153 (Ill. App. Ct. 1999).

90. Coady v. Harpo, Inc., 308 Ill. App. 3d 153 (Ill. App. Ct. 1999).

91. Ann-Margret v. High Society Magazine, 498 F. Supp. 401 (S.D.N.Y. 1980).

92. See Matthew A. Chivvis, "Consent to Monitoring of Electronic Communications of Employees as an Aspect of Liberty and Dignity:

Looking to Europe," 19 *Fordham Intell. Prop. Media & Ent. L.J.* 799 (2009) (employers should ask explicit consent from employees before monitoring their workplace communications, in order to respect their liberty and dignity); Michael L. Rustad & Sandra R. Paulsson, "Monitoring Employee E-Mail and Internet Usage: Avoiding the Omniscient Electronic Sweatshop: Insights from Europe," 7 *U. Pa. J. Lab. & Emp. L.* 829 (2005) (enacting an Electronic Monitoring Act will make American companies more competitive with European companies); Jake Spratt, "An Economic Argument for Electronic Privacy," 6 I/S: *J.L. & Pol'y for Info. Soc'y* 513 (2011) (personal privacy and e-commerce will be improved by enacting comprehensive electronic privacy laws).

93. United States v. Jones, 132 S. Ct. 945 (2012).
94. Florida v. Jardines, 133 S. Ct. 1409 (2013).
95. McBurney v. Young, 133 S. Ct. 1709 (2013).
96. Pike v. Hester, 2013 U.S. Dist. LEXIS 99625 (D. Nev. July 9, 2013).
97. Northwestern Memorial Hospital v. Ashcroft, 362 F.3d 923 (7th Cir. 2004).
98. McKenzie v. Foley, 1995 Kan. App. Unpub. LEXIS 268 (Kansas Ct. App. Aug. 11, 1995).
99. Ehling v. Monmouth-Ocean Hospital Service Corp., 872 F. Supp. 2d 369 (D.N.J. 2012).
100. Fraley v. Facebook, 2013 WL 4516819 (N.D. Cal. Aug. 26, 2013).
101. Eagle v. Morgan, 2013 U.S. Dist. LEXIS 34220 (E.D. Pa. Mar. 12, 2013).
102. Wiest v. E-Fense, Inc., 356 F. Supp. 2d 604 (E.D. Va. 2005).
103. Neeley v. Wells Fargo Fin., Inc., 2012 U.S. Dist. LEXIS 168669 (M.D. Fla. Nov. 28, 2012).

7. The First Amendment Bubble, Absolutism, and Hazardous Growth

1. See David Copeland, *The Idea of a Free Press: The Enlightenment and Its Unruly Legacy* p. 15 (Northwestern Univ. Press 2006); Michael Kent Curtis, Free Speech, "The People's Darling Privilege": *Struggles for Freedom of Expression in American History* p. 36–37 (Duke Univ. Press 2000).
2. Cato's Letter No. 32, *Reflections Upon Libelling* (1721).
3. Frederick Schauer, "The Role of the People in First Amendment Theory," 74 *Cal. L. Rev.* 761 (1986).
4. 491 U.S. at 541.
5. Bollea v. Gawker Media, 2012 U.S. Dist. LEXIS 162711 (M.D. Fla. Nov. 14, 2012), quoting Anonsen v. Donahue, 857 S.W.2d 700 (Tex. App. 1993).
6. Clift v. Narragansett Television, 688 A.2d 805 (R.I. 1996).
7. Anderson v. Blake, 2005 U.S. Dist. LEXIS 25654 (W.D. Okla. Oct. 21, 2005).
8. Ibid. Emphasis added.

9. Anderson v. Blake, 2006 U.S. Dist. LEXIS 8454 (W.D. Okla. Feb. 9, 2006).

10. Anderson v. Suiters, 499 F.3d 1228 (10th Cir. 2007).

11. Peckham v. New England Newspapers, 865 F. Supp. 2d 127 (D. Mass. 2012).

12. Branzburg v. Hayes, 408 U.S. 665 (1972).

13. In re Inquest Subpoena (WCAX), 890 A.2d 1240 (Vt. 2005).

14. Indianapolis Newspapers v. Junior Achievement of Central Indiana, 963 N.E.2d 534 (Ind. Ct. App. 2012).

15. http://arnesvenson.com/theneighbors.html

16. Foster v. Svenson, 41 Media L. Rep. 2564 (N.Y. Sup. Ct. 2013)

17. Catherine Wagley, "Arne Svenson: The Neighbors," www.photographmag .com (Feb. 1, 2013).

18. Clift v. Narragansett Television, 688 A.2d 805 (R.I. 1996).

19. Chris Cole, "Website The Dirty Flourishing with New Scandals," *Arizona Republic* (Aug. 2, 2013).

20. Anthony Lewis, reviewing Randall P. Bezanson, *How Free Can the Press Be?* (Urbana: University of Illinois Press 2003).

21. www.aejmc.net/law/FirstPlace.pdf. Emphasis added.

22. "Law and Policy Notes," Fall 2010, www.aejmc.net.

23. California Penal Code § 647 (j)(4)(A) (2013).

24. www.leginfo.ca.gov.

25. Bartnicki v. Vopper, 532 U.S. 514, 541 (2001).

26. Eric Schulzke, "California Lawmakers Target 'Revenge Porn' but Miss, Critics Say," *Deseret News* (Sept. 8, 2013).

27. Emily Bazelon, "Why Do We Tolerate Revenge Porn?" www.slate.com (Sept. 25, 2013).

28. Deirdre Dlugoleski, "We Are All Journalists Now," *Columbia Journalism Review* (May 20, 2013).

29. Bob Giles, "Mainstream Media and the Survival of Journalism," www.neiman.harvard.edu (Fall 2005).

30. Scott Gant, *We're All Journalists Now: The Transformation of the Press and Reshaping of the Law in the Internet Age* (New York: Free Press 2011).

31. Eric Deggens, "Snowden's Leaks Force Media Self-examination," www.poynter.org (July 3, 2013).

32. David Sirota, "Meet the 'Journalists Against Journalism' club!" www.salon .com (July 2, 2013).

33. Digital Music News v. Superior Court, 2014 WL 1912587 (Cal. Ct. App. May 14, 2014); In Re Domestic Drywall Antitrust Litigation, 2014 WL 1979310 (E.D. Pa. May 15, 2014).

34. Tim Arango, "In Scandal, Turkey's Leaders May Be Losing Their Tight Grip on News Media," *N.Y. Times* (Jan. 11, 2014).

35. Reuters, "Turkey Keeps YouTube Block Despite Court Rulings" (Apr. 10, 2014).

36. Citizens United v. Federal Election Commission, 530 F. Supp. 2d 274 (D.D.C. 2008).

37. Citizens United v. Federal Election Commission, 558 U.S. 310 (2010).

38. "President Obama on Citizens United: 'Imagine the Power This Will Give Special Interests Over Politicians,'" www.whitehouse.gov (July 26, 2010).

39. Editorial, "Awash in Money," *Roll Call* (Jan. 27, 2010).

40. See, e.g., Richard L. Hasen, "Citizens United and the Illusion of Coherence," 109 *Mich. L. Rev.* 581 (2011); Robert Weissman, "Let the People Speak: The Case for a Constitutional Amendment to Remove Corporate Speech from the Ambit of the First Amendment," 83 *Temple L. Rev.* 979 (2011).

41. United States v. Stevens, 559 U.S. 460 (2010).

42. Paula Reed Ward, "Supreme Court to Hear Appeal of Man Jailed for Dogfight Videos," *Pittsburgh Post-Gazette* (Oct. 4, 2009).

43. Kathleen Parker, "Crush Animal Cruelty; The Next Step Is Up to Congress," *Washington Post* (Apr. 25, 2010).

44. Marie Price, "U.S. Supreme Court Chief Justice John Roberts Court Expands Free Speech, Narrows Reach of Establishment Clause," *Journal Record* (July 29, 2011).

45. Sorrell v. IMS Health Inc., 131 S. Ct. 2653 (2011).

46. Jamie Raskin, "'Citizens United' and the Corporate Court," *The Nation* (Oct. 8, 2012).

47. Rebecca L. Brown, Phelps Lecture on First Amendment Law, "Freedom of Speech 2.0," Tulane University Law School, Feb. 8, 2012.

48. McCutcheon v. Federal Election Commission, 134 S. Ct. 1434 (2014).

49. Michael D. Sullivan, "Selling the First Amendment to a Jury," *Communications Lawyer* (Nov. 2012).

50. State of the First Amendment: 2013, First Amendment Center, www.firstamendmentcenter.org (July 2013).

51. Donald Gillmor, *Power, Publicity, and the Abuse of Libel Law* (Oxford: Oxford University Press 1992).

52. Haas Publishing Co. v. Indiana Department of State Revenue, 835 N.E.2d 235 (Ind. Tax Ct. 2005).

53. Greenstein v. Greif Co., 37 Media L. Rep. 1225 (Cal. Ct. App. 2009).

54. United States v. Smith, 2013 WL 6576791 (S.D.N.Y. Dec. 4, 2013).

8. Drawing Difficult Lines

1. Williams L. Prosser, "Insult and Outrage," 44 *Cal. L. Rev.* 40 (1956).

2. Rodney A. Smolla, "Will Tabloid Journalism Ruin the First Amendment for the Rest of Us?," 9 *DePaul-LCA J. Art & Ent. L.* 1 (1998).

3. White v. Nicholls, 44 U.S. 266 (1845).

4. Holden v. Minnesota, 137 U.S. 483 (1890).

5. Mutual Film Corp. v. Industrial Commission of Ohio, 236 U.S. 230 (1915).

6. Near v. Minnesota, 283 U.S. 697 (1931).

7. 376 U.S. 254 (1964).

8. Time, Inc. v. Hill, 385 U.S. 374 (1967).

9. Ibid.

10. New York Times Co. v. United States, 403 U.S. 713 (U.S. 1971) (Black, J., concurring).

11. Minneapolis Star & Tribune Co. v. Minnesota Commissioner of Revenue, 460 U.S. 575 (1983).

12. Smith v. Daily Mail Publishing Co., 443 U.S. 97 (1979).

13. Nelson v. McClatchy Newspapers, Inc., 936 P. 2d 1123 (Wash. 1997).

14. See, e.g., Miranda v. Byles, 2012 Tex. App. LEXIS 8897 (Tex. Ct. App. Oct. 25, 2012).

15. Restatement (Second) of Torts § 652D, cmt. g.

16. Lee Bollinger, *Uninhibited, Robust, and Wide-Open* (Oxford: Oxford University Press 2010).

17. Draft Report, "Promoting Responsible and Professional Reporting on Corruption on the Basis of the United Nations Convention against Corruption: A Guide for Governments and Journalists," United Nations Office on Drugs and Crime (Draft of 26 July 2013).

18. See, e.g., Katherine Mangan, "In Remarks to College Leaders, New York Times Editor Describes Upheaval in News Business," www.chronicle.com (June 10, 2008).

19. Jessica Bruder, "Is the Death of Newspapers the End of Good Citizenship?" *Christian Science Monitor* (Nov. 11, 2012).

20. Ibid.

21. Dean Starkman, "Tracking Digital-Era News Quality Declines," *Columbia Journalism Review* (Jan. 14, 2014).

22. Home News v. Department of Health, 677 A.2d 195 (N.J. 1996).

23. RonNell Andersen Jones, "Litigation, Legislation, and Democracy in a Post-Newspaper America," 68 *Wash. & Lee L. Rev.* 557 (2011).

24. Peter Osnos, "These Journalists Spent Two Years and $750,000 Covering One Story," *Atlantic* (Oct. 2, 2013).

25. Steven Waldman, "The Information Needs of Communities: The Changing Media Landscape in a Broadband Age," www.fcc.gov (June 2011).

26. Ibid.

27. Pete Hamill's preface, *Shaking the Foundations: 200 Years of Investigative Journalism in America,* (New York: Nation Books 2003), Bruce Shapiro, ed., p. vii.

28. Cohen v. Cowles Media Co., 501 U.S. 663 (1991).

29. Citizens United, 558 U.S. 310.

30. Zacchini v. Scripps-Howard Broadcasting Co., 433 U.S. 562 (U.S. 1977).

31. Cohen v. Cowles Media Co., 501 U.S. 663 (U.S. 1991).

32. E.g., Time v. Firestone, 424 U.S. 448 (1976), Wolston v. Reader's Digest Ass'n, Inc., 443 U.S. 157 (1979).

33. Erik Sass, "Public Trust in Newspapers Dips Again," www.mediapost.com (June 17, 2013).

34. Bruce Sanford, "Don't Shoot the Messenger" (New York: Free Press 1999).

35. Andy Kohut, "Pew Surveys of Audience Habits Suggests Perilous Future for News," www.poynter.org (Oct. 4, 2013).

36. Andrew Beaujon, "New Bit.ly Map Tracks Media Popularity in Real Time," www.poynter.org (Oct. 3, 2013).

37. Jon Bruner, "The Interactive Media Map: America's Most Influential News Outlets," www.forbes.com (Mar. 22, 2012).

38. Michael D. Sullivan, "Selling the First Amendment to a Jury," *Communications Lawyer* (Nov. 2012).

39. Elizabeth Landau, "Shhhh . . . Some Secrets You Might Need to Keep," www.cnn.com (Nov. 5, 2012).

40. Ibid., comment by pmichner.

41. Restatement (Second) of Torts § 652D, cmt. g.

42. Restatement (Second) of Torts § 652D, cmt. h.

43. Ronald Krotoszynski, Jr., "The Polysemy of Privacy," 88 *Ind. L.J.* 881 (2013).

44. Harper & Row v. Nation Enters., 471 U.S. 539 (1985).

45. Haynes v. Alfred A. Knopf, 8 F.3d 1222 (7th Cir. 1993).

46. Clifford Christians, "Social Dialogue and Media Ethics," 7 *Media Ethics* 182 (2000).

47. Neil Richards, "Reconciling Data Privacy and the First Amendment," 52 *U.C.L.A. L. Rev.* 1149 (2005).

48. Leviston v. Jackson, 980 N.Y.S.2d 716 (N.Y. Sup. Ct. 2013).

49. See James Whitman, "The Two Western Cultures of Privacy: Dignity Versus Liberty," 113 *Yale L.J.* 151 (2004).; Guy E. Carmi, "Dignity Versus Liberty: The Two Western Cultures Of Free Speech," 26 *B.U. Int'l L.J.* 277 (2008); Rex D. Glensy, "The Right To Dignity," 443 *Colum. Human Rights L. Rev.* 65 (2011); Ronald J. Krotoszynski, Jr., "The Polysemy of Privacy," 88 *Ind. L. J.* 881 (2013); Scott J. Shackelford, "Fragile Merchandise: A Comparative Analysis of the Privacy Rights for Public Figures," 49 *Am. Bus. L.J.* 125 (2012).

50. Krotosynzski, "The Polysemy of Privacy," 88 *Ind. L.J.* at 907.

51. Article 8, European Convention on Human Rights, Right to Respect for Private and Family Life.

52. Paul Tweed, *Privacy and Libel Law: The Clash with Press Freedom* (West Sussex: Bloomsbury Professional 2012), p. 103.

53. Tom Welsh, Water Greenwood & David Banks, *McNae's Essential Law for Journalists* (Oxford: Oxford University Press 2005) p. 390.

54. Michael Birnbaum, "In Germany, Angela Merkel Photos Show 'Secret Family Life' of Chancellor," *Washington Post* (Apr. 6, 2013).

55. Sarl Louis Feraud International v. Viewfinder, 489 F.3d 474 (2d Cir. 2007).

56. David Li, "France's 'First Lady' Hospitalized after Reported Presidential Fling," *New York Post* (Jan. 12, 2014).

57. "Actress Julie Gayet Gets $20,000 Judgment against Tabloid Linking Her to President Francois Hollande," *Reuters* (March 27, 2014).

58. Opinion, "Ordering Google to Forget," *N.Y. Times* (May 13, 2014).

59. Gavin Phillipson, "The 'Global Pariah', the Defamation Bill and the Human Rights Act," a chapter in *Modern Defamation law: Balancing Reputation and Free Expression* (D. Capper, ed.) (Belfast: Queens University Belfast Press).

60. Ashley Messenger, "What Would a 'Right to be Forgotten' Mean for Media in the United States," *Communications Lawyer* (June 2012).

61. Philip Patterson, Lee Wilkins, *Media Ethics: Issues and Cases* (Boston: McGraw Hill 2008).

62. See, e.g., Suzanne LaBarre, "Why We're Shutting Off Our Comments," www.popsci.com (Sept. 24, 2013).

63. "Post Industrial Journalism: Adapting to the Present," p. 3, quoting Lord Northcliffe.

64. Restatement (Second) of Torts § 652D, cmt. g.

65. Skilling v. United States, 130 S. Ct. 2896 (2010).

66. Winters v. New York, 333 U.S. 507 (1948).

67. Snyder v. Phelps, 131 S. Ct. 1207 (2011).

68. See, e.g., Oao Alfa Bank v. Center for Public Inquiry, 387 F. Supp. 2d 20 (D.D.C. 2005).

69. DeSirey v. Unique Vacations, 2014 WL 272369 (E.D. Mo. Jan. 24, 2014).

70. Marshall McLuhan, *Understanding Media: The Extensions of Man* (New York: McGraw Hill 1966).

71. Ibid.

72. Bill Kovach and Tom Rosenstiel, *The Elements of Journalism* (New York: Three Rivers Press 2007).

73. Search done using search technology available on amazon.com May 18, 2014.

74. Melvin Mencher, *News Reporting and Writing* (New York: McGraw Hill 2011).

75. Lexis search for "privacy" done in the Cases database on May 18, 2014. There were 141,417 results.

76. Robert M. O'Neil, *The First Amendment and Civil Liability* (Bloomington: Indiana University Press 2001).

77. Erwin Chemerinsky, "Rediscovering Brandeis's Right to Privacy," 45 *Brandeis L. J.* 643 (2007).

78. Erwin Chemerinsky, "In Defense of Truth," 441 *Case W. Res. L. Rev.* 745 (1991).

79. Lior Jacob Strahilevitz, "A Social Networks Theory of Privacy," 72 *U. Chi. L. Rev.* 919 (2005).

80. Daniel Solove, "Teaching Information Privacy Law," www.prawfsblawg .blogs.com (May 10, 2005).

81. Lee Rainie, Sara Kiesler, Ruogu Kang, Mary Madden, "Anonymity, Privacy, and Security Online," Pew Internet and American Life Project, www.pewinterest.org (Sept. 2013).

82. Report on Amy Gajda done by private investigator as part of research on file with author.

83. N.S.A. Examples Social Networks of U.S. Citizens, *New York Times* (Sept. 28, 2013).

84. Jay Rosen, "A Most Useful Definition of Citizen Journalism," www.pressthink.org (July 14, 2008).

85. Jay Rosen, "Lefty Journalism Professor Tries to Discredit the Tea Party by Passing Along Sensational Footage to His Buddies at the Times!!!" www.pressthink.org (Oct. 28, 2011).

86. Mary-Rose Papandrea, "Citizen Journalism and the Reporter's Privilege," 91 *Minn. L. Rev.* 515 (2007).

87. Sonja R. West, "Awakening the Press Clause," 58 *UCLA L. Rev.* 1025 (2011) (preserving the Press Clause requires narrowing the definition of "the press" and embracing press exceptionalism)

88. See, e.g., Xcentric Ventures v. Borodkin, 934 F. Supp. 2d 1125 (D. Ariz. 2013); In re January 11, 2013. Subpoena, 75 A.3d 1260 (N.J. Super. 2013).

89. J.O. v. Township of Bedminster, 77 A.3d 1242 (N.J. Super. Ct. 2013).

90. Service Employees International Union v. Professional Janitorial Service, 415 S.W.3d 387 (Tex. Ct. App. 2013).

91. United States v. Bayer Corp., 2013 U.S. Dist. LEXIS 124928 (D.N.J. Aug. 28, 2013).

92. 735 ILCS 5/8-901 (2013).

93. 735 ILCS 5/8-902 (2013).

94. Sonja R. West, "Press Exceptionalism," 127 Harv. L. Rev. ___(2014).

95. Morgan Weiland, "Congress and the Justice Dept's Dangerous Attempts to Define 'Journalist' Threaten to Exclude Bloggers," www.eff.org (July 23, 2013).

96. Morgan Weiland, "Why Sen. Feinstein Is Wrong About Who's a 'Real Reporter,'" Electronic Frontier Foundation, www.eff.org (Aug. 9, 2013).

97. Debra J. Saunders, "Real Reporters Cannot Be Shielded from Real Insanity," *San Francisco Chronicle* (Sept. 29, 2013).

98. Jay Rosen, "PressThink: An Introduction," www.pressthink.org (Sept. 1, 2003).

99. Bollinger, *Uninhibited, Robust, and Wide-Open.*

100. Michael D. Sullivan, "Selling the First Amendment to a Jury," *Communications Lawyer* (Nov. 2012).
101. See, e.g., Roy L. Moore and Michael D. Murray, *Media Law and Ethics* (New York: Routledge 2012).
102. See, e.g., Cohen v. Cowles Media, Co., 501 U.S. 663 (1991).
103. www.deadbeatlink.com
104. Martha Nussbaum, "Objectification and Internet Misogyny," in *The Offensive Internet* (Cambridge: Harvard University Press 2010), p. 68.
105. Lyrissa Barnett Lidsky, "Silencing John Doe: Defamation and Discourse in Cyberspace," 49 *Duke L.J.* 855 (2000).
106. Yochai Benkler, *The Wealth of Networks* (New Haven: Yale University Press 2006).
107. Danielle Keats Citron, Cyber Civil Rights, 89 *B.U. L. Rev.* 61 (2009).
108. Daniel Solove, "Speech, Privacy, and Reputation on the Internet," in *The Offensive Internet* (Cambridge: Harvard University Press 2010).
109. 17 U.S.C. § 512 (2010).
110. Jim Henson Productions, Inc. v. John T. Brady & Associates, 687 F. Supp. 185 (S.D.N.Y. 1994).
111. Michael D. Scott, Scott on Privacy § 4.37 (3d ed. 2013).
112. Edward Carter, "Argentina's Right to be Forgotten," 27 *Emory International L. Rev.* 23 (2013).
113. Eric Barendt, *Freedom of Speech* (Oxford: Claendon Press 1985), p. 190.
114. See, e.g., Doree Lewak, "Lawsuit Over Negative Yelp Review," *N.Y. Post* (Mar. 23, 2014).
115. Style Blog, "Can Katherine Heigl Really Sue Duane Reade for Tweeting Her Photo? Yes, and Here's Why," *Washington Post* (Apr. 11, 2014).
116. Jay Rosen, "If Bloggers Had No Ethics Blogging Would Have Failed, But It Didn't. So Let's Get a Clue," www.pressthink.org (Sept. 18, 2008).
117. "A Blogger's Code of Ethics," www.cyberjournalist.net (Apr. 15, 2003).
118. Verne Kopytoff, "Bloggers Disinclined toward Suggestion of Net Civility: Proposed Code of Conduct Stirs Up a Hornet's Nest Online," *San Francisco Chronicle* (Apr. 10, 2007).
119. Gannett Co. v. Anderson, 2006 WL 2986459 (Fla. App. Oct. 20, 2006). It was eventually reversed on statute-of-limitations grounds.
120. www.rcfp.org.
121. Donald Gillmor, *Power, Publicity, and the Abuse of Libel Law* (Oxford: Oxford University Press 1992).
122. Debra Cassens Weiss, "Average Hourly Billing Rate for Partners Last Year Was $727 in Largest Law Firms," *ABA Journal* (July 15, 2013).
123. Scholz v. Boston Herald, 2013 Mass. Super. LEXIS 93 (Mass. Sup. Ct. June 25, 2013).
124. "[S]uppose a senator's administrative aide tells you that the senator is about to resign, but asks that you not divulge his role in reporting the story . . .

you [must] come as close as possible to telling the listener just why the source is believable." There is no mention of finding a second source. Brad Kalbfeld, *Associated Press Broadcast News Handbook: A Manual of Techniques & Practices* 90 (2001). See also Kathleen O'Toole, "Journalists Discuss Clash of Ideals, Reality in Their Business," www.stanford.edu, Stanford News (July 2, 1997) ("Under competitive pressure, many news organizations have given up traditional rules such as having two sources of attribution. . . .").

125. A. O. Scott, "Critic's Picks: Man with a Movie Camera," www.nytimes.com (Oct. 3, 2011).

126. Prince v. Viacom, 2008 U.S. Dist. LEXIS 32092 (S.D. Tex. Apr. 18, 2008).

Acknowledgments

I owe many people thanks for their help with this book.

To the scholars, practitioners, and journalists who have helped me think about this subject in important ways through their work and otherwise from the very beginning and through completion of this book, especially Sherry Lee Alexander, Anita Allen, Samantha Barbas, Eric Barendt, Tom Bivins, Bryna Bogoch, Clay Calvert, Linda Campbell, Ed Carter, Erwin Chemerinsky, Cliff Christians, Danielle Citron, Erin Coyle, Richard Davis, Devin Desai, Eric Easton, Anthony Fargo, Ted Glasser, Catherine Hancock, Catherine Hardee, Walt Harrington, Woody Hartzog, Steve Helle, Jennifer Henderson, Elizabeth Hindman, Anne Hoag, Chris Hoofnagle, Kirsty Hughes, RonNell Anderson Jones, Andrew Kenyon, Sue Kieffer, Jane Kirtley, Ron Krotoszynski, Lili Levi, Lee Levine, Anthony Lewis, Lyrissa Lidsky, Dahlia Lithwick, Rich Martin, Barry McDonald, Lisa McElroy, Helen Nissenbaum, Ari-Matti Nuutila, Paul Ohm, Michael Olivas, Mary-Rose Papandrea, Don Pember, Gavin Phillipson, Joel Reidenberg, Neil Richards, Amy Kristin Sanders, Paul Schwartz, Dan Solove, Larry Solum, Eugene Volokh, Stephen Ward, Russell Weaver, Keith Werhan, Sonja West, Kyu Ho Youm, and Diane Zimmerman.

This book also benefited from many discussions with colleagues, both on-the-formal-schedule and not, at conferences around the world: the annual Privacy Law Scholars Conferences in Berkeley and Washington; the Defamation and Privacy: Comparative Law, Media, and Public Speech Workshop at the University of Melbourne; the International Privacy Law Conferences at Clare College, University of Cambridge; the Silicon Flatirons Cable Academic Workshop; Law and Society conferences in Honolulu and Boston; the Washington University First Amendment Roundtable; the Law in the Age of Media Logic Conference at the Oñati International Institute for the Sociology of Law; the Israeli Law and Society Association Conference; the Privacy Discussion Forum at Johannes Gutenberg University in Mainz; the Summit on Freedom of the Press in the Twenty-First Century; the Tulane Law School Faculty Scholarship Symposium; annual meetings of the Association for

Education in Journalism and Mass Communication; and academic conferences at Brigham Young University Law School, the University of Colorado Law School, and the University of Georgia Law School. Many thanks, too, to the anonymous reviewers who reviewed my initial book proposal and a manuscript draft and made this book stronger.

Thanks too to the students at Tulane Law School, who helped with research for this book. Special thanks to my research assistants, who helped specifically and significantly with this project: Dominique Fasano, Laura Fink, Ian Gunn, Liz LaVance, Mia Lindell, Joanna Martin, Parmita Samanta, Graham Williams, Kelsey Zeitzer, and Micah Zeno.

Thanks also to following students and former students who helped with research in other important ways: Chris Arkin, Carys Arvidson, Caitlin Baroni, Caroline Bordelon, Khalil Bou-Mikael, Nolen Boyer, Catherine Burnett, Dominique Caamano, Shannon Chapman, Michelle Chatelain, Rachael Chenoweth, Rebecca Cobbs, Richard Crowson, Dornisha Davis, Lori Dowell, Mariel Dumas, Myranda Elliott, Marcus Foster, Bryanna Frazier, Justine Geiger, Zachary Glimcher, Rodney Golden, Jillian Hanneken, Jordan Howes, Jesse Hudson, Spencer Joffrion, John Krolik, Matthew Landry, Deirdre MacFeeters, Maxwell Malvin, Margaret Manns, Meagan Mariano, Megan McVeagh, Eliza Meltzer, Marlie Merwin, Lauren Michel, Tyler Minick, Nicole Morris, Alex Onstott, Kyle Oxford, James Perelman, Emilie Pfister, Justin Pierre-Louis, Caitlin Poor, Kyle Pruner, Marshall Rader, William Reily, Michael Riess, Alana Riksheim, Krista LaFave Rosolino, Addie Rubino, Alison Sher, Mitchell Tedesco, Mark Vessio, Alston Walker, Bri Whetstone, Kristen Wilson, Peter Wilson, and Brittany Wolf. Thanks too to Lindsay Gus and Ashley Mango, my undergraduate research assistants; to the students in my Spring 2014 Information Privacy class, who worked through a draft chapter with me; and to my Information Privacy and Torts students over the years at Tulane Law School and the University of Illinois College of Law. Thanks also for administrative help from Kathy Trainor and Gail Nelson.

Special thanks to Jean McDonald, whose critical mind and sharp pen made this book better, to Katie Ostler for editing assistance, and to Lili Levi, Lyrissa Lidsky, Michael Meyer, Keith Werhan, Ed Carter, and Len Gajda, who read the manuscript or multiple chapters and offered extremely helpful comments. Thanks also to Amanda Watson, who cheerfully and quickly found obscure texts for me.

Thanks to Elizabeth Knoll for invaluable guidance and support.

And, finally, thanks above all to Dave, Michael, and Matthew, my wonderful family. I love you with all my heart and always will.

Index